T0333331

THE MATCH OF THE CENTURY

THE MATCH OF THE CENTURY

OF THE

CENTURY

ENGLAND, HUNGARY, AND THE GAME THAT CHANGED FOOTBALL FOREVER

MATT CLOUGH

The
History
Press

First published 2022

The History Press
97 St George's Place, Cheltenham,
Gloucestershire, GL50 3QB
www.thehistorypress.co.uk

British Library Cataloguing in Publication Data.
A catalogue record for this book is available from the British Library.

ISBN 978 0 7509 9814 7

Typesetting and origination by The History Press
Printed and bound in Great Britain by TJ Books Limited, Padstow, Cornwall.

Trees for Life

CONTENTS

1

THE ENGINEER
AND THE COUNT

The past is never dead. It's not even past.

William Faulkner

Spanning the glittering, aquamarine waters of the Danube, in the shadow of the imposing Hungarian Parliament in the beating heart of Budapest, there stands a bridge. Amid the Hungarian capital's architectural splendour, the Széchenyi Chain Bridge stands alone in its alchemy between form and function. Not only a connection between the ancient conurbations of Buda and Pest either side of the Danube, the Chain Bridge, flanked at either end by a pair of formidable stone lions, is a work of art. It owes its almost two centuries of existence principally to two men.

In many respects, William Tierney Clark and Count István Széchenyi were unlikely bedfellows, sharing little aside from a relatively close proximity in age. Clark, from Bristol, lost his father early in childhood and by the age of 12 was apprenticed to a millwright so he could learn a trade and begin providing for his family. Through hard work and some star-crossed meetings, Clark found himself rising swiftly through the ranks at West Middlesex Water Works.

In eras past, the destiny for those like Clark, forced from education in order to provide, was generally a life of drudgery, of little ambition beyond scrabbling to make ends meet. However, he was the personification of the rising tide of industrial prowess sweeping Britain in the early to mid-nineteenth century. After centuries of a strict class system, the promise of the Industrial Revolution went some way to finally breaking down barriers. Britain needed innovators and brilliant minds to help push boundaries, and quickly found that the lower classes were every bit as likely to produce them as the upper classes were. It was a time of nearly unprecedented opportunity in Britain's history to that point, and men like Clark were the chief beneficiaries.

Before long, his brilliant mechanical mind was focused upon the singular problem with which he would make his name – bridges. His crowning achievement in Britain was Hammersmith Suspension Bridge, the first suspension bridge to span the Thames, which melded engineering brilliance with artistic flair, thanks to a neoclassical design. This meeting of style and substance was typical of many of the Industrial Revolution's greatest achievements and, combined with the vast news-spreading capabilities of the British Empire, played a critical role in making Britain not only the workshop of the world, but the envy of much of it too.

By the completion of Hammersmith Bridge, Clark's appearance was replete with many of the features that have come to be associated with his time. Typically clad in black, he boasted bristling sideburns that helped bring some volume to an otherwise sallow, almost sickly face that was well accustomed to an austere expression.

Széchenyi, who arrived in Britain in 1832 on a fact-finding mission, hoping to learn all he could from Britain's sudden explosion of industrial vigour, did not possess such an unassuming appearance. A receding hairline of jet-black hair was accompanied by a chinstrap beard that brought to mind a Jacobian ruff. An impressive moustache sat atop his lip. Remarkably, none of these features were his most notable; that accolade went to a pair of mesmerically thick eyebrows which lent him an air of sombre wisdom.

It was a striking appearance that befitted a striking man. Born into enormous wealth and privilege, Széchenyi, the youngest of five children, could have easily lived out his life in opulent indolence. Instead, he joined the army at 17 and conducted himself with distinction during the Napoleonic Wars before travelling through Europe to glean insights into how he could help to modernise and improve life in his homeland of Hungary. He would ultimately be instrumental in the introduction of everything from critical railway infrastructure and steam navigation to milling and even horse racing.

He was fanatical about bringing British innovations home, but few stoked his imagination as Clark's Hammersmith Bridge did. Széchenyi rhapsodised that the bridge was far more than just a solution to a problem;

it was, in fact, a creation of 'astounding appearance', a construction with the capability to 'overwhelm the senses, and to deprive man of his judgement'.[1] At the time, the vast River Danube rolled between two cities, Buda and Pest, and no permanent structure connected the two metropolises. Gazing upon Clark's structure across the Thames, Széchenyi knew he had found the solution for spanning the river and laying the foundations for modern-day Budapest.

Széchenyi and Clark began liaising frequently and before long a plot was hatched. Széchenyi set about persuading the Hungarian Parliament of the project's merits, while Clark busied himself with designing his masterpiece. After years of carefully navigating bureaucratic channels more treacherous than the ice flows that drifted down the Danube in winter, ground was finally broken in 1840, and the bridge opened nine years later. Appropriately for such a grand tour de force, the final stages of the bridge's construction coincided with a tumultuous epoch in Hungary's history, as they fought for independence from Austria and the Habsburg Empire. At several points, the almost-finished bridge was threatened, never more so than when Austrian troops attempted to destroy it in order to halt the advancing Hungarian forces, only for the officer charged with demolishing the bridge to accidentally use the explosives on himself. The survival and completion of the bridge, denoting as it did a huge symbolic step towards modernity for Hungary, served as an apt metaphor for the revolution. Though the Hungarians were eventually defeated, the groundwork had been laid for the spirit of Hungarian nationalism which would play a critical role in the country's future.

The Széchenyi Chain Bridge remains as a timeless reminder of the relationship between Hungary and Britain – and a core difference between the national characters of the two nations. For Hungary, there was no shame at all in seeking help from others in order to advance their personal cause; gleaning advice from outside could help to avoid long and often painful learning curves. At the same time, as the British Empire's diaspora was spreading the gospel of Britain and her innumerable innovations far and wide, a more insidious aspect was being ingrained within the national psyche at home: a stubbornness, an assumption of unending supremacy, an arrogance that lent itself to an unwillingness to learn from elsewhere. The British Empire was unrivalled in expanse and power – what could anyone else possibly have to offer it?

Half a century after the completion of the Chain Bridge, another cultural exchange between the two nations was taking place. The glamour of the British Empire's unfettered power had translated to a rampant strain of Anglomania across Austria and Hungary, where the well-to-do equated British fashion, art and culture with status. This trend was so prevalent that even British exports considered working class and gauche at home were elevated and given a rarefied air by the time they reached Budapest or Vienna.

This was the case when an exciting new ball game named football arrived, close to the turn of the twentieth century. The game had its theoretical origins in the minds and quadrangles of Cambridge and Oxford but was given physical life in the muddy quagmires and on the begrimed cobbles of the north of England and Scotland. By the time football was being exported elsewhere, the British upper classes were already turning their backs on it.

The British elites deemed football's simplicity, and the resulting fervid adoption of the game across the working-class strongholds within northern England and Scotland (the traditional Saturday 3 p.m. kick-off time was codified in response to the time factories let out, giving the workers enough time to make it to the grounds), as reasons to denigrate and dismiss football. By time word of the game reached the coffee shops on the banks of the Danube, the class distinction had been diluted and lost and the Hungarian establishment and proletariat alike were swiftly in thrall to the new sport.

The very act of exporting the game, and the biases that were lost along the way, triggered the first rift between the British and Hungarian versions of football. In Britain, the game, associated with the mill towns and mines of places like Manchester, Bolton, Newcastle and Sunderland, was arrogantly assumed to be of no intellectual merit, and anyone who disagreed was treated with suspicion or outright hostility. In Hungary, it was viewed with the same respect as a piece of high culture and was regarded with intellectual rigour. The same men who, in Britain, were mocked for believing there could be more to the game than the fundamentals, were welcomed to countries like Hungary with a sort of hushed reverence, their words and ideas pored over like religious manuscripts or ground-breaking literature. This intellectual esteem for the sport would remain fundamental to generations of Hungarian football players, coaches and fans.

Men like Clark had been born at a unique point in Britain's modern history when the gifted could rise to the top, regardless of status or circumstance, but by the time football emerged, the Industrial Revolution was emitting its dying embers, and with it the possibility of upward movement was being replaced by a return to a more stratified society of haves and have-nots. Though it would take decades to coalesce, it was this shift, this closing off of opportunity, this attempt by those already satisfied with their lot to lift up the drawbridge behind them to prevent others from crossing it, that would play a critical role in the eventual decline and collapse of the British Empire. The same insidious pattern would be mirrored across the board rooms and training pitches of football clubs across England, as well as in the corridors of power in the Football Association's (FA) headquarters at Lancaster Gate.

The Chain Bridge was partially destroyed during the catastrophic, bloody siege of Nazi-occupied Budapest by the Soviet Red Army during the Second World War, before being rebuilt and reopened in 1949 to stand once again as a testament to Hungary's strength and resilience, its willingness to learn, and a commitment to pragmatism mixed with aesthetics. At the same moment, the exact same qualities could be found in the country's remarkable national football team, a team that synthesised a mechanically engineered, almost forensic approach to the science of football with an effervescent, joyous beauty in a manner never before seen on a football pitch. Over the following years, despite enormous pressure and political strife, the team would conquer all before them, before being granted an irresistible opportunity to prove themselves in the ultimate way. In November 1953, the Hungarian team emerged from behind the Iron Curtain and took up the mantle of attempting to become the first team from beyond the British Isles to defeat England on their home soil.

In their way stood an England team that, like Britain during the post-war disintegration of the empire, was facing a reckoning. Their proud, undefeated home record remained the hook upon which all expectations, all esteem and all assumptions of supremacy were hung. The pool of players the FA had to pick from was formidable – league winners, cup heroes, two future England record goal scorers, another who would become the first to reach 100 caps for his country, and arguably the most famous player on the planet. Yet, after finally bowing to the global tide and expanding their horizons beyond a narrow obsession with the home nations, the venerated status of the England national team was under threat like never before, particularly following a disastrous maiden World Cup.

Once the afterglow of the Allied victory in the Second World War had waned and the triumphant street party bunting had been taken down, Britain had been left to survey a scene of utter devastation: nearly half a million dead, cities levelled by the Luftwaffe, an economy propped up by American aid (an unthinkable prospect just years before), rationing not only still in effect but more stringent than during the war itself. The empire was crumbling. India had achieved independence in 1947 and was shortly followed by Ceylon and Brunei, while other colonies and dominions laid the groundwork for eventual independence. Though it would take the Suez Crisis in 1956 to truly underline just how diminished Britain's standing in the new world order was, there was no question that the empire was faltering badly. At a time when the English people were looking to their football team more than ever as a beacon of hope and an affirmation of Britain's status despite mounting evidence to the contrary, the pressure upon the players had never been greater.

★ ★ ★

The day of 25 November 1953 dawned with a scene that could just as easily have belonged to the Victorian London of Arthur Conan Doyle or Robert Louis Stevenson as it did the post-war era. Heavy overnight rain had left the streets slick and glassy, upon which ghostly apparitions of the buildings towering above them were reflected. The rain had given way to a cloying, nearly impenetrable fog against which the gas-lit street lamps strained. Cars rolled steadily past commuters swaddled in overcoats, hunched against the cool autumn air. Less than ten years before the Beatles inaugurated a decade of psychedelic technicolour, this was England in sepia, in many respects unchanged from the early 1900s.

Maintaining the status quo was precisely what the England team sought to achieve that day. Teams had arrived from the Continent amid great fanfare before, and the Three Lions had always thwarted their ambitions. It was imperative that they did so once again.

Excitement and anticipation was at fever pitch as the teams walked out onto the famous Wembley Stadium pitch for what the newspapers were calling 'The Match of the Century'. West versus East, capitalism versus communism, the masters versus the students, the old guard versus the upstarts, the British Empire versus a satellite of the Soviet Union, tactical stagnation versus innovation, Stanley Matthews, Billy Wright and Alf Ramsey versus Ferenc Puskás, Sándor Kocsis and Nándor Hidegkuti. It all rested on the outcome of England versus Hungary. All that remained for them to do was play.

2

THE OLD MASTERS

The story of Britain in the first half of the twentieth century is one of tumult and upheaval. The nation entered the 1900s with an unprecedented expanse of empire, a rich cultural reputation and a renown as the workshop of the world. It wasn't simply goods that the empire exported around the globe, but ideas and inventions. Victorian-era Britain had given the world the telephone, the rubber tyre, the modern form of the postal service and thousands of other innovations that had greased the wheels of commerce to an unprecedented slickness.

In 1900, there was no reason to suspect that anything on the horizon could challenge Britain's pre-eminent position, aside from the fear that the empire had grown so vast that defending it all could stretch resources to breaking point, even as the nation allocated more than half of all public spending to imperial defence.[1] Queen Victoria remained on the throne, demand from other nations for British coal and textiles continued to boom as other countries desperately attempted to keep up with the unassuming little island in the north Atlantic, and Britain continued to produce brilliant individuals, capable of keeping foreign theatres packed to the rafters, their readers enraptured and their factories firing.

One British invention, codified in 1868 after a glacial formation over centuries (as far back as the 1300s, Edward III had been moved to ban it in order to have his subjects focus on archery to aid Britain's cause in the Hundred Years War),[2] was less trumpeted, at least by the upper-middle and upper classes who tended to act as gatekeepers for what was and wasn't exported across the empire. By the 1900s and 1910s, however, this particular creation could not be stopped by any border, natural, political or otherwise, nor could it be held back by those who deemed it a pursuit of low worth and questionable moral value.

It may have taken hundreds of years to reach the point where the English Football Association formalised it and twelve trail-blazing clubs organised the first coordinated league season (in 1888), but from then on, association football spread like a virus, a sporting epidemic that took root in any host it could, hopping from person to person, port to port, field to field, until it had enveloped the globe. This proliferation was charged by the sport's accessibility (anything could be – and invariably was – scrunched up and substituted for a ball) and its deceptive simplicity, which masked endless complexities, combinations and possibilities.

Within a matter of decades, football in Britain went beyond what any sport had previously achieved in terms of popularity and devotion. In the words of esteemed writer Arthur Hopcraft, football had become:

> … not just a sport people take to, like cricket or tennis or running long distances. It is inherent in the people. It is built into the urban psyche, as much a common experience to our children as are uncles and school. It is not a phenomenon; it is an everyday matter.[3]

The effect was mirrored across the globe. From Liverpool to Lisbon, Cambridge to Calcutta, Bolton to Belo Horizonte, Blackburn to Budapest, football fanned out like wildfire.

Nowhere was impervious. The game's most fervent apostles in the first decades of the twentieth century were British soldiers, stationed in every far-flung outpost of the empire, which by 1910 included New Zealand, numerous Caribbean and Pacific islands, Nigeria, British Guyana and, of course, India. Even in the fleeting moments of calm amid hails of gunfire, billowing acrid smoke and the stench of death, thoughts quickly turned to football, most famously in no man's land on the Western Front at Christmas 1914, when a brief halt in the unfathomable carnage of the First World War saw British and German soldiers seize the opportunity to play impromptu matches.

These brief minutes of levity between warring soldiers were far from the first examples of football between nations, standing in as a proxy for far more serious disputes. Almost as soon as the rules of association football had been codified, the prospect of international matches had been raised. England took on Scotland in the first international in 1872, watched by 4,000, which ended 0-0 despite England fielding seven forwards and Scotland five. For the next three decades, England's international schedule would remain entirely within the confines of the British Isles but would expand in frequency with the advent of the Home Championship, which began in 1883 and crowned a winner annually.

It wasn't long, however, before this isolation began to chafe. By 1907, England had won the Home Championship on fourteen occasions, Scotland had won eleven and Wales one. A general lack of competitiveness and the repetition of England playing the same three teams meant that interest was stagnating, with home crowds rarely exceeding 30,000, a number that had barely moved since the mid-1890s. The time had come for England to cast her net further.

In 1908, the national team embarked on their first ever foreign tour, playing Austria (twice), Hungary and Bohemia, all then part of the Austro-Hungarian Empire. News of the Danubian fervour for football had reached British shores and inspired England's choice for their first ever non-British opponents. However, all three opponents would swiftly come to understand that enthusiasm alone was not enough to earn parity with England's team of full-time professionals. Over the course of the four games, England earned an aggregate victory of 28-2.

England's early forays abroad were more important for their role in spreading the gospel of the sport rather than as sporting encounters. Though the games were of great interest abroad, at home they were regarded far more coolly, oddities that, from a competitiveness perspective, offered far less than a match with the Scottish did. Almost subconsciously, the England national team began to take on the same aura of benevolent superiority that had been used to justify Britain's imperial expansion, the idea that those nations and their people, who had been subsumed and subjugated, no matter how brutally, were far better off with the British example than left to their own devices.

The tours also fired the imaginations of a new type of British travel-ler. Missionaries had been criss-crossing the globe in the name of countless causes and creeds for centuries, and the British Empire was no stranger to their likes. Some were well meaning (if misguided), attempting to teach the world the story of Christianity and what they felt was the only route to salvation. Others were less altruistic. The religious dogmatism of some was transmuted into racial and eugenical theories that, in turn, lent credence to some of the worst atrocities to occur in the name of the British Empire, with infamous figures such as Cecil Rhodes acting with ruthless impunity in the belief that the accident of their British birth gave them an inherent precedence.

It was with a far more benign mission that men began to set sail from British shores in the early 1900s to help spread the gospel of football. In the words of Rory Smith, these were the men 'who taught the world how to beat England at their own game'.[4] William Garbutt, a former player, graduated from working on the Genovese docks to eventually become the godfather of Italian football management. Jack Greenwell, a miner from County Durham, travelled to Barcelona, first to play for the club and then manage them, eventually establishing them as one of the great forces of Spanish football. Jimmy Hogan, another former pro, travelled through Europe, planting seeds in the Netherlands, Switzerland, Austria and Hungary.

Even with these philanthropic figures exporting the British standard of tactical organisation and coaching, it would take until the late 1920s for Continental European nations to begin to catch England. In 1923, England failed to beat a Continental team for the first time, being held 2-2 by Belgium. Six years later, in Madrid, England finally lost their unbeaten record against mainland European teams, going down 4-3 to a spirited Spain. The *Athletic News* commemorated the occasion with a front-page headline announcing 'England's First Fall', but set the tone for future coverage of England's defeats to foreign opposition by focusing on mitigating factors (in this case, the long domestic season and the intense Spanish heat).

Just as it appeared that a truly competitive international landscape was emerging, the decades-long head start enjoyed by the home nations finally expended, the British FA took a fateful decision. The first World Cup was due to be played in Uruguay in 1930, but the British teams wouldn't be there, having withdrawn from FIFA, first in 1919, then more permanently in 1928, ostensibly in an argument over the precise parameters of amateurism in the game. A more cynical interpretation of the timing of events is that England and their British neighbours, rather than countenance the idea that they might no longer sweep all comers aside, simply picked up their ball and went home. It would take the best part of twenty years before they returned to the fold. In the meantime, the home nations enjoyed a splendid isolation which allowed England to pick and choose their opponents and carefully cultivate their continuing claim of supremacy.

It wasn't just on the football pitch that, after leading the way for so long, Britain suddenly appeared to be retreating. Victory in the First World War had come at a grave cost. Hundreds of thousands of British men had perished in unimaginable conditions. Those who gave the orders to send wave after wave of men out of their trenches into a hail of machine-gun bullets and certain death were typically upper class, cloistered behind miles of barbed wire and blissfully unaware of both the futility of their orders and the bloody carnage they were responsible for. Huge swathes of those who died hailed from Ireland, India and elsewhere in the empire. Those who returned home to tell their tales did so with renewed determination that they be afforded the right to self-governance and freedom from the yoke of Britain's oppressive rule in exchange for their sacrifice.

The war also came with tremendous economic ramifications. Even as the Treaty of Versailles awarded Britain yet more territory, marking the high-water point of the empire's expanse with rule over a quarter of the people on Earth, the hiatus in Britain's global export business had ended its reign as the workshop of the world and seen nations such as the USA and Japan amass huge naval power. Before the war, David Lloyd George had pondered if the economic comforts afforded by the empire had bred complacency, a nation of 'footballers, stock exchangers, public-house and music-hall frequenters'.[5] The rapidity of the empire's decline following the war seemed to confirm the Welshman's thesis.

The obstinacy of the officer class, when faced with irrefutable, bloody evidence that their modes and methods were woefully outdated, was to become a leitmotif of imperial thinking. This stubbornness pervaded everything from British attitudes to the people they ruled over, even as they became increasingly restless, to the loss of economic supremacy in staple industries such as textiles following the war. Many in Britain, from the leaders in Parliament, to the newspapermen, to the man on the street, simply wouldn't countenance the idea that the sun could be setting on the British Empire. The same thinking was prevalent at the FA's Lancaster Gate headquarters in their attitudes towards the national team, for which they refused to hire a manager, preferring instead to pick the team by a committee that invariably quarrelled, compromised and relied on guesswork.

Even without the World Cup to provide definitive evidence, the England team appeared to be heading for a reckoning, sooner or later. No longer could they travel to the Continent on an end-of-season tour and expect the red carpet to be rolled out by an awestruck team of opposing amateurs who would be duly crushed by a cricket score. During the 1930s, there were defeats abroad to France, Czechoslovakia, Austria, Belgium, Switzerland and Yugoslavia. In 1934, England returned to Budapest, the scene of their first forays abroad back in 1908 and 1909, where they'd won 7-0, 4-2 and 8-2. The intervening years, however, had reduced the gulf between the two nations dramatically, and two second-half goals gave the Hungarians a famous victory. The result was greeted in Britain with the obligatory combination of pessimism – the *Daily Mirror* lamented a 'severe blow' to the 'prestige of English Soccer' – and justifications, with the newspapers arguing that the pitch was 'like iron', dust affected the players, the heat was unseasonable and the ball was lighter than the English were accustomed to.

In 1936, for only the second time since the war, England lost more games than they won in a calendar year. The English, however, held steadfast in their belief that they remained the apogee of international football, emboldened by a pattern of vengeance that emerged during this period. Though they could be defeated away from home, often (it was claimed) after being handicapped by external factors ranging from lax refereeing, to travel fatigue, to unfamiliar climate, to alien food, at home England remained imperious against Continental opposition. In 1931, two years after they fell in their first ever defeat to Continental opposition in Madrid, England crushed *La Roja* 7-1. Czechoslovakia and Hungary were both defeated in return matches in England. France, who arrested a run of eight straight defeats to England with a win in Paris in 1931, were then beaten at White Hart Lane and Stade Olympique de Colombes in the following years.

There were also signal performances, the strength of which could not be denied by even the most fervent of Anglophobes and critics of the team. One came in Berlin in 1938, with a match that lives on in infamy. Before kick-off, the English players were press-ganged by British diplomats into offering a ceremonial fascist salute to the crowd and gathered German dignitaries, including Rudolf Hess, Joseph Goebbels and Joachim von Ribbentrop, an indication of the growing political cachet of the game.

What is less clearly remembered is that England came away 6-3 winners after a stirring performance against the cream of not only German talent, but the remnants of the 1930s Austrian *Wunderteam*, following Germany's annexation of their neighbours. The *Guardian*'s somewhat condescending write-up of the game was typical of the imperialist mindset, reminding its readers that the progress made by the German team was a direct result of Britain's benevolence in sending ambassadors abroad decades earlier. The *Sports Argus* followed suit, declaring that England's win, along with a victory for Jimmy Hogan's Aston Villa over a German select team, had shaken 'the foundations of the international football world', before conceding that thanks to Britain's tireless missionary work, 'the pupil is now almost, if not quite, the equal of the teacher'.

The German press were simply enchanted, with *Fussball Woche* consoling themselves that their nation's defeat had come at the hands of football's true 'unparalleled champions'. A year later, a 2-2 draw with reigning two-time World Cup winners Italy in Milan underlined the Three Lions' claim to still be the best in the world.

Within months of these games against Germany and Italy, Britain would find herself locked in a very different and altogether more consequential battle with the two countries. For the second time in the twentieth century, Britain would emerge from a global conflict the winner, but bearing the hallmarks of having achieved a pyrrhic victory. The First World War had stretched the empire to breaking point, causing the first significant tears to appear. The Second World War accelerated the process, ripping apart the very fabric.

Nations that had sent their men to fight and die for Britain under the banner of opposing tyrannical fascism now demanded that they be afforded the basic rights that they had been fighting in the name of. America's assistance during the war came contingent on Britain decolonising once the conflict was over, and two years after D-Day, India, the jewel in the empire's crown and the key domino in the break-up of the empire, had her independence. More than twenty different nations would follow over the coming years. Those that weren't granted their independence peaceably looked to take it by force. Over the next decade, both Britain and France would fight increasingly desperate – and bloody – battles in the vain hope of preserving their empires.

The war, though ending in an Allied victory, had also made it clear that some parts of that alliance were more equal than others. At Yalta, Winston Churchill had been reduced to a junior partner, a glorified spectator watching on as the USA and Soviet Union carved up the spoils of the conflict and remade the global stage with themselves at the very centre. To add to the indignity, France and Britain, for centuries two of the world's greatest superpowers, found themselves reduced to relying on vast sums of American aid to help rebuild their flattened cities and tattered economies.

3

POMP AND CIRCUMSTANCE

To be a follower of football in Britain immediately following the Second World War was to survey a landscape every bit as devastated as the smouldering ruins of the country's bombed-out cities. Dozens of players were killed on active duty, while countless more lost the best years of their careers. Clubs were in various states of financial ruin, their previously healthy coffers emptied by the loss of crowds, who feared gathering en masse and didn't want to risk doing so only to see rag-tag teams of guest players (many First and Second Division sides resorted to fielding well in excess of 100 players during the war years).

Manchester United would play their home fixtures at the Maine Road home of their bitter cross-city rivals Manchester City, until 1949, after Old Trafford was all but levelled by German bombing raids. Miraculously, no football league clubs succumbed to financial oblivion, though many resorted to effectively shutting down during the war, not partaking in even the hastily organised wartime leagues due to the small number of hardy souls still willing to brave live games not coming close to covering the costs of hosting a match.

Club directors and owners could at least take solace in the fact that once the horrors of the Second World War abated, they could look forward to returning to a state of affairs that had never been so good. The 1938 season had seen the third-highest average First Division attendance in history. Attendances for the national team when playing at Wembley dwarfed those of the national rugby and cricket teams, even as the metropolitan elites of London continued to denigrate football as existing on a lower intellectual and cultural plane than the traditional fare of Twickenham and Lord's. What's more, attendances had surged following the hiatus caused by the First World War, with returning soldiers and those who had remained at home alike desperate for a return to normality and finding it in the weekly, working-class ritual of going to the match. There was nothing to suggest the same pattern wouldn't repeat itself.

When football did finally resume amid a burst of post-war euphoria, there had been an undeniable changing of the guard. In the twelve seasons before the Second World War had broken out, Arsenal, managed first by Herbert Chapman and then George Allison, had won five titles, while Everton, inspired by the absurd goal-scoring feats of Dixie Dean, had won three. It would take a decade before another pair of dominant, dynastic teams – Matt Busby's eponymous Babes at Manchester United and Stan Cullis' irrepressible Wolves – emerged. In the void came a footballing morass in which eight different teams would win the next nine championships. The twin mechanisms of the maximum wage, which disincentivised players from agitating for moves to earn more money, and the retain-and-transfer system, which wedded players' registrations to their club and prevented them from obtaining free transfers after the expiration of their contracts, helped encourage this egalitarian state of affairs, as the clubs who had come through the war less financially scathed than others weren't able to hoover up talent from less-monied teams.

And there was plenty of talent to hoover. Even as fans mourned the loss of many of the heroes of the pre-war years, it was impossible to resist the excitement that built around the new crop of players who emerged, moulded by their time serving in the forces and guesting for clubs and armed forces teams.

Few league debuts in history can have been greeted with such fanfare and anticipation as Tom Finney's. Having begun his career during the war years and turned in some eye-catching performances in the 1945–46 FA Cup, which resumed a year before the leagues did, Finney had to wait only four weeks after his first league appearance for Preston North End before he received his maiden England cap. It was to be the start of a glittering career, in which Finney haunted the dreams of the myriad defenders who attempted to stop his surging runs. As if to underscore football's status as the working-class game, Finney supplemented his wages throughout his career by working as a plumber, earning him the immortal moniker of the 'Preston Plumber', with his teammates often referred to less charitably as Finney's 'ten drips'.

A few miles south, in Bolton, where the outstanding forward of the late 1930s, Tommy Lawton, had been raised, Bolton Wanderers discovered their own enduring talent, plucked from Lancashire's coalfield, named Nat Lofthouse. A bulldozing centre-forward with an innate finishing ability, Lofthouse formed a lifelong friendship with Finney, and the pair would eventually share the goal-scoring record for the national team.

On the coast, Blackpool's answer to Lofthouse came in the form of Stan Mortensen, a less physical but no less predatory goal scorer, while Newcastle United had Jackie Milburn as their marksman. In Yorkshire, English football's first South American star arrived in the form of Barnsley's inside-forward George Robledo, a Chilean who would go on to achieve legendary status with Newcastle.

The counterbalance to this infusion of attacking skill and power came in the form of a new class of outstanding defender, no better exemplified than Wolves' Billy Wright and Southampton's Alf Ramsey. Wright, a dominating, powerful defender of great versatility, would become the first England player to amass more than 100 caps, a remarkable feat given the national team typically only contested between seven and nine fixtures a year during his career.

Ramsey, meanwhile, lacked Wright's raw physical attributes but was feted for his unparalleled reading of the game and the tactical inquisitiveness that this ability engendered. This was only heightened when, in 1949, Ramsey was bought by Arthur Rowe's Tottenham, whose daring push-and-run style distinguished them from the direct English norm and saw Spurs win the league in their first season back in the top flight, in Ramsey's second year at White Hart Lane. With the W-M formation used universally in the English leagues, placing little emphasis on the centre of the pitch, the left- and right-half remained relatively unglamorous positions designated to indefatigable workhorses, who were tasked with racing back and forth between the defence and attack for 90 minutes. Few players did so with such gusto and verve as Jimmy Dickinson, Mr Portsmouth, who would set a record for league appearances for a single club that has only been broken once.

It wasn't only in the playing department that fresh blood was being introduced. The post-war era dawned with Manchester United a slumbering giant that hadn't won any significant silverware since 1911 and had spent most of the 1930s in the Second Division. In their quest to return to their earlier halcyon days, the club turned to the untested pairing of Matt Busby, who had made his name starring for United's two biggest rivals, Manchester City and Liverpool, as manager and Jimmy Murphy as chief coach. Even after the initial success the two enjoyed with the team they built shortly after the resumption, few could have predicted the seismic impact Busby would go on to have on the British game.

For a lucky few who had debuted before 1939, the war hadn't robbed them of their best playing years. Blackpool's defensive rock Harry Johnston remained an enormously reliable presence who won the FWA Footballer of the Year for 1951. A year earlier, the same accolade had been received by Joe Mercer, who had moved to Arsenal from Everton and captained the Gunners to league and FA Cup success.

At the other end of the pitch, Tommy Lawton remained the benchmark for strikers across the league, even as players who had grown up idolising him were now playing against him. Lawton moved to Chelsea, where he picked up where he had left off, scoring twenty-six times in thirty-four games and re-establishing himself as the undisputed owner of the England No. 9 shirt.

Of course, no player exemplified the transition from interwar to post-war period in English football more than Stanley Matthews. Before the war, Matthews had been one of the biggest draws in the league, mesmerising crowds and humiliating defenders with his acceleration and trademark body swerve. Matthews was 30 in 1945 and had lost what, for most players, would have been his prime years. Despite helping draw punters to England wartime internationals with unerring consistency, it was felt that his career would soon be on an inextricable downward trajectory, particularly with his style of play being so reliant on bursts of pace and deft skills, both the domain of younger players.

Nonetheless, even with the assumed waning of his magic, Matthews continued to attract fans in their droves. Matthews' force of character, aided by his popularity, meant he was one of the few players of the time who was able to successfully agitate for a transfer, something that won him no fans in the national team selection committee, which comprised largely club chairmen. Moving to Blackpool in 1947, he was asked by his new manager Joe Smith if he thought his 32-year-old legs could stand the rigours of two more years of first-class football. Smith, like millions of others, would soon be forced to reckon with Matthews' apparent footballing immortality.

Matthews may have been capable of overcoming the loss of his prime, but countless others were left with a yawning gap in their careers filled with could-have-beens. England and Arsenal captain Eddie Hapgood, one of the great full-backs of his day, was 30 as the war broke out and never played a first-class game again. Another Arsenal star, prolific centre-forward Ted Drake, was only 27 in 1939, but his career was ended by injury almost as soon as football returned after the hostilities. T.G. Jones, Everton's Welsh defender considered by many the best there had ever been, returned to find the Toffees' championship-winning team dismantled and himself subject to bitter accusations of feigning injury to avoid wartime matches. Then there were the footballers who didn't come home at all. Bolton captain Harry Goslin and Liverpool player Tom Cooper were just two of dozens of professional players killed during the conflict.

★ ★ ★

While club football staggered to reassert itself, English fans could at least look to their national team with a continued sense of pride. Though the FA and British government were yet to have their eyes opened to the rich vein of diplomatic possibilities football offered, the role that the national football team was nonetheless already playing as a tool for patriotism and as a proxy for Britain's former economic and military successes abroad was unbounded.

Appropriately enough, given their increasing role within British foreign policy, the England national team were controlled almost entirely, via the FA, by men who had been schooled in the unimpeachable might, righteousness and divine purpose of the British Empire. This mindset tended to encourage a unique degree of arrogance, entitlement and, above all, a nationalistic streak that often lurched beyond pride into jingoism and a self-serving, infantilising belief that because of the sheer vastness of the empire and the role Britain had played in the world order, there was nothing she could learn from any other nation, even as she plundered these nations' resources.

This belief could be detected in every class and creed in Britain, though it unquestionably grew more pronounced within the higher echelons of society, and by the 1940s, it was entrenched beyond all reproach. Football was, in the words of Bob Ferrier, an 'old man's game, run by a class philosophically opposed to anything new'.[1]

Post-war Britain would quickly become the scene of pitched battles between this establishment and those who recognised the writing on the wall for Britain's status and the need to modernise, favouring collaboration over colonisation. In the FA's case, this man was Stanley Rous, the organisation's secretary. A former FA Cup final and international referee, Rous was unusual in an association populated largely by businessmen and grandees in that he had direct experience of the game as it was played on the pitch. During the chaos of the war, the forceful, strong-willed Rous began to scheme about how he could encourage some long-overdue modernisation of the FA and the national team.

With the unfettered supremacy that England had enjoyed over all opposition beyond the British Isles for the first four decades of international competition now under threat, the impetus was on England to evolve. Almost immediately, Rous faced opposition from those in the FA who wanted no alteration to the decades-old status quo that had granted them the golden combination of huge power over the running of the game and the national team with very little accountability. Rous was hardly a radical – legendary football scribe Brian Glanville characterised him as 'a snob and authoritarian', who seemed 'almost embarrassed' that his professional elevation in the world 'all depended on young men in shorts running about muddy fields'[2] – but he was, compared to the men surrounding him, at least enterprising. Before long, he was focused on two areas that would enable the England team to evolve, albeit at a glacial pace compared to foreign teams.

Firstly, Rous brought an end to England's self-imposed isolation. After their withdrawal from FIFA in the 1920s, the British nations had been marooned, largely keeping it within the family by contesting the annual Home Championship and engaging in sporadic foreign tours. The upshot of this was that England missed the first three World Cups, despite a speculative invitation from FIFA to participate in the 1938 competition, a proposition that Rous was amenable towards but one that he couldn't persuade the rest of the FA to accede to.

In 1946, however, Rous' campaign achieved success. England, along with the other British teams, re-joined FIFA, paving the way for their participation in their first truly international competition. Immediately, the 1950 World Cup became an enormous draw, even allowing for the fact that it would take place in Brazil and thus entail an arduous journey for European teams. Setting all arrogance aside, there had been an undeniable sense that without the British teams involved, the first three World Cups had been somewhat lacking in legitimacy; the reverence that the game's progenitors were held in meant that winning the World Cup without British teams was not enough to be truly considered World Champions.

Rous was also agitating for a remarkably basic concession from the FA to bring England into line with just about every other major footballing nation of the time – installing a manager. Teams such as Italy and Austria had already demonstrated the benefits of having forceful managers unafraid to put their stamp on their sides, both achieving enormous success during the 1930s. England, meanwhile, had remained a shapeless mass of players chosen on the whims of the FA's selectors and sent out without so much as a focused training session or pre-match pep talk, something which had astonished Italy's legendary manager Vittorio Pozzo.[3]

As with so much about the organisation of the national team, there was more than a whiff of arrogance about the resistance to a managerial figure. Other nations may need their best players to be told what to do, but an Englishman who was good enough to receive a cap for his country was presupposed to be at the very pinnacle of the sport; surely there was no wisdom a manager could hope to impart on such a player.

Rous, however, had seen the light, his epiphany coming when he himself had acted as a de facto manager for the team during the war, an experience that convinced him of the benefits of a degree of autocracy in the team's organisation. Despite the natural English aversion to dictators and dictatorships (something which has been connected theoretically to Britain's status as an island affording it greater security and therefore less fear of invasion than other nations),[4] Rous believed passionately that, in Ferrier's words, until the team 'had a Cromwell, not a cabinet', they would continue to relinquish their previous supremacy.[5] That England teams pre-Second World War had enjoyed such a long run of success was testament to the ability of the players, the relative rawness and naivety of foreign opponents, and to the omnipresence of the W-M formation, which meant that England were generally facing teams set up in a familiar manner. In a sense, England in those early decades were akin to a virtuoso orchestra without a conductor and with only one piece of music in front of them. For a time, it was an effective formula. However, no matter how wonderfully they performed, sooner or later their sound would become monotonous, their chosen piece of music out of touch with contemporary trends, and the musicians hopelessly ill-prepared if asked to perform something new.

Rous' selection for the England team's first ever manager was a bold one. The 33-year-old Lancastrian Walter Winterbottom had never held the role of a team manager and had only enjoyed two seasons of professional football with Manchester United before a spinal ailment ended his career. He and Rous had first met on a coaching course run by Jimmy Hogan.[6] During the war, Winterbottom had served with the RAF and excelled in a role that saw him coach physical trainers. It was this experience and passion for instruction that won him the England job. The FA under Rous had attempted to run coaching courses for aspiring trainers and managers in the past, with little success, and Winterbottom's position as manager was concurrent with his job as the FA's Director of Coaching. Winterbottom himself felt the latter responsibility, in which he was far more comfortable and familiar, took precedence above the former, an indication of just how negligible the role of England manager was perceived to be when it was first conceived.

Winterbottom's lack of experience and amenable, genteel personality were also key in leveraging his appointment past the FA's selection committee, and likely satisfying Rous' own aspirations as well. Appointing a more seasoned coach would have risked ceding power to the manager, something neither Rous nor the factions of the FA that he found himself constantly at odds with would tolerate. Winterbottom's age and short playing career would ultimately become two of the chief weapons used to undermine him, not least by his own players, many of whom subscribed to the pre-war opinion that those selected to play for England represented the very cream of the crop, who couldn't be taught anything by even vastly successful managers, let alone one whose playing career had ended almost before it began. Tommy Lawton referred to him disparagingly as 'that PT teacher', while Raich Carter found Winterbottom's training drills juvenile and Matthews felt the man in the managerial role to simply be 'irrelevant'.[7]

At a time when there was little to differentiate managers tactically and England remained blessed with a remarkably skilled group of players, the most productive sort of manager for the national team would have been a rabble-rousing ex-pro, someone who had been there and done it with England and could empathise with his charges, putting an arm around the shoulder of those who needed it and delivering stirring, Churchillian oration to fire his men up before they went into battle. Alas, Winterbottom did not fit this bill, preferring an analytical, didactic approach to coaching which, while forward-looking for the time, found little truck with players who had grown up being told that there was little sophistication or nuance about football. Indeed, the snide, classist assumption that football lacked any academic merit, rooted in the imperial belief in masters and servants had, by the 1940s, infected even the players whose mental capacity it slighted the most.

The other major hindrance to Winterbottom during his long tenure as manager was a caveat inserted by Rous' opponents before he was appointed. Winterbottom would be the manager, in charge of coaching the team for the short moments each season when the squad came together. However, despite Rous lobbying for Winterbottom to be given full control, the FA's selection committee, made up of as many as nine FA officials and club chairmen, would retain control over which players Winterbottom had to work with. At best, Winterbottom could hope for a compromise: he would learn to suggest a team in the full knowledge that it would never pass the selection committee unscathed, on the logic that having been instantly overruled on some players, he stood a better chance of being given more leeway with others.

Even so, Winterbottom would be frequently frustrated by the committee, particularly with their proclivity to effectively blacklist a player if he endured a nervy debut or put in one particularly bad performance, and their selection of players based purely on reputation. He would recall on one occasion, after a spirited debate about which two goalkeepers to select, the committee finally reached their conclusion, at which point he asked who among them had seen either of them play in the flesh. Not a single committee member raised his hand.[8]

The urbane Winterbottom was joined in his low opinion of the committee by the more assertive Rous, who famously denigrated them as a group of 'retired butchers, greengrocers, builders, motor-dealers, brewers and farmers', whose lofty opinions of their own expert knowledge of football were entirely unwarranted.[9]

The arrangement wasn't without precedent. Indeed, many of the chairmen who served on the committee held similar sway over player selection at their clubs. However, it would ultimately prove Winterbottom's most invidious hurdle, as time and again he was forced to change teams for petty or asinine reasons, or to use inferior or ill-suited players, all the while never knowing who he'd have at his disposal the next time the squad was decided. In total, 159 players received their debuts under Winterbottom during his 139 matches in charge, a truly remarkable figure that speaks to the almost unworkable degree of churn he had to deal with.

★ ★ ★

Despite this often-poisonous atmosphere, Winterbottom and his patron Rous could scarcely have asked for a better beginning to England's first managerial experiment. While Britain remained on her knees following the war, the England national team was a picture of health, losing just once in the first eighteen official internationals after football resumed. Winterbottom was helped by the fact that even with the selection committee's endless tinkering, the team remained relatively settled by virtue of a truly remarkable crop of talent that even the most curmudgeonly selector could do little to argue against.

Nowhere was this more evident than when Winterbottom's men travelled to Lisbon in 1947 to play their first ever match against Portugal. The Portuguese were an emerging footballing nation and were enjoying their best run of form in the country's history, having recently beaten France, Spain and Ireland twice. However, at the Estádio Nacional in May, the *Seleção* were given a stinging reminder of just how far they had to progress before they could consider themselves as having joined international football's top table.

England's forward line was simply irresistible. Centre-forward Tommy Lawton netted four times. Not to be outdone, Stan Mortensen, making his debut at inside-right, bagged four of his own. In the other inside-forward position, Wilf Mannion, Middlesbrough's 'golden boy', failed to score but was instrumental in setting up attack after attack. The big revelation, however, came in the wing positions, where Stan Matthews and Tom Finney featured concurrently for the first time. Both nominally right wingers, the two had been interchanged since Finney's debut, but the move to allow Matthews to continue in his usual position with Finney on the left was an epiphany. The 10-0 scoreline was made all the more resounding by the fact that the Portuguese swapped the regulation ball for a smaller, more familiar one at half-time and also made two illegal substitutions as their players succumbed to the sheer elemental power of the English play. It was little surprise that England's shell-shocked opponents chose to forgo the customary post-match banquet.

Better was to come. A year later, England's by now traditional end-of-season tour of the Continent took them to Turin to face Italy, still reigning World Champions by dint of no World Cup having taken place since 1938 and in the process of building a formidable side based upon the remarkable *Il Grande Torino* team. Winterbottom and his players had every reason to anticipate a tough afternoon but could at least take solace in the fact that in the five matches they played in between the Portugal rout and the visit to Italy, they had won four and scored sixteen times. The same five forwards who had torn Portugal to shreds lined up against the Italians, whose reputation as a physically powerful, defensively effective team was etched in stone even then.

It took just 4 minutes for cracks in that facade to appear, however, when England's Blackpool contingent combined to open the scoring. Matthews played in Mortensen, who then drifted towards the touchline. With both his teammates and the opposition expecting a cut back, Mortensen took his chance, rocketing a shot past the near post from an impossibly acute angle. It was the sort of stunning goal that oozed both consummate skill and an irrepressible confidence, and it proved symptomatic of the rest of the match. Though the game was far more even than the Portugal match had been, England's attack, later remembered by Matthews as the best forward line he'd been a part of, remained simply unstoppable. Aided by outstanding performances from goalkeeper Frank Swift and centre-half Neil Franklin, England registered a stunning 4-0 win.

The Italians responded with the same paroxysms of despair as the Portuguese had, firing the head of their football association in response to the defeat. Despite Italy having had numerous good chances, including a goal ruled out for a somewhat dubious offside, the match did much to embolden the opinion among the English FA and press that while technically gifted, teams from abroad simply lacked the requisite thrust in their attacks and shooting ability to conquer England and the other home nations. For all their swift, short passing and meticulous build-up play, they rarely had a player willing to simply blast the ball home as Mortensen had memorably done.

Brian Glanville, writing several years later, supported this thesis, opining that 'the chief difference between Britain and the leading Continental countries was in shooting, an art which no team beyond the British Isles had yet succeeded in mastering. Latins and Central Europeans were alike in their ambition to walk the ball into the goal.'[10] This was, of course, an oversimplification, largely borne of the less direct passing of foreign teams and England's advanced defensive organisation that meant foreign strikers rarely got within shooting distance of the English goal. Nonetheless, it was symptomatic of the sort of misguided reasoning for England's superiority that was ingrained in the national footballing psyche.

Winterbottom's tenure could have scarcely enjoyed a more propitious beginning for all concerned. He had survived with the sword of Damocles suspended above his head, as the selectors and rivals of Rous had looked for any opportunity to brand the implementation of a team manager as a failure. Rous had been vindicated, his first major innovation as FA Secretary, Winterbottom's appointment, apparently paving the way to success in his second, the termination of England's splendid isolation from FIFA and the World Cup. For their part, Winterbottom's and Rous' detractors still found they wielded the power behind the throne, selecting players as they had always done.

★ ★ ★

Above all, England's results had been excellent. Finney would proffer, without a shred of self-aggrandisement, that England's resounding victory over Italy had a 'very good claim to be the highpoint of the English game' beside England's World Cup success in 1966.[11] As remarkable as the Turin triumph was, what was even more stunning was how quickly the England team's fortunes faded from the moment they left the sun-kissed pitch of the Stadio Comunale di Torino to the appreciative applause of the Italian fans.

The first worrisome signs came within twelve months of the signal victory over Italy, as England suffered a 3-1 home defeat to Scotland, only the second time that the noisy neighbours from north of the border had triumphed in England since their famous 5-1 win in 1928 with a team subsequently dubbed the 'Wembley Wizards'. As with the Italy match, the game was closer than the scoreline perhaps suggested, only this time Walter Winterbottom's team were on the wrong end of the good luck, having come up against Scottish goalkeeper James Cowan in inspired form.

However, just one year before there had been a sense that no matter what stood in England's way, attempting to stop the team's forward line was destined to be a doomed enterprise. The sudden evaporation of England's attacking power owed much to the break-up of the group that had decimated Portugal and Italy. The critical loss was of Tommy Lawton, who exited the international stage with a speed nobody could have anticipated, making what proved to be his final England appearance in the match immediately following the famous Italian victory.

Though still just 28 and rapidly closing in on the national team goal-scoring record, Lawton's international career effectively ended when he made a British-record transfer to Notts County of the Third Division. The controversy surrounding the move and the lack of visibility his new club had saw Lawton quickly recede from prominence in the press and the minds of the selectors. Winterbottom, for his part, did not mourn the loss of Lawton as profusely as he could have. The two men had never seen eye to eye, their relationship never truly recovering from Lawton's stinging suggestion that Winterbottom could never hope to improve the players he managed.

In his place came Jackie Milburn who, despite his legendary goal-scoring exploits for Newcastle United would never quite feel comfortable donning the No. 9 shirt of England and would only be awarded thirteen caps across seven years. Wilf Mannion's international career didn't come to quite such a screeching halt, but he had attracted the ire of the English footballing establishment by attempting to force through a transfer away from Middlesbrough in 1948, subsequently missing six months of football while on strike. Though he would appear sporadically for England until 1951, his gradual exclusion by the selectors was heavily influenced by their wish to make an example of Mannion's behaviour.

Beyond the break-up of England's formidable yet fleeting forward line of the immediate post-war years, the more foundational cause for England's sudden mortality was the improvement of their opponents. Though few Continental teams had recovered as quickly as England had following the war, after four years they were ready to ask questions of the game's creators once again.

Years of refinement and developing their own brands of football, combined with decades of English arrogance and complacency (aided and abetted by the weisenheimers in the FA), had meant the gap had closed. Defeat to Scotland didn't illustrate this, but the loss England suffered to Sweden in the next match did so in abundance. Though the leading force in Scandinavian football and winners of the Olympic gold the year before (not that England's impending debut in the coming World Cup had done anything to discourage their antipathy towards any form of championship that didn't involve them), Sweden had posed little opposition to England in the past, conceding four on each of the three previous meetings between the two nations. However, they stunned England 3-1 in Stockholm, a win that owed much to the English influence: the team's coach, George Raynor, was a Yorkshireman, perhaps the ultimate epitome of the nomadic British expat coach of the first half of the twentieth century. His brief, unspectacular playing career in England meant he lacked the reputation and relationships needed to get a foot in the door at English league clubs – coaching ability and ideas simply weren't part of the equation. Abroad, however, it was a different story.

If Winterbottom's ascendancy to the lofty position of England manager seems, by modern standards, unlikely, Raynor must have woken up each day during his three spells in charge of the Swedish national team and pinched himself, wondering how he had ended up in such an illustrious role in Scandinavia after a nondescript coaching career that had previously seen him overseeing Aldershot's reserves. Raynor owed his role with Sweden to Rous, who had spotted him coaching Iraqi players as part of his service during the Second World War and had recommended him when Sweden were seeking a coach. Despite his lack of experience, Rous' word and the cachet of simply being an Englishman who had played professionally were enough to secure Raynor the position.

Energetic, engaging and a passionate advocate for the benefits of coaching, Raynor likely would have endured a similarly fraught and unproductive relationship with the England players as Winterbottom. With Sweden, however, he found a group of men who possessed unquestionable talent (not least the 'Gre-No-Li' triumvirate of Gunnar Gren, Gunnar Nordahl, and Nils Liedholm, all of whom would go on to star in the Italian Serie A) but were unburdened by decades of antipathy towards the concept of coaching. By the time England travelled to the Swedish capital, Raynor had been in his post for the best part of three years, and his coaching methods and infectious enthusiasm had borne fruit. Though Raynor and Winterbottom's teams wouldn't meet again for seven years, their respective careers would dovetail in illuminating fashion in the meantime.

Two games later, in England's first match of the 1949–50 season that would culminate in the World Cup in Brazil, an even more calamitous milestone was reached at Everton's Goodison Park. By 1949, England had played over 100 home internationals, yet remarkably had never been defeated by a team other than Scotland or Wales, with whom enough footballing character and heritage was shared to lessen the blow of the losses. Of those nineteen defeats, the bulk had come against Scotland, and most dated back to a bygone era. By the late 1940s, England had been defeated at home just four times in over twenty years. Even accounting for England's early advantages in international football, it was a remarkable record, and one the country was justifiably proud of.

Few reckoned that unbeaten accolade to be under serious threat, particularly not on a muggy September day in Liverpool, where England faced the Republic of Ireland. It was only the second meeting of the two nations, with England having triumphed 1-0 in Dublin, three years earlier. As they arrived on Merseyside, cheered by thousands of the Irish immigrants who populated the city, the Irish players had plenty of reason for trepidation. Though boasting a majority of Football League-based players, including Manchester United captain Johnny Carey, the Republic's post-war record made for grim reading. They had won only four of their fourteen matches since the end of the war, losing the other ten. They did at least arrive in England on the back of a win, 3-0 over Finland, but their opponents were hardly the toughest of tests; they had not won a game since 1939.

35

The pre-match omens appeared to have been accurate as England came within inches of opening the scoring inside 30 seconds. That set the tone for an almighty barrage, but the longer Ireland held out, the more belief their players seemed to gain. Soon, they were daring to break out in attack whenever they managed to stymie one of England's assaults, and they took the lead in the 32nd minute via a penalty from Aston Villa's Con Martin. Stung into action, England ratcheted up the pressure, hitting the bar and squandering a number of glorious opportunities as Ireland defended manfully. With 5 minutes remaining and every English outfield player pushing forward, Peter Farrell, playing at his home ground, was played through on goal to wrap up an incredible 2-0 victory.

It was a bitter blow. The *Daily Herald*'s Clifford Webb wrote gravely that 'bleak, black history' had been written in the Goodison mud. The *Daily Mirror* worried about how such a feeble display would translate to the upcoming World Cup. *The Times* declared that 'for England this was nothing short of a major disaster and they only have themselves to blame for it'. In the following months, the FA and the press would variously spin the result so as to mask the loss of England's proud record; they now had never lost to a *Continental* foreign team on home soil nor had ever truly lost to a foreign team *at home* because the match had taken place at Goodison, not the veritable fortress that was Wembley's Empire Stadium. Remarkably, others effectively subsumed Ireland into the United Kingdom for the purposes of keeping England's defeats strictly within the confines of the British Isles. Within a matter of a few short months, performing mental gymnastics to retain the sanctity of the English national team's prowess would become an awful lot more difficult.

★ ★ ★

England approached the 1950 World Cup with a mixture of apprehension and self-possession. They would be in uncharted waters, playing their first ever World Cup in the alien climes of Brazil. The Three Lions had never even played a South American nation, let alone travelled to the continent. However, they could seek comfort in the knowledge that the game had been inculcated by British expats in South America just as it had in Continental Europe, leading them to the belief that England would encounter little that was out of the ordinary.

There was also little question that both England and the teams they would be facing still bought into the nation's legendary mythos. Even considering the recent setbacks against Sweden and Ireland, the Portugal and Italy successes were still fresh in the memory, and the bookies considered them favourites for the tournament. Prior to the World Cup team travelling, an England B squad had been sent to tour North America. To the amazement of everyone but his detractors in the FA, Stanley Matthews was chosen to tour with this team as they completed a set of haphazard fixtures (one opposing team arrived with not enough players and were hammered 19-1, despite England loaning them Nat Lofthouse and Tim Ward), rather than for the squad travelling to Brazil. Thanks to the outcry over his exclusion, Matthews was eventually flown to Brazil to link up with the full team, having played several games and travelled thousands of miles with the B team. It was the sort of organisational mishap that jarred with the rarefied air with which many in the FA carried themselves and didn't exactly bode well on the eve of perhaps the stiffest test of England's mettle in their history. There was, at least, some good news from the North American tour – the B team, despite travelling the width of the continent and back again, had comfortably dispatched the ramshackle USA side that would be in England's group in Brazil.

Matthews had fallen out of favour with the selectors following the loss to Scotland, and his repeated omissions were indicative of a changing of the guard in the England team. Having been blessed with several almost undroppable stars in the post-war years, and therefore limited meddling from the selection committee, Winterbottom was now faced with increasing bureaucratic interference on the topic of team selections from men such as Arthur Drewry.

Drewry was one of the few selectors to escape Rous' ire and would eventually rise to the lofty position of President of FIFA, but it wasn't without some raised eyebrows that a man who had made his money as a fishmonger and who chaired a Grimsby team that would end the following season dead last in the Second Division was presiding over critical decisions at England's first ever World Cup. With the generation of players who'd established themselves before 1939 being phased out, England's teams now took on a far less-settled appearance.

Of the twenty-one-man squad chosen to travel to Brazil, only six had more than fifteen caps to their name (including Matthews, whose last-minute inclusion came too late for him to play in England's first match). Five players had five appearances or fewer, and another five had never played for their country.

Some omissions, however, couldn't be helped. Mere months before the World Cup, Neil Franklin, the experienced centre-half rated by many of his contemporaries as the best England possessed, had stunned the footballing world by walking out on Stoke City and joining Bogotá in Colombia. A rebel association that paid no heed to existing contracts, Colombia had been banished by FIFA and the transfer brought an even more decisive end to Franklin's international career than Lawton's shock decision to drop down two divisions.

Franklin's move was motivated by the lucrative wages he was promised (he once told Finney that their clubs were 'taking fortunes off people who want to see us play. We should be getting more of that money. It's a scandal.'),[12] and the FA's selectors saw no option but to severely punish such a transgression against the system of indentured servitude that the English game was built upon. Even after returning to England after less than two months, disillusioned with life in South America, Franklin would never again pull on the white shirt of England, and the remainder of his career was spent languishing in the lower divisions. As was the case with Lawton's vacated centre-forward position, the loss of Franklin as the pivotal central defender in the back three would bedevil Winterbottom and the selectors for years to come.

There were still, however, plenty of sources for optimism in the England ranks. Finney, Mannion and Mortensen, who had recorded a remarkable nineteen goals in eighteen matches, all remained in the frame. At the back was Spurs' cerebral, set-piece specialising defender, Alf Ramsey. Further ahead was Wolves' domineering half-back and team captain Billy Wright, who would receive a record thirtieth consecutive cap and extend his streak of playing in every single Winterbottom side in England's first game of the competition against Chile. Wolves' status as a rising force in the English game under the tutelage of Stan Cullis, who liked his teams to play in a relentless attacking style, saw both goalkeeper Bert Williams and outside left Jimmy Mullen also come into the team, the latter in place of Matthews.

Things got off to a promising start in Brazil, as England produced a competent, if unspectacular, 2-0 win against Chile, the first South American nation they had ever faced. Next was the USA, participating in their third World Cup. Despite this experience, and almost having caused an upset in their first match against Spain, when they had clung desperately to a 1-0 lead until Spain netted three times in the final 10 minutes, England were overwhelming favourites. In an era when vastly lopsided scores were commonplace in such an international competition (Group F was decided by a single match between Uruguay and

Bolivia, which the former won 8-0), there was no greater mismatch than that between the USA and England. The USA were fielding a team cobbled together with journeymen semi-pro players, three of whom weren't even US citizens, with virtually no experience of playing together. So dim were the USA's prospects that just a single member of the American press made the long trip to Belo Horizonte. Bill Jeffrey, the US coach, said before the match that his team were 'sheep ready to be slaughtered',[13] apparently without any hidden agenda of trying to inspire his charges.

If the Sweden and Ireland defeats had slowed the momentum of Winterbottom's England, what happened next brought it to a screeching halt. England, still without Matthews after Drewry had overruled Rous and Winterbottom and elected to field an unchanged team, had rarely enjoyed such overwhelming domination of a match, but it was all for naught.

Despite rattling the woodwork on numerous occasions, bringing a series of outstanding stops from US keeper Frank Borghi and spurning countless gilt-edged chances, England simply couldn't find a way past virtually the same US team that had been comfortably seen off by the touring England B team just ten days before. So remarkable was England's profligacy that there was a degree of inevitability about the goal scored by Haitian-born Joe Gaetjens with one of the USA's only forays forward just before half-time. The second half continued in much the same vein, with England laying siege to Borghi's goal, yet contriving to miss chance after chance. By the time Italian referee Generoso Dattilo blew the full-time whistle, England were resigned to the most extraordinary of defeats.

The *Guardian* called it 'probably the worst display ever by an England side', while the *Daily Herald*'s Clifford Webb deemed it the 'biggest shock in the history of international football'. So dumbfounded by the display was Winterbottom that he hosted a special demonstration upon the team's return to British shores for members of the FA, to illustrate the sheer improbability of contriving to miss so many chances. Winterbottom wasn't laying the blame at the door of specific players, but rather attempting to show that England had come undone thanks to nothing more insidious than a streak of incredibly bad luck.

Though Winterbottom was acting understandably out of an instinct of self-preservation, his demonstrative excuses for England's shortcomings were emblematic of the proclivity for shirking responsibility that ran right through English football. It was these types of excuses that would ultimately prove the national team's undoing. Defender Bill Eckersley offered a more laconic explanation for England's failures, commenting, 'The only reason we lost was that the other teams scored more goals than we did.'[14]

England still had the opportunity to keep their tournament alive with victory over Spain, but even the return of Matthews to the team couldn't inspire England. Spain had both luck and some highly dubious refereeing decisions on their side as they won 1-0 and brought England's South American adventure to a premature end.

★ ★ ★

It was a watershed moment in the history of English football, but only in retrospect. The ignominious exit from the country's first World Cup and the startling lack of preparation evinced by Matthews' hasty spiriting down to Brazil ought to have been sufficient to wake the FA and the national team from their stupor. However, several factors meant that what should have been a great epiphany about how the England team was being run would actually prove to be a grave missed opportunity.

Firstly, technology and travel at the time meant that the embarrassment at the World Cup, and the USA match in particular, received far less coverage than games at home would have. Limited members of the Fleet Street press had made the arduous trip across the Atlantic, and a famous tale alleges that when the US result was wired home, some writers believed it to be a typo, with England presumably having won either 10-0 or a more modest 10-1. What's more, at a time when football still jostled with cricket for supremacy as England's premier sport, particularly among the middle classes who wrote the newspapers, the England cricket team had suffered an equally shocking home series defeat to the West Indies.

The cricket team, arguably a more potent symbol of Britain's imperial might than the football team at that point, naturally attracted the greater headlines (the *Daily Herald*'s headline was 'England lose by one goal and 326 runs'.) Nonetheless, the press the team did receive was damning. The *Daily Herald*'s Clifford Webb called the episode the 'blackest chapter in England's football history', while in the *Daily Mirror*, John Thompson railed against the 'smug[ness]' which had led England to not bother to arrive in Brazil until the last minute and then find themselves 'outstripped – both in football ideas and in technical ability' on the pitch.

Another element that helped to spare England's blushes was, ironically, the fact that they had been defeated by, of all countries, the USA. Had England fallen to somewhat stronger opposition, there would have been a greater acceptance that England's reign as Europe's supreme footballing force was under considerable threat. Instead, it was so inconceivable that the might of England had succumbed to a rag-tag group of semi-professional players that there was nothing to do but chalk the whole misadventure in Brazil up as ill-fated from the beginning, with the mitigating factors of travel, unfamiliar food and an alien climate meaning that there were no important or lasting insights to be gleaned from a period of introspection. It was a fanciful conclusion that all involved would soon come to rue.

4

THE YOUNG
PRETENDERS

The British Empire entered the twentieth century with an unbridled faith that while other rival superpowers may have been on the rise, Britain remained as untrammelled as ever. The same could not be said for the grand old Habsburg Empire.

The British Empire was a veritable industrial machine, keeping its subjects and interests in line with a ruthless, mechanical precision. The Habsburg Empire, meanwhile, which in 1900 comprised vast swathes of modern-day Austria, Hungary, Czech Republic, Croatia, Slovakia, Slovenia, Romania, Bosnia, Ukraine and Poland, was an antiquated relic, creaking worryingly as it attempted to combine mothballed ancient traditions with a heady mix of ethnicities, religions and nationalities. In the late 1800s, the Austrian Chancellor had described the key to managing the empire as a matter of 'preserving all the nationalities of the Monarchy in a state of balanced and well-modulated discontent'.[1] In fact, by the twentieth century, even the Habsburg name was an anachronism; the empire had, since 1867, been officially known as the Austro-Hungarian Empire, a compromise designed to keep the upstart latter nation in check.

Hungary had, up to that point, been one of the more unlikely thorns in the Habsburg side. A predominantly agricultural nation, Hungary had risen up against their colonial overlords in the 1840s, and only an intervention by Russia had prevented independence. It would not be the last time that Russia and Hungary would be involved in such a bloody skirmish.

By the time of the 1867 Compromise, Hungary was primed and ready to demonstrate its worth to the wider world beyond the suffocating confines of the empire. Hungarian inventors were responsible for the Rubik's Cube, the soda fountain, the Biro pen and a type of lightbulb. Franz Liszt composed some of the century's most influential music. And in Budapest, Hungary's capital city, they had a metropole that was soon to become the envy of the rest of the world. By 1914, the city would boast a population of 1 million people and iconic architecture including the Parliament Building, Europe's largest stock exchange and countless Gothic and Baroque churches, not to mention numerous bridges spanning the glittering expanse of the Danube, which swept through the heart of the city.

The Parliament Building had been based on London's Palace of Westminster, a fitting tribute, given the two-chamber structure of the Hungarian Parliament owed a debt to Britain's House of Commons and House of Lords. These were far from the only examples of Hungary borrowing from Britain. Like the rest of the globe, by the mid-1800s Budapest was taking cues from London in countless ways. British engineers, fresh from helping to eradicate cholera at home, arrived to advise and aid in the construction of a modern drainage system. Railways suddenly meant that produce from the Hungarian plains could now be exported abroad. Numerous buildings were based upon the designs of British architects. Without British inventions and interventions, it's hard to imagine Hungary finding the gumption to rise up against Habsburg rule.

The Hungarian love affair with Britain did not end with civic infrastructure. As was common during the late Victorian period, the three-quarters of the world not subsumed into the British Empire viewed trends and fads emanating from London as the height of sophistication and sought to mimic them. One such example was the sport which had swept Britain and was, by the early 1900s, staking a claim as England's most popular pastime.

The metropolitan elites of Budapest and Vienna took to football with a fervour that was sorely lacking in the upper classes of England, where the game's popularity among the working classes tainted it in the eyes of the upper crust. Budapest, famed as a melting-pot city, with countless ethnicities and religions living within close quarters, found in football a language that all its diverse citizens could understand. Though the game became rampantly popular among the Hungarian working classes, thanks to its simplicity and lack of costly equipment, the middle classes, unlike many of their British equivalents, retained their interest in the game. What followed was a 'coffee house culture', with Budapest's famed cafés soon hosting impassioned debates about players, styles and tactics. This ongoing intellectual inquisitiveness about the sport in Eastern Europe contrasted with the British belief that the game had been effectively perfected as soon as the rules were codified and represented one of the first major divergences in football's genealogical pool.

A greater willingness to learn was all well and good, but it would take years to bear fruit. In the meantime, Hungary would receive some harsh lessons. England's 7-0 win in Budapest on their first foreign tour in 1908 remains the Hungarian national team's joint-heaviest defeat. They lost by the same scoreline to Great Britain in their first taste of competitive tournament football in the 1912 Olympics. However, among these defeats was incontrovertible proof that a bright future lay ahead for the national team as a result of Hungary's early and fanatical adoption of the game. They shared a tumultuous rivalry with Austria, routinely beat both Bohemia and Germany, and enjoyed resounding victories against a number of other European teams. They won the Olympic consolation tournament following their defeat to Britain and, a week later, played two games in Moscow against the Russian team, who they hammered 12-0 and 9-0.

While Hungary's national team showcased the country's natural aptitude and enthusiasm for the sport, it was at club level where the next evolutionary step would occur. With the English league system scarcely two decades old, it was already set in its ways to such an extent that an intrepid band of British football missionaries felt they had to travel abroad in order to have their voices heard. Hungary was one of the countries that embraced such figures, whose belief in the power of coaching and tactics meant they could offer much to the nascent football culture.

One such figure was John Tait Robertson, a Scotland international who enjoyed a successful career before moving into management, first with Chelsea, then with Glossop. He was hired to manage Magyar Testgyakorlók Köre (MTK), and though his stay was brief, the coaching foundations he laid, with an emphasis upon the Scottish short-passing style as opposed to the more direct English model, led MTK to a league and cup double.

Without doubt, the most influential visitor from the British Isles, however, was Jimmy Hogan. Hogan's desire to coach abroad had been fired by his experience on a tour of the Netherlands with Bolton Wanderers. Seeing that the locals' enthusiasm for the game remained undimmed despite their obvious disorganisation compared to English teams, Hogan vowed to return to show them how to play. What followed was a peripatetic tour across Europe, during which time Hogan established himself as British football's most devoted apostle and, in the words of Jonathan Wilson, 'arguably the most influential coach of all time'.[2]

Hogan would take over MTK shortly after Robertson had departed and oversaw the most sustained period of success in the club's history, as his focus on organisation and football theory gave his charges an enormous advantage. His achievements with MTK also saw him tasked with taking charge of the Hungarian national team on a sporadic basis.[3] Between MTK and the national team, Hogan laid the groundwork of Hungary's footballing identity.

Ironically, despite Hogan's roots, it was his intervention that drove an ideological wedge between his native British (and specifically English) football and that of his adopted homes. He impressed upon both Hungary and Austria his philosophy of winning through holding possession and passing the ball, starving the opposition of opportunities to create chances of their own, rather than risk ceding possession with long, direct passes.

English football, meanwhile, was wrestling with the greatest tactical disruption the sport had yet faced. In 1925, FIFA, under pressure from the English FA, who feared a decline in goals would soon hit them and their clubs in the pocket as bored crowds turned to other leisure pursuits, altered the offside rule. English football soon adjusted, introducing an extra defender to help compensate for the greater freedom forwards now had, a development decried as representing a shift away from entertainment and into a results-first business. Hungary, meanwhile, saw no reason to recalibrate.

The less-pragmatic path proved no less profitable. Throughout the 1920s and 1930s, they continued to develop as an international force, benefiting from frequent matches in competitions such as the Central European International Cup, which forced Hungary to keep pace with the rest of the Continent as it collectively emerged from the long shadow cast by the British teams.

Football was blossoming across Europe, as was its cultural cachet; nations now looked to their football teams for matters of national pride that far outweighed the actions of the eleven men on the pitch. For Hungary, proof of their strength and virility as a nation had taken on an entirely new level of importance following the First World War. Inexorably dragged into the conflict by virtue of their coupling with Austria and alliance with Germany, Hungary emerged from the war defeated and chastened having, in the words of historian Norman Stone, come 'off worst of all the defeated Central Powers'.[4] In total, Hungary lost two-thirds of its territory and more than

50 per cent of its pre-war population. To compound matters, there were military restrictions and astronomical reparations demanded, leading to hyperinflation and the nation becoming the most indebted in Europe as they sought to rebuild.[5] It was a dramatic fall from grace for the newly independent country, and into the void, acting as a beacon of nationalist price, came football.

In May 1934, Hungary took on England for the first time since 1909, amid incredible excitement, and beat them 2-1 in front of more than 30,000 in Budapest. Later that same month, Hungary defeated Egypt in the Magyars' first-ever World Cup tie, before narrowly losing to Austria in the quarter-finals. Four years later, in Paris, they exceeded that achievement, reaching the World Cup final, where they suffered a noble defeat against reigning champions Italy amid rampant speculation that Benito Mussolini had strong-armed Hungarian Regent Miklós Horthy into letting Italy win 'for the good of fascism'.[6]

Though many of the team, which included stars such as György Sárosi, Pál Titkos, and Gyula Lázár, would see their international careers curtailed by the Second World War, the legacy of the class of 1938 would be immeasurable. For football-obsessed youngsters across the country, the national team had, by reaching the very pinnacle of the international game, brought to life and made flesh the stories of Hungary's past glories, her former role as global kingmaker within a vast empire. The synaptic connection being made across the country, as the eleven Hungarian players walked out onto the pitch of the Stade Olympique de Colombes, was clear – football equalled glory.

★ ★ ★

In 1948, the job of marshalling the generation of players who had been inspired by the heroics at the World Cup a decade before fell partially to Gusztáv Sebes. On paper, Sebes appeared to be a somewhat unlikely candidate for involvement in the three-man committee charged with running the team. There were plenty of other coaches who had garnered greater managerial experience and enjoyed more successful careers. MTK's coach Márton Bukovi had managed abroad and achieved famous victories over illustrious opponents such as Liverpool in exhibition games. Béla Guttmann, who managed both Újpest and Kispest immediately following the war, would later go on to coach Benfica, who he led to two successive European Cups before leaving under a cloud and infamously cursing the club, vowing they would never again win European silverware (a curse which, despite Benfica subsequently reaching eight European finals, has held true).

However, both Bukovi and Guttmann's success and reputations counted against them when it came to the national team. Bukovi could be blunt and was tactically innovative; he would not stand to be told what to do or how to deploy a team under his command by any external party. Guttmann was a combustible character, managing no fewer than twenty-five separate managerial spells in his forty-year career as a coach, and rarely lasting longer than two years at a single club. He would famously claim that spending more than two seasons in a single job was incompatible with success – not that he always had a say in the manner or timing of his departure from some of his clubs.

What the ruminative, inscrutable Sebes had in his favour was less tangible than supreme coaching credentials or a glittering trophy cabinet from his playing days. The son of a cobbler, his modest playing career had been punctuated by a spell in France where, as well as playing for a factory team, he had been a prominent trade unionist while working as a fitter in a Renault factory. Throughout his life, he had held strident communist views and, as a result of his unionism in Paris, had developed outstanding diplomatic skills. He was able to read a room and know when to pull back in negotiations – and when to push forward. Ordinarily, these skills would have positioned an intelligent, hardworking man like Sebes ideally for a role in politics, not football. Fortunately for him, however, the two were becoming less and less distinguishable from one another in post-war Hungary.

If the First World War had dealt a catastrophic blow to Hungary, the Second World War threatened to prove fatal. The country had attempted to walk the vanishingly thin line between the warring sides and remain above the fray, before eventually siding with Germany when promised a restoration of much of the territory lost in the wake of the earlier conflict. Hungarian Prime Minister Pál Teleki was so distressed by this development that he wrote, 'We have become breakers of our word … [and] taken the side of scoundrels', before shooting himself.[7]

For a time, it appeared that Hungary had elected to join the winning side, but when Hitler decided to renege on his pact of non-aggression with the Soviet Union, the war took a decisive turn. As the tide began to shift, Hungary's support of Germany wavered, and eventually, in 1944, Hitler had had enough of their prevarications. Germany invaded, and Hungary endured a months-long occupation, during which German troops began viciously implementing the Final Solution upon the country's sizeable Jewish population.

Hungary was then the stage for a brutal siege, as the Red Army took Budapest by force, at the cost of some 160,000 lives (including 40,000 civilians). Every bridge crossing the Danube was destroyed, water and electricity supplies were cut, buildings were levelled. Those that remained standing were in varying states of disrepair, including several that had German gliders, crashed after failed missions to resupply the besieged troops, embedded high in their walls.[8]

Following the Allied victory, the destiny of Hungary was intended to be handled by both the Soviets and the UK, but backroom geopolitical machinations meant that it ultimately fell solely into Russia's sphere of influence. In the months that followed, the Soviets aimed to keep up appearances by holding ostensibly free (yet, behind the scenes, heavily meddled with) elections in the hope that the Hungarian people would opt for Soviet-style communism of their own volition. For the Hungarian people, the situation bore a grim resemblance to what had happened after the First World War. Instead of reparations, the country had to contend with the rapacious Red Army, who consumed huge quantities of the country's already-meagre supplies, raping and pillaging as they went. It wasn't long before the country was once again gripped by severe hyperinflation, with the Hungarian mint producing notes equivalent to 100 quintillion pengő before the currency was completely abandoned in favour of a new one, the forint.

Despite their best attempts to convince the Hungarian people that all of the ills befalling them and their country could be resolved if only they embraced communism, by 1947 patience in the Kremlin was running thin. The elections had not yielded the victory for the Soviet-backed parties that the USSR had desperately hoped for in order to vindicate their claims of democratic expansion. Several prominent Hungarian communists, chief among them Mátyás Rákosi, who had spent fifteen years in prison for attempting to organise a Hungarian Communist Party in the 1920s, began to turn the screw. Legitimate members of the presiding Smallholders government were forced out and replaced with men more willing to bend to the wishes of Moscow and Hungary's Muscovite communists. Any pretence of democracy was cast aside in exchange for Rákosi's strong-arm 'salami' tactics.[9] Never was this more evident than when Rákosi forced the resignation of Prime Minister Ferenc Nagy by threatening to kidnap Nagy's son while the minister was out of the country.

Over the next few years, Rákosi took complete control of the country, with his dictatorship coming to mirror the worst excesses of other Soviet satellites, rigging elections (the Rákosi-led coalition of parties won a somewhat suspicious 96 per cent of the vote in 1949),[10] conducting farcical show trials, incessantly warring with rivals for power and enforcing collectivism on the country, no matter the cost. Independent farmers were placed into collective groups in an attempt to regulate food production, a move which ultimately achieved the opposite by forcing out effective farmers and leading to widespread food shortages. By 1953, only a quarter of Hungary's rich arable land was in use.[11]

This chaos and poverty was underscored by an omnipresent fear. In total, Rákosi's government is suspected of having imprisoned more than 300,000 opponents (more imagined than real) and having been responsible for thousands of deaths. A popular joke at the time darkly commented that Rákosi's Hungary had three classes – those who had been in prison, those who were in prison and those who would soon be in prison.[12]

As a government who took their cues directly from Joseph Stalin's example, Rákosi's regime sought to achieve absolute control over how they and the country were perceived. While the fascist regimes of pre-war Italy and Germany had whipped up nationalistic fervour, Rákosi instead aimed to tamp it down, fearing that excessive pride among Hungarian people was a threat to his autocracy, particularly following Yugoslavia rising up against the Soviet Union. Future goalkeeper Gyula Grosics described life in Hungary at the time as living 'under a very radical regime that used many weapons, including intimidation, to impose its vision. It included attempting to undermine our national identity and our sense of ourselves.'[13]

★ ★ ★

In centuries past, nations had sought to prove the superiority of their people and ruling ideologies through displays of brute force on the battlefield. The nuclear age, however, had already changed that. Though the phrase 'mutually assured destruction' wouldn't be coined until 1962, the logic behind it had been crystalised as soon as the Soviet Union detonated their first atomic bomb in 1949, far sooner than commentators in the West had felt possible. After dropping the bombs on Hiroshima and Nagasaki, the USA and its allies had enjoyed almost unmitigated power. When the Soviets achieved parity, the world was plunged into a terrifying nuclear stalemate.

With the cataclysmic, worldwide conflict that the twentieth century had already twice borne witness to now rendered an exercise in self-destructive lunacy, both the USA and the Soviets were awakened to a new type of warfare. The Cold War would be fought with weapons in Korea and Vietnam, but it was just as much a battle of soft power. Both sides were utterly convinced of the righteousness of their cause and the immoral evil of their opponents, and both now looked to the burgeoning new aspects of culture as areas in which to hammer home their positions.

One of the key battlegrounds was sport. For millennia, sporting conflict has been used as a proxy for war, recognised as a way of enabling one person, team or nation to prove their superiority over an opponent without necessarily resorting to bloodshed. The Ancient Olympics, though only contested between Greeks, were still imbued with political import due to athletes representing different city-states, which were frequently at war with one another. One competitor, Sotades, was said to have switched allegiance from one tournament to the next after receiving a bribe, such was his new state's eagerness to harness his abilities to further their claim of greatness. In more recent times, as international travel had become increasingly straightforward, sport's role as a weapon of foreign policy had taken on a greater importance.

The controversial 'bodyline' Ashes cricket series of 1932–33 led to so much ill feeling between Australia and England about the latter's perceived overly aggressive and unsporting tactics that it put significant strain on relations between the countries. Trade between the two suffered, and a statue of Prince Albert in Sydney was vandalised and had its ear knocked off. It took their combined efforts in the Second World War to reunite the two cousin nations.

Even more infamously, Adolf Hitler used the 1936 Olympic Games in Berlin to showcase both the might and splendour of the German nation – and his insidious views on racial supremacy, as he barred Jewish athletes from representing the home country. Hitler's use of sport as propaganda would backfire in humiliating fashion, first, when Jesse Owens won gold at the games, and two years later, when African-American boxer Joe Louis despatched German fighter Max Schmeling in the World Heavyweight Championship, shattering the Nazi belief that the result was preordained thanks to Schmeling's Aryan superiority.

The USA and the Soviets were no different in recognising sport's importance. Under Stalin's rule, the Soviet Union conducted huge, bombastic 'sport parades' designed to showcase the communist supermen and women to the masses. The Soviets didn't participate in the 1948 Olympics, instead choosing to send observers to the London games to head off any possibility of embarrassment in future games. They would finish second to the USA in 1952 and would gain the most medals in the next four games.

Two of the climactic Cold War battles between the USA and the Soviet Union came via sport. The first took place on ice, when a team of US amateurs miraculously beat the full Soviet team in ice hockey, just about the only team sport that both countries could claim to have a shared passion for, at the 1980 Winter Olympics. The second came on the chess board, when Bobby Fischer defeated Russian Boris Spassky in the 1972 World Championships in a contest dubbed 'The Match of the Century'. Another Soviet chess grandmaster, Garry Kasparov, would later call Spassky's defeat 'a crushing moment' for the Soviet cause.[14] American muscle had triumphed over Russian brawn; American mind had won out against Russian brainpower.

Football was not immune to such political influence. The 1934 World Cup in Italy was, like the Berlin Olympics, used by Benito Mussolini as a showcase for the political superiority of fascism. Mussolini ensured that the games were not only a showcase of fascism's organisation, but a sporting demonstration too, as he allegedly intervened to guarantee that eventual champions Italy received favourable referees for their games. After Italy won the competition again in 1938, once again under a cloud of suspicion about off-field influences, Mussolini's press officer made clear the connection between football and the destiny-driven nationalism of Mussolini's regime: Italians 'shook and still shake with joy when seeing these thoroughbred athletes, that overwhelm so many noble opponents, such a symbol of the overwhelming march of Mussolini's Italians'.[15]

In the same year, England played their notorious match against Germany before which they delivered the one-armed fascist salute. The FA and Foreign Office agreed that the salute would be appropriate as a show of appeasement, even as the players themselves resisted (one, Bert Sproston, told Stan Matthews that Hitler was 'an evil little twat')[16] and the spectre of Continental war loomed ever closer. It remains one of the most egregious episodes in the history of the England national team.

After the war ended, and as the Iron Curtain descended over Eastern Europe, a travelling Dynamo Moscow team arrived in Britain for a brief tour, leading to what Brian Glanville described as a 'national frenzy' on a scale never aroused before.[17] Dynamo wasted no time in delineating the contrast between their style and that of the British teams. Coach Mikhail Yakushin explained that 'the principle of collective play is the guiding one in Soviet football' and committed a cardinal sin when he declared that Stanley Matthews' individualism would have made him incompatible with the Dynamo team.[18]

The visitors drew with Chelsea and crushed Cardiff before defeating a heavily reinforced Arsenal team featuring Matthews and Stan Mortensen, before finally being held by Rangers. Dynamo returned home triumphant and were the subjects of a Russian musical comedy which held them up as incorruptible heroes laying bare the decadence of the West.[19]

Back in Britain, the excitement surrounding the tour had been replaced with bitterness, with the British feeling that Dynamo had been an international-strength side in disguise and had benefited from some highly dubious refereeing. Dynamo, meanwhile, argued that they'd been afforded inadequate accommodation and the Arsenal game, with Matthews and Mortensen as ringers, had effectively featured an England XI. For George Orwell, the tour's potency as a propaganda weapon was obvious, and potentially disastrous: 'Sport is an unfailing cause of ill-will, and that if such a visit as this had any effect at all on Anglo-Soviet relations, it could be to make them worse than before.'[20]

★ ★ ★

Rákosi's regime, following the Kremlin's lead, was acutely aware of sport's potency as a tool of propaganda and persuasion. Football was, by a distance, Hungary's favourite sport, and by 1949, with Rákosi in full charge of the country, it was becoming clear that the generation of players coming of age together were capable of more than just providing a useful distraction to the Hungarian people; they could help to demonstrate, on an international stage, that the communist system produced the most virile, athletic, exciting football players. As Grosics stated, 'The state was very keen to push sport as a way of advertising to the world the success of the communist system, and the emergence of the Golden Squad was a part of that.'[21]

Sebes' communist credentials positioned him perfectly in Hungary's new political climate. In 1948, he was appointed head of a three-man coaching committee charged with managing the national team's affairs, and he also chaired the country's Olympic Committee. When he oversaw Hungary's fourth-placed finish at the London Olympics that same year, it enhanced his reputation in the eyes of Rákosi's government and lent further credence to the importance (and, for the government's means, usefulness) of sport to the Hungarian nation.

The team that Sebes' committee inherited in 1948 were already showing signs that they were capable of elevating Hungary's respectable standing in international football. The first indication had come in Hungary's first two post-war games, a double header against fierce rivals Austria over the space of two days in August 1945. The games took place in a Budapest that had been shattered by the war and occupation by first the Germans, then the Soviets. The players were eager to participate not simply for prestige and pride, but because playing meant they were guaranteed room and board for a week.

Hungary won both games, and one of those players so eager to secure a roof over his head was an 18-year-old debutant named Ferenc Puskás. Over the next decade, the stocky, domineering forward would become perhaps Hungary's greatest living hero.

From those two signal victories, Hungary would go from strength to strength. Between 1945 and when Sebes' committee assumed the management of the team in 1948, the only teams to beat Hungary were Austria and Italy, while the Magyars registered huge wins against the likes of Romania, Luxembourg and Bulgaria. In 1947, the bulk of their fixtures were in the Balkan and Central European Competition, which they won comfortably with a perfect record in their four matches.

These were their final games under coach Tibor Gallowich, to whom Sebes was an assistant. Gallowich had overseen an infusion of new talent into the team, including the eccentric, yet brilliant goalkeeper Gyula Grosics and Puskás' childhood best friend, half-back József Bozsik, as well as giving a bit part role to the versatile, cultured forward, Nándor Hidegkuti. After Gallowich's departure from the role in early 1948, the Sebes-led committee took over the team.

While this socialist approach to team management was in keeping with the political milieu enveloping Hungary, it quickly became evident that having three men managing the team wasn't conducive to success. There were high points, including a 9-0 demolition of Romania and a 6-2 rout of Poland in front of 40,000 in Warsaw, but the Hungarians narrowly scraped past a weak Czechoslovakian team, drew with Albania and, most damagingly, lost to an unremarkable Bulgarian team in November. By that point, the management committee, despite consisting of three close friends in Sebes and coaches Gábor

Kléber and Béla Mandik, had succumbed to arguments and disagreements about the best way to set up the team.

The Bulgaria loss was the final straw. All three men resigned their posts and Sebes' political manoeuvring ensured he was reappointed as the sole man in charge at the beginning of 1949. With Rákosi's communists on the verge of taking complete control of the country, the abandonment of the collective approach to managing the national team was a reminder that although the Magyars would become a critical tool in the promotion of communist ideology in Hungary and beyond, their success was owed to a decidedly less egalitarian approach.

Though he was a committed communist, Sebes was also a pragmatic and wily operator. He had made a compelling case that attempting to make joint decisions in charge of the national team was folly; ultimately, in order to make progress, the team would need to dance to a single tune. Now he had sole command, the next stage in his plan would involve exploiting the newly implemented communist framework to begin building a formidable team.

★ ★ ★

In 1947, Hungary had lost 3-2 in Turin to Vittorio Pozzo's Italy in a match that has gone down in the annals as one of the most unique in international football history – not for the scoreline, but for the team selection. Despite Italy suffering indifferent form since the resumption of international football following the war (including their humbling against England in Turin), there was something special happening behind the scenes, in large part thanks to another Hungarian, Torino technical director Ernő Erbstein.

Under his direction, Torino had built one of the most remarkable teams European football had ever known, an all-Italian machine known as *Il Grande Torino*. Torino won the first four Serie A championships after the Second World War, and their success was simply impossible to ignore for the national team. The match against Hungary represented the apex of Torino's contribution to the *Azzurri*, with every single outfield player being drawn from the Turin club. In an age when national teams had even less time to practise with one another than they do in the modern era, Italy benefited enormously from having a core of players who were not only exceptional individuals but had the opportunity to hone their chemistry by playing, week in, week out with one another.

As well as Pozzo, Sebes was also inspired by the work of Hugo Meisl and his Austrian *Wunderteam* of the 1930s, which had relied on players drawn from Austria Wien and a small number of neighbouring clubs and had reaped the rewards of the team's enhanced familiarity within the squad. Sebes made the idea of following these teams' example central to his plan for the Hungarian national team. In a cruel twist of fate, just as Sebes was launching his project of emulating *Il Grande Torino*, their time as a team was cut tragically short, as almost all the players and Erbstein perished in a plane crash on their return from an exhibition match against Benfica on 4 May 1949.

In the management committee's final game in charge, the chastening defeat to Bulgaria, the Hungary team had consisted of players from no fewer than six different clubs. Sebes sought to address this immediately, and it wasn't long before his political instincts alerted him to the perfect opportunity. As part of the communist policy of nationalisation, MTK were swiftly taken over by the secret police.

With one of Hungary's biggest teams already spoken for, the natural choice for Sebes' proving ground seemed to be Ferencváros, at that point Hungary's most successful club. However, the club had long been associated with right-leaning tendencies, putting them at odds with Rákosi and the Hungarian Working People's Party. At one stage, the Hungarian authorities attempted to ban Ferencváros from playing altogether, so fervent were the suspicions that the club was becoming a hive of anti-communist sentiment. They were eventually forced to change their name, abandon the traditional green strip and was barred from playing at home, after one too many matches saw their supporters exploit their anonymity to voice their anti-Soviet feelings.

Sebes instead turned his attention to Kispest. In late 1949, the club from the outskirts of Budapest was taken over by the Ministry of Defence and became the team of the army, renamed Honvéd, 'Defenders of the Homeland'. The name may have begun as a reference to the armed forces, but over the coming years, it would come to take on another meaning as Honvéd began supplying the lifeblood of the national team.

While Honvéd lacked the profile and prestige of MTK or Ferencváros, the fact that it was a traditionally smaller club wasn't without advantages. A relative paucity of supporters made them more malleable and meant little opposition to Sebes implementing his plans. Not that Honvéd or their coach, Ferenc Puskás Senior, were likely to have complained. Now, as the team of the army, Sebes could conscript anyone eligible for national service and give them the choice of serving their time as a member of the Honvéd team or wasting years of their career in a desolate border post. As hard as some players found it to leave their boyhood clubs, taking the Honvéd option wasn't a difficult choice. The extraordinary powers that Sebes wielded were akin to giving a child free rein in a sweet shop.

There were two other critical reasons for Honvéd's selection as Sebes' proving ground: József Bozsik and Ferenc Puskás. Lifelong friends, these two were destined to carry their playing partnership from the dusty scraps of vacant land, known as *grunds*, dotted around Kispest, to the very peak of the sport.

The relationship between Puskás and Bozsik was the sort of unlikely friendship that can only find root in childhood. The two were near polar opposites in terms of personality. Puskás was a natural leader, possessing unshakeable self-confidence, twinned with arrogance, humour, fearlessness and, of course, the footballing ability to lead by example. He was fiercely loyal to his teammates and would never fail to come to their aid, on and off the field, as he did in one early match when Bozsik succumbed to a fit of pique after being kicked one too many times and threatened to simply walk off, only for Puskás to talk him around.

This episode, however, was an exception. Unless suffering from the untoward attentions of an opponent, Bozsik was far more reserved, despite being a year and a half older than his bolshy comrade. Given the amount of time the two spent together, it's entirely possible that Bozsik simply got used to his friend doing enough talking for the pair of them. They were next-door neighbours as children and had developed a system of wall knocking to let the other know when they wanted to play a quick game, which was practically every day. The two developed such a passion for football that, by the time they were juniors for the Kispest youth team, watching the first team play at home was no longer enough, and they regularly resorted to donning their tracksuits and attempting to sneak into grounds to watch away matches, once going so far as to dig their way under a perimeter fence to get in.

Football made the trials of life in occupied Hungary bearable. First the Nazis, then the Soviets brought terror during their occupations. Long queues to get even the most basic of commodities were commonplace. Puskás remembered emerging from the cellar where he hid to escape the fighting and running straight to a football pitch after the German forces had been driven out of Budapest.

By the time the war was over, both Puskás and Bozsik had already made their debuts for Kispest. While it was the former's prolific goal-scoring from the inside-forward position that immediately attracted attention, Bozsik was already displaying an unflappable control of the centre of the pitch, usually as a right-half, orchestrating attacks and breaking down the opponents' efforts in equal measure.

Puskás made his debut for Hungary in their first games after the war, while Bozsik would be forced to wait until 1947 before receiving his first cap, a delay that some felt was due to his measured, cerebral play being mistaken for indecision and mental lethargy. It was only when one came to recognise how rarely Bozsik relinquished possession, how often he could pick the precise moment to deliver a clinical, inch-perfect pass, that his true value was evident. As with their contrasting personalities, the subtleties of Bozsik's play could not be attributed to Puskás' style, which was part explosive power, part mesmeric skill, and all utterly bombastic.

By the time the national team selected Bozsik for his debut, his close friend already had eight caps and nine goals to his name. Built solidly and, as some would unkindly point out, somewhat squat, even at an early age, Puskás was sometimes derided as being little more than a physical, bullying forward. However, this description does him a grave injustice. Before he was even out of his teenage years, it was clear that as an attacking force, he had it all – acceleration, balletic balance, intelligence, strength and a predatory eye for goal. Yet, it was the attributes he possessed in spite of his unathletic appearance that truly set him apart. His first touch was rarely less than immaculate, and even if it was, he appeared to possess a sort of psychic command over the ball that could turn poor control into a moment of seemingly divine inspiration.

Such natural talents had bestowed upon the young Puskás a certain arrogance that irritated some, particularly early teammates who quickly tired of the young upstart's barked orders and muttered complaints when the ball failed to find him. An early display of such hubris came in 1948 while the equally pugnacious Béla Guttmann was in charge of Kispest, having replaced Puskás' father as coach. Dismayed by what he deemed as unnecessarily aggressive play from his own player, Mihály Patyi, Guttmann ordered him from the field. Puskás, not agreeing with his manager, told Patyi to stay put. A psychological tug of war ensued, and Patyi eventually bowed to his young teammate instead of his manager. A chastened Guttmann quit his post immediately after the match.

Puskás' confidence served him well as his abilities singled him out for some uncompromising treatment from opponents. During the 1948 defeat to Bulgaria, which signalled the end for the three-man coaching committee, Puskás lashed out at two defenders after they had repeatedly fouled him. After the match, when a Hungarian official had admonished him for his conduct, Puskás had no qualms with telling the man what he thought of his criticism. He was swiftly banned from club competitions for several months and from the national team for a season.

In justifying the decision to ban Hungary's new star, an editorial in the newspaper *Nepssport* claimed he hadn't given his all for the national team's cause (a particularly grave accusation given that he was 'a sportsman of the people's democracy proceeding towards socialism'). Even more sensationally, the editorial claimed Puskás had blackmailed the team into giving him preferential treatment by threatening to defect.[22] In fact, Puskás had been made a lucrative offer to join Italian giants Juventus after Hungary's 3-2 defeat to the Torino-inspired Italy in 1947, but had turned the move down for fear of repercussions at home against his family, particularly due to their German heritage.[23] Never one to back down, Puskás explained in his own editorial, 'I did behave badly in Sofia, but I was extracting just revenge for the kicking I was getting'.[24] Neither ban was actually upheld; Puskás was already too critical to his country's cause. It would not be the only time that the Hungarian authorities' ideological bark would prove greater than their bite when it came to the national team.

By the time the army was looking to take charge of a team and give Sebes a centralised point around which he could pool his players, Puskás and Bozsik alone were enough to make Kispest the club of choice. Once Kispest had become Honvéd and Sebes had been given carte blanche to begin constructing a national team in miniature, the next question was which players would be brought into the fold.

There's little doubt that the inspiration for Sebes' use of Honvéd owed much to both Pozzo's Italy and Meisl's Austria teams. However, to describe Sebes as merely aping the two illustrious managers is to do him a gross injustice. Both Pozzo and Meisl had identified a pooling of talent at specific clubs and had reasoned that, while there may have been better players available elsewhere, the synergy generated by selecting more players from Torino or Austria Wien outweighed pure ability. In many respects, both were fortunate to have had such rich seams to tap into; in the case of Pozzo, he had the Hungarian Erbstein to thank. Sebes, meanwhile, did not take charge of Hungary to find the Honvéd core ready and waiting. Instead, he recognised who his key players were and worked to move them together, in effect, reverse engineering what Meisl and Pozzo had been handed by serendipity.

This campaign of 'Honvédisation' wasn't an easy one. Sebes wielded great power and influence within the Hungarian government, but he wasn't omnipotent. He knew that any wasted resources, any lost time, any missteps, would count against him. It is only with hindsight that the Honvéd situation can be viewed as an unmitigated benefit to the national team. At the time, it contributed to the pressure on Sebes being far beyond what was typical for a national team manager. Nobody was more aware than the politically shrewd Sebes that the favour he enjoyed with the government in 1949 would quickly evaporate were his team to fail to reach their increasingly evident potential. That pressure would only become more acute after his team got off to a less-than-auspicious start in the first game under his lone guidance.

★ ★ ★

Though the Magyars would be playing away, in Prague, they would be facing a Czechoslovakia side who had been bottom of the 1948 Balkan Cup table at the point it was abandoned, losing all four of their games, including to Hungary in Budapest. The team that Sebes initially proposed was a bold one, featuring a front five consisting of László Budai, Sándor Kocsis, Ferenc Deák, Puskás and Zoltán Czibor. Of the five, only Puskás wasn't a teenager, and only he and Deák had been capped more than once. It was a daring selection, one that demonstrated Sebes' willingness to put his neck on the line in spite of the intense political scrutiny he was under.

The proposed selection bore a striking resemblance to what would become recognised as the strongest starting XI of the future Golden Team. Of the five forwards who would start against England in their famous meeting in 1953, only Deák would not feature from the five who Sebes picked, a testament to the remarkable foresight the manager possessed.

Sebes' bold choices, however, were deemed far too radical by the Hungarian Football Association, who, like Sebes, were alert to the increasingly blurred lines between their jurisdiction and those in Rákosi's orbit. They felt that to field such an inexperienced line-up would leave Hungary exposed, as the young forwards all sought to leave their mark and focused too much on attacking. They lobbied Sebes to reconsider, and the new manager eventually acquiesced, starting Deák and Puskás but restoring team captain Ferenc Szusza to the line-up and generally giving the team a more solid, experienced appearance.

This conservatism backfired in spectacular fashion, with the match ending in an embarrassing 5-2 defeat to the Czechs. The defeat, naturally, stung Sebes, but it would prove to be a watershed moment. From then on, Sebes would countenance no interference. He was the team's manager, and the one whose reputation – and more – was on the line. With such jeopardy, he would live and die by his convictions. The next match, against Hungary's long-time football-ing nemesis Austria, would be played with *his* team – if he was going to lose, he was at least going to do it on his terms. Fortunately for Sebes and Hungary, losing was about to become a very rare occurrence indeed.

Unbowed by the prospect of a raucous crowd of 50,000 Hungarians watch-ing on and the fact that, despite having managed a single game, his position was bound to come under serious scrutiny should his team suffer their first home defeat to their old foes in almost twenty years, Sebes selected his desired forward line. Puskás and Deák remained, at inside and centre-forward respec-tively, but Sebes handed debuts to wingers Budai and Czibor, and only a second cap to Kocsis. He was warned the line-up was too youthfully exuberant and liable to pell-mell attacking – but Sebes refused to see this as a bad thing. As future star Nándor Hidegkuti would recall, a gung-ho self-belief always permeated the Hungarian forwards of the period: 'We used to joke with our defenders sometimes: "Don't worry if you let one in, we'll score two." That's how we felt.'[25] Why worry about defence if the forward line was capable of scoring at will?

It was games like this meeting with Austria that gave rise to this belief. By the time referee Jaroslav Vlček blew the full-time whistle, Puskás had helped himself to the third hat-trick of his fledgling international career, Deák had netted twice and Kocsis had got in on the act as well. The final score – Hungary 6, Austria 1 – was the biggest margin of victory that the Magyars had ever enjoyed over their old rivals. It was a display that completely vindicated Sebes' faith in his youthful team selection, and also served as an early notice of what would become both the trademark of the team's style and their most devastating weapon.

5

THINKING THE
UNTHINKABLE

While the hand-wringing about England's abysmal showing in their first World Cup continued in earnest, the recriminations for the embarrassment in Brazil would not stretch to any meaningful analysis of England's on-field tactics. The country's status as the world's foremost footballing power may have come into question, even in the minds of some of the most patriotic supporters and FA officials, but the system the team deployed on the pitch remained sacrosanct.

The English may have had an over-inflated view of the strength of their national team, but from a tactical standpoint, there was no question about the influence they had had on the game. Early football in Britain had been marked by a sort of antediluvian, primordial chaos. The first ever international, played between Scotland and England in 1872, had seen the English line up with what most closely resembled either a 1-1-8 or a 1-2-7, making the 2-2-6 deployed by the Scottish appear positively suffocating in its conservatism.

It wasn't long, however, before a standard formation evolved from the early experiments. By the 1890s, teams all over Britain were setting up in a 2-3-5 formation, supposedly first inspired by the success of Cambridge University's team (the formation was known as the Cambridge pyramid as a result) with two defenders (designated as 'full-backs'), three midfielders ('half-backs') and five forwards, comprising of two wingers, two inside-forwards and in the middle, a centre-forward.

For several decades, the 2-3-5 would hold the key to the international successes of teams from Britain. Other nations may have had players with equal or even better athletic attributes or more potent raw ability, but only British players were schooled so rigorously and uniformly in a single formation. To most countries at the time, the idea of players growing up with a set position – other than goalkeepers – was a total anathema. Decades before any sort of pre-match preparations or analysis of the opposition became commonplace, foreign teams facing England found themselves in comparative disarray when met with the Three Lions' well-drilled 2-3-5.

The emergence and canonisation of the 2-3-5 occurred as Britain was producing its first generation of footballing missionaries, such as John Tait Robinson and Jimmy Hogan. A motley group of those looking to make a quick windfall, former players who had failed to find continued employment in the Football League, and those who were simply evangelical about football, these men would travel around the globe and help bring the British brand of football to an enthusiastic audience. A common belief these expats shared was in the efficacy of coaching, of taking raw players and improving them, of thinking tactically, all of which were sneered at in Britain. This was truer for nobody more than Hogan. Early in his playing career, he had realised that his way of thinking, of analysing the reasons for the unique ebb and flow of a match, made him an outlier. For most of his contemporaries, the question of formations and tactics had been answered once and for all by the 2-3-5. Time spent trying to think of different ways to do things was time wasted. Hogan disagreed.

Together with his mentor and friend, Hugo Meisl, Hogan discussed and debated the tactical foundations on which football had been constructed, and helped to create what became known as the 'Danubian style'. Still largely modelled on the 2-3-5, this new philosophy borrowed from the Scottish brand of short passing and encouraged a generally looser interpretation of the set roles of the players.

As the system was adopted and adapted by Hogan's MTK team, the rest of the Hungarian league, inspired by MTK's newfound success, followed their example. Before long, the Hungarians and Austrians were playing with what Jonathan Wilson describes as closer to a 'W-W' formation, with the inside-forwards positioned closer to the half-backs in midfield and the centre-half somewhat withdrawn, closer to the full-backs.[1]

The purpose of this deeper centre-half wasn't for destructive, defensive purposes, but to allow a creative playmaker to sit back, freed from the congested morass of the midfield, and orchestrate his team's attacks. This was one of the first major tactical divergences in the history of football. Many other nations would simply follow the British style for decades to come, but in the south-east corner of Europe, the Danubian playing philosophy took root and, in Italy, eventually evolved into Vittorio Pozzo's *metodo* style, which can, in turn, trace its genealogical impact through to the Dutch school of Total Football in the 1970s and the *tiki-taka* of twenty-first-century Spain and Barcelona.

★ ★ ★

The Danubian strain of the 2-3-5 kept the formation alive in mainland Europe. In Britain, meanwhile, it met an abrupt end in the mid-1920s, the victim of a rule change that rendered it almost incompatible with effective defending. The system that would replace it would survive almost as long in England as the 2-3-5 and would mark the final footballing era in which one single formation dominated so utterly.

By the early 1920s, football was firmly established as a prolific money-making business, and was well on its way to indisputably becoming England's most popular sport. In 1920, the Football League had added a Third Division. Three years later, the number of clubs expanded again to finally spread the gospel of league football to the south of the Midlands properly. The same year, the Empire Stadium at Wembley, designed in a pseudo-Indian style in homage to the Empire's jewel in the crown, was opened and inaugurated when a reputed 300,000 watched Bolton Wanderers triumph over West Ham United in the FA Cup Final.

However, despite such demonstrable forward progress, the FA were worried that the footballing boom would not last if the current state of the game persisted. Average First Division crowds had hit a peak in 1921 but had dropped by more than a quarter by 1924. The FA pinpointed the cause of this drop-off as the gradually dwindling supply of the sport's key currency – goals. The four seasons between 1920 and 1924 had been the four with the lowest average goals per game on record. Without exciting, goal-filled matches, the FA reasoned, attendances would continue to fall, and gate receipts with them.

In an uncharacteristic moment of proactivity, the FA lobbied FIFA for a change to the rules, which was granted in time for the 1925–26 campaign. From then on, only two players (including the goalkeeper) were required to be between the attacker and the goal for the attacker to be rendered onside, replacing the previous rule that had required three players. Overnight, the number of goals exploded. In the 1924–25 season, the First Division saw 1,192 goals, at an average of just over two and a half per game. The next year, after the rule was altered, there were 1,709, more than an extra goal per game, aided chiefly by those teams whose defences coped less than admirably with the rule change. In one of the more remarkable examples, Cardiff City succumbed to Sheffield United 11-2 on New Year's Day, 1926, yet the Bluebirds still ended up conceding fewer goals than the Blades that year.

While many teams and players suffered often comical lapses in comprehension of the new rule, one thing remained constant: Huddersfield Town retained their First Division title for a third year running. Town were a new team, having only been founded in 1908, and had won their three titles despite having been in the top flight for just six years. Their success was owed to one man, their manager, Herbert Chapman. A journeyman amateur as a player, Chapman had risen through the footballing pyramid and arrived at Huddersfield in 1920, having cut his managerial teeth at smaller clubs, where he had had the autonomy to make tactical alterations and tweaks as he pleased. Chapman was an exceedingly rare example of a manager who occupied the same school of thought as Hogan and other believers in tactics yet had broken into English football's upper echelons. He was an impassioned believer in teams having playing philosophies, and he developed certain basic movements which he then sought to implement by recruiting the right sort of players. At a time when most managers would have considered buying players in order to suit a system putting the cart before the horse, Chapman recognised the benefits of moulding his squad to suit his tactics.

Chapman left Huddersfield before their third title success, but there was no question to whom the credit for their treble was owed. His move, to Arsenal, coincided with the change to the offside rule, and it was at Highbury where he developed his most innovative idea yet, aided by veteran signing Charlie Buchan. Using the 2-3-5 as the template, the first change was one of necessity, dropping the centre-half back into the defensive line with the full-backs, thereby compensating for the offside rule change (despite this shift, the tag of 'centre-half' remained, creating a quirk of nomenclature that persists to this day).

Other teams would recognise this need, too, and Chapman's Arsenal would suffer at the hands of teams who had implemented the defensive centre-half more effectively, such as when they were battered 7-0 by Newcastle United. Chapman, however, was only getting started. While most managers in the First Division were content with having plugged that one particular leak, Chapman recognised that teams were now playing with three defenders, two midfielders and five forwards. None of the firepower had been lost by moving the centre-half backwards, but a team's ability to funnel the ball forward effectively and keep hold of possession in central areas had been cut by a third.

Over the course of the next five seasons, Chapman tweaked his formation until it performed in the manner he desired. His chief innovation was to abandon the traditional front line of five, instead dropping the inside-forwards further back to form a quadrilateral in the centre of the pitch with the two remaining half-backs, enabling Arsenal to rapidly and effectively transition from defence to attack. When other teams' defences won back possession, they were often reduced to lumping the ball forward in hope rather than expectation, a development that many purists derided as sounding the death knell for exciting, short-passing based, attacking football of earlier eras. Chapman's Arsenal could funnel the ball from the back three, to the half-backs, to the inside-forwards, to the forward three. The name given to the formation mirrored this structure – the W-M.

Understandably, such an upheaval took time to bed in. Just as the rigidity and organisation of the 2-3-5 had been an advantage to England in the early days, as soon as any flexibility was required, it became a marked disadvantage, with players having to unlearn lifelong habits in the middle of their careers. By 1930, however, Chapman had the squad he needed. Arsenal won the league four seasons out of five between 1930 and 1935. Chapman wouldn't live to see Arsenal win the final title – just as his team appeared unstoppable, the chief architect of their success and the most impactful tactician that English football had known died suddenly of pneumonia.

It wasn't long before the rest of the Football League were copying Arsenal and their W-M. It's tempting to think that had Chapman lived, he would have gone hunting for the next evolution to give his team an edge once again. Without him, strategic innovation all but disappeared from the English game, and British football once again entered a period of tactical stasis.

★ ★ ★

By the 1950 World Cup, the W-M was omnipresent. The global standardisation of the laws of the game meant that every country was affected by the 1925 offside rule changes, and all had to adapt. As had occurred with the 2-3-5, many countries simply copied the English solution. However, in the countries where the 2-3-5 had already been adapted and changed, this was not such a simple process. In Hungary and Austria, where the game had developed a distinctive brand, the W-M was fiercely debated and discussed, demonstrative of a football culture in the two nations that was far more inquisitive than in Britain. Arthur Rowe, the former Tottenham Hotspur and England centre-half, was invited to Budapest to give a series of lectures proselytising the W-M. Yet in the late 1930s and early 1940s, many Hungarians were still resistant to the change, fearing that such a defensive shift would reduce the centre-half, the beating heart of the team's creativity, to little more than a stopper, stymying the flowing passing of the Danubian style. National team captain György Sárosi went so far as to pen an open letter arguing against adopting the system into the Hungarian game.[2] It would take until after the Second World War for the pragmatism of the W-M to finally prevail over the passion for the old Danubian 2-3-5, but the spirit that imbued the latter would not be forgotten.

There are several explanations for why the 2-3-5 and W-M remained in vogue for so long, and why so few were willing to experiment with ways to counteract either formation. In England, there was undoubtedly a degree of anti-intellectualism that pervaded the game, with those willing to think outside of the box like Jimmy Hogan and his ilk finding their opportunities limited in favour of those less likely to rock the boat by asking searching questions. For the best part of seventy years, every player in Britain had grown up playing in either a 2-3-5 or a W-M. To upend that was to enter the unknown, force players from their comfort zone and risk a painful, difficult period of transition while others were free to continue ploughing the same furrow.

It was a risk that few chairmen, board members and owners were willing to take, particularly with the ever-growing financial investment in the game. Indeed, in one of Hogan's two managerial roles in England, at Aston Villa, he was told by his chairman, 'I've no time for all these theories about football. Just get the ball in the bloody net; that's what I want.'[3]

Shortly before England's climactic meeting with Hungary in 1953, the *Daily Herald* football correspondent Clifford Webb recounted musing that England were continually finding themselves outplayed by Continental opponents 'because in 90 years our only new idea has been the stopper centre-half'. The club owners and chairman he was with couldn't argue with Webb's claim. Instead, they could only justify English football's torpidity by saying, 'You can't introduce new ideas into League matches. It might cost points.'

The same logic that led to the change in the offside rule in 1925 still applied – those with money at stake in the sport wanted it looked after. The W-M had many limitations, but it did ensure that two of the most venerated aspects of the British footballing spectacle – the power struggle between the centre-half and centre-forward, and the winger's freedom to run at an isolated full-back – were present in abundance. Just how successful Stanley Matthews would have been had he not had a full-back to dance past, we will never know, but it brought punters through the turnstiles, and that was what the owners wanted.

The traditional hierarchical structure of British clubs did little to help usher new formations in. By the 1950s, almost all clubs in the Football League had a manager or secretary manager, who dealt with transfers as well as the general running of the football side of the operation. Meanwhile, a head coach looked after training the players he was given and tried to impart some rudimentary wisdom that might give his side the edge over the next team they faced.

This disconnect between manager and coach typically meant that the Chapman approach of building a squad to suit a particular playing style was impossible and left a void between the two roles where tactical decisions lay. It's little coincidence that as the likes of Matt Busby at Manchester United began to exert control over both the administrative and playing aspects of the club, so too did the tactical walls begin to tumble.

Earlier exceptions did exist. Following his lectures in Hungary, Arthur Rowe returned to England and took charge of Spurs, where he would pioneer a fast-paced style known as 'push and run'. However, even as writers like Brian Glanville hailed Rowe's innovations as post-war British football's 'first bold tactical experiment',[4] it existed firmly within the rigid framework of the W-M.

Then there was the simple philosophical problem that tactics had been so stagnant, so unshifting, that thinking about them in the abstract and wielding them as a weapon to be utilised just as a new signing would was akin to thinking the unthinkable, particularly in the arrogant British imperial mindset. It seems remarkably naive to us in hindsight, but by the 1950s, football in England had been based on two formations for over six decades. Without the change to the offside law, it's unlikely that the 2-3-5 would have morphed into the W-M. It simply wasn't an area that many of those capable of making a difference in the English game gave any thought to. It was for this reason that anyone who dared challenge the status quo, no matter how gently, was akin to the one-eyed man, capable of becoming king in the kingdom of the blind.

★ ★ ★

Eastwards, in Hungary, attitudes were different. The same spirited arguments and intellectual curiosity that greeted the introduction of the W-M had not abated after Chapman's formation had finally been adopted. Just as a multitude of factors contributed to the English refusal to engage critically with the idea of tactics, so too were a variety of elements at play as to why the Hungarians were willing to examine these footballing fundamentals.

In England, football competed with cricket and rugby, both of which were held in higher regard by the elites. Indeed, the famous origin story of rugby, in which William Webb Ellis cleverly exploited a loophole in the rules of football by catching the ball and running with it, contains traces of the academic snobbery with which football was treated. These elites were liable to sneer at the idea that a sport so popular among the working classes could have any intellectual merit.

In Hungary, the game was treated with far greater intellectual respect. As Rory Smith explains, the sport had been imported on a wave of Anglophilia and was viewed as 'just as sophisticated' as other British imports, fashion and culture.[5] The trend of fans dissecting the games they'd just watched in the coffee houses on the banks of the Danube had never abated.

There was also a degree of humility in the Hungarian attitude towards the sport that was sorely lacking in Britain. They had been exchanging coaches and the ideas they carried with them with other nations for decades and weren't embarrassed about admitting the immense debt the sport in Hungary owed to foreign wisdom and influence. Figures like Jimmy Hogan weren't written out of history or treated as embarrassing secrets; they were venerated. In Britain, and England particularly, the attitude held towards football was similar to that which enveloped many of the nation's greatest exports and had its roots in the country's formerly pre-eminent position in the world. Britain had been responsible for inventing modern football, so the very idea that any nation outside of Britain could improve upon it was treated with derision.

The hurdles that prevented outside-the-box thinkers such as Jimmy Hogan finding ready employment in England were far less abundant further east. Hungary welcomed foreign coaches and Hungarians who had gone to coach abroad alike, and many Hungarian coaches relished the opportunity to learn their trade abroad. By the time Béla Guttmann returned to his home country and had his run-in with the young Ferenc Puskás at Kispest in 1948, he had already managed in Austria, the Netherlands and Romania, as well as playing for several years in the USA. Árpád Weisz, before he and his family perished in Auschwitz-Birkenau, became the first foreign coach to win the Italian championship with Internazionale, and remains the youngest coach to have won a *scudetto*. Dori Kürschner won titles in Germany and Switzerland and an Olympic silver medal as a coach of the Swiss national team (alongside Hogan and Teddy Duckworth), before becoming a semi-mythical figure in Brazil, introducing the country to the Hungarian interpretation of the W-M and setting the foundations for the incredible success of the *Seleção*.

Such foreign escapades weren't restricted to professional coaches. Even Dracula himself, famed Hungarian actor Bela Lugosi, spent much of his time between film shoots in Los Angeles lending his name and his money to the promotion of football on the west coast of the USA. Unlike Hogan and many of his contemporaries, who found their success translated to nought in the eyes of English chairmen only interested in experience within the narrow confines of the Football League, Hungarian coaches who had been abroad were greeted with open arms by clubs who were keen to see how their manager's foreign escapades might find new cracks in the armour of their old rivals.

One of the men who arrived home in Hungary in the years between the Second World War and the beginning of Gusztáv Sebes' reign as national team manager was Márton Bukovi. Bukovi was the very epitome of the Hungarian footballing nomad. After playing in Italy, he moved to Ferencváros and received eleven caps for the Hungarian national side before finishing his playing career at FC Sète, in France. His coaching career then took him to Yugoslavia, where he managed Građanski Zagreb for several years before the Second World War, winning two league titles before the club was dissolved and replaced by the post-war communist regime as retribution for their having participated in a fascist-backed wartime league. Bukovi remained coach of the replacement club, Dinamo Zagreb, and it was here that he would develop the tactic that would transform the Hungarian game and, by extension, the very fabric of football.

By the time Građanski was replaced by Dinamo, Bukovi was, like most in Eastern Europe, utilising the W-M, but he hadn't blindly adopted it. He had initially used a system that Jonathan Wilson describes as far closer to the Italian *metodo*, the modified 2-3-5 that had its genus in Hungary and Austria.[6] This formation had seen his Zagreb team crush Liverpool 5-1 in a friendly. This match, and a return tour of England, opened Bukovi's eyes, both to the virtues of the English W-M, and to the fact that even the slightest variation on it could deeply unsettle teams that stuck as rigidly to it as English sides did. Armed with this knowledge, he waited until Dinamo faced their local rivals Lokomotiva in a match to decide the Zagreb Championship to unleash a new weapon.

Not one to downplay his own achievements, Bukovi later described the match as 'not an ordinary game for the football in our country – nor, I dare say, for the world'.[7] Dinamo won the game, in large part thanks to their centre-forward repeatedly dropping out of the front five and effectively acting as a link between the half-backs and the inside-forwards, in the area of the pitch that today would be occupied by an attacking midfielder. The opposing centre back, so used to having his opponent mere yards from him for the entire 90 minutes, was at a loss. If he followed the centre-forward, he quickly found himself in alien climes, closer to the halfway line than his own penalty box, reducing Lokomotiva's defence to two men who were quickly overwhelmed by the four remaining Dinamo forwards. If he stayed put, the centre-forward had copious amounts of room in which to receive and distribute the ball. To Lokomotiva's players, there seemed to be no answer. Though Bukovi's assessment of the match lacked hubris, nobody could argue with its central truth. The world of football had never seen anything like it.

In 1947, Bukovi returned to his home country to manage MTK, which emerged from the Second World War a shadow of the force they had previously been. Before 1940, they had only finished outside of the top three in Hungary twice. However, the club had been banned from playing during the war due to its historic Jewish roots. In the three seasons after the conflict, they had limped to two sixth-place finishes and a fifth with a relatively weak squad. In Bukovi's first year, it again finished sixth, before improving rapidly. In the next three years, Bukovi nurtured a squad that featured Nándor Hidegkuti, Mihály Lantos, and Károly Sándor, leading them to third and second place twice. This improvement in form and the loss in 1949 of the team's stony-faced Romanian forward Norberto Höfling was enough to convince Bukovi that the time had come to give the tweak of the W-M that he had trialled in Zagreb a more rigorous test.

When Höfling left for Lazio, Bukovi was left without a player who fitted the billing for the physical centre-forward role. Instead, he looked to two players, neither of whom possessed the robustness to battle with the centre-half, but who both compensated with other skills. The first was Péter Palotás, who made his debut for both MTK and the national team in 1950, aged 21. The young phenom would vie for the centre-forward berth with Nándor Hidegkuti, a versatile forward, capable of playing on the wing, at inside-forward or in the centre. Seven years older than Palotás, Hidegkuti had been capped by the national team eight times. There was, however, a sense that despite his consistently excellent goal-scoring record for MTK, his chances for international stardom may have already passed.

Though future accounts would typically peg Hidegkuti as one of the two or three best players of the Hungarian golden team generation (invariably behind Puskás), nobody would have believed he would earn such a lofty billing when he arrived at MTK in 1946, after spending the early years of his career at the minor clubs of Elektromos FC and Herminamezei AC, where he was known as a talented but limited player (it was Bukovi who spotted that Hidegkuti's inability to last 90 minutes in games was due to his being anaemic, rather than a lack of fitness).[8]

Hidegkuti made his national team debut in 1945, but had then spent two years in the wilderness, before enjoying some sporadic appearances, generally at inside-forward, between 1947 and 1950. In Hidegkuti's way stood the likes of Puskás, Sándor Kocsis and, at centre-forward, Ferenc Deák. Just two months older than Hidegkuti and blessed with a natural predator's instinct, by the time Sebes took sole charge of the team in 1949, Deák had eighteen goals in twelve appearances, while Hidegkuti had a comparatively paltry seven in seven (five of which had come in his first two caps, both seven-goal wins over Romania and Bulgaria). Even after Bukovi came in at MTK, feats such as firing the club to second place in 1948–49 with twenty-six goals in twenty-eight league games could not force Hidegkuti past Deák, who was the Nemzeti Bajnokság I's top goal scorer three times in the first five post-war seasons, including in 1948–49, when he scored an absurd fifty-nine goals for Ferencváros. In 1949, Deák's position in the national team seemed utterly unassailable.

Now Palotás was challenging Hidegkuti for both the Magyars and for his club, his chances of an international career seemed to be disappearing. Bukovi was now proposing, in effect, a lifeline for Hidegkuti's long-term prospects as a member of the Hungarian national team, though neither he nor his manager yet knew it. While many forwards of Hidegkuti's experience would have balked at being asked, aged 27 and supposedly at the very peak of their powers, to reinvent themselves, Hidegkuti approached the idea with an open mind.

Almost as soon as Bukovi and Hidegkuti reached their understanding, fate intervened in a manner that nobody had anticipated. Swiftly following Rákosi's communists taking complete control of the country in the elections of May 1949, the political climate, already cool towards any vocal non-communists, turned decidedly frosty. For some, such as the dyed-in-the-wool communist Sebes, this development undoubtedly enhanced their careers. For the forthright Deák, just like his club, the historically right-of-centre Ferencváros, it was a hammer blow.

A former slaughterhouse worker who had become one of the best players in the country, Deák had little interest in communism or pretending he wasn't enjoying his success. When he was arrested for a drunken brawl, Sebes did little to hide his contempt for his player. Eventually, Deák's outspokenness led to him being banned from the national team, and unlike the ban levied at Puskás in 1948, about which a great show was made before it was quietly disregarded, Deák's ban was permanent. Deák's ideologically motivated exile was cruel, yet it would ultimately prove to be a moment of remarkable good fortune for Sebes, Nándor Hidegkuti and the national team.

6

MR SEBES, IT'S TIME WE ARRANGED A MATCH

In 1950, Hungary contested a shortened league season in order to allow them to adopt a calendar year season format and thus synchronise with Russia, just one of countless indications of the sway the Soviet Union now held over the country. It was yet another reminder to Gusztáv Sebes that his job encompassed far more than just being a mere football manager. He was now responsible for the architecture and performance of one of the most critical propaganda weapons that Mátyás Rákosi's government possessed. Academic Péter Fodor has suggested that the importance of sport was particularly acute in Hungary, where the country's success at both the 1938 World Cup and the Berlin Olympics wedded the Hungarian people to sporting success.[1] To fail to continue in this tradition would be a tacit suggestion that the communist system had failed to deliver what pre-war capitalism had done.

If that wasn't enough additional pressure on Sebes, it was becoming clear that the generation of players he had under his charge was exceptional. Rákosi would soon establish regular and direct communication with the manager, repeatedly reminding the coach of what was at stake, and what the potential repercussions could be if Hungary dared to lose. There was now a significant political interest in the team, not only in Hungary but in the wider Soviet Union, which watched, hawklike, over every satellite in its orbit to monitor how they were – or weren't – promoting the Soviet cause to the wider world.

Sebes' stock was high after the thumping success over Austria with the youthful, attacking line-up in his second match in sole charge of the team. For his third match, the team travelled to Italy, whom they had last beaten in 1925 and subsequently endured a fifteen-match winless run against. Hungary were unable to break that streak, drawing 1-1, but it was a creditable result, nonetheless. Less impressive, though by no means a disaster, was the 2-2 draw against George Raynor's Sweden in Solna that followed. The Magyars then returned to winning ways by demolishing Poland 8-2 in Debrecen, with the soon-to-be-ostracised Ferenc Deák netting four times.

In these matches, Sebes was willing to experiment with his team selection and the precise mechanics of their play. Against Italy, for example, the headlong attacking style they'd utilised against Austria was replaced by a more measured approach that enabled the team to retain defensive solidity.

While he was still trialling different line-ups and putting the players through their paces, this period was also a showcase of the coach's political shrewdness. Throughout his time with the national team, Sebes would focus on specific fixtures that he knew carried additional clout for Rákosi and the government. It was a delicate balancing act, as he couldn't afford to simply throw away a single match, even if it was in service of a greater goal. Nonetheless, it was a method that he would utilise to enormous success.

Hungary's next match, in Vienna in October 1949, was one of those key fixtures. Neither they nor Austria had beaten the other away from home for twelve years, and Sebes and his players were absolutely determined to emphasise that their convincing win over *Das Team* earlier in the year in Budapest had not been a fluke.

Played before 65,000 impassioned Austrian fans at the national Praterstadion, the match teetered back and forth. Hungary, playing with four of the five forwards who had torn Austria apart five months before (Zoltán Czibor, who had turned 20 in between the two games, was replaced by Sándor Zsédely), found themselves 1-0 down after just 2 minutes, but came roaring back to lead 3-1 before half an hour had been played.

Austria's star, Ernst Ocwirk, was of especial interest to the Hungary players. Nicknamed 'clockwork' by the British press, Ocwirk was, even by 1949, something of a throwback, a centre-half who placed far more emphasis on creativity than the increasingly defensive duties associated with the position in the British style W-M. The quality of his methodical, quarterback-esque long-range passing was so exceptional, however, that the loss of a defensive presence was worth the trade-off. Ocwirk's ability to pick out teammates with raking passes and to control the ebb and flow of a match was unparalleled for the time, and the Hungarians knew they had to deal with him.

Before the match, Sebes had demonstrated his burgeoning understanding of his players' individual psyches. The manager explained to the team that he had wanted to assign the all-action Ferenc Puskás the job of man-marking the Austrian playmaker, but he hadn't wanted to give the Honvéd star such a disciplined role and so asked Deák to fulfil the defensive obligation instead. For the irascible Puskás, the implication that he couldn't be trusted to perform such a regimented task was like a red rag to a bull, and he stuck doggedly to Ocwirk throughout the match, which had been Sebes' intention all along. How effective this stratagem was is debatable, as Austria came back to equalise at 3-3, but it certainly did no harm to Puskás' offensive performance, as he netted a hat-trick, including the winning strike, which made the final score 4-3.

It was a result that truly signalled Hungary's credentials to the wider footballing world, and their potential as a tool of propaganda to Rákosi's government. So well received was the result that the Hungarian players were granted a 600 forint pay bonus, designated as 'calorie money' that they could use to help keep their strength up. What role these extra calories played in the team's next three matches, all of which were won 5-0, is difficult to say. By the third of these games, against Czechoslovakia in April 1950, Sebes was beginning to establish his favoured line-up and unearth what would grow into the *Aranycsapat*, Hungary's 'Golden Team'.

Nándor Hidegkuti played his second match in a row, in what was the beginning of a sustained run in the team. At this stage, he was still very much a creative utility forward within the attacking line, yet the outstanding support work of the 'old man', as he was teasingly called by his younger teammates, was crucial in enabling the emerging stars of the national side to flourish.

Sándor Kocsis had made his debut in 1948 and had properly broken into the team in mid-1949. Despite being only 21, by 1950 Kocsis had been a regular in the Ferencváros team for several years. In spite of Deák's prodigious goal-scoring rate, Kocsis had been able to emerge from his shadow as a goal scorer in his own right, in part thanks to an outstanding heading ability that wouldn't have been out of place in the aerially oriented English game and earned him the nickname 'Golden Head'.

Few club or national teammates were willing to argue with the vocal Puskás, but Kocsis, despite being younger and typically quite reserved, had the selfish streak required of all first-class goal scorers and had no qualms about standing his ground with Puskás. László Budai would quip that teams with both Puskás and Kocsis needed to play with two balls, due to the unshakeable conviction both had that they should receive the pass in every attack.[2]

The rivalry between the pair didn't stop off the pitch, or even with them. Kocsis' family were known to denigrate Puskás' reliance on his left foot compared to Kocsis' ambidextrousness. Kocsis' mother even allegedly went so far as to complain to the Sports Ministry that Puskás earned more than her son, an accusation that wasn't without risks, given the suggestion that a degree of un-communist remuneration was taking place.

All of this could have led to an early, bitter falling out between Kocsis and Puskás. However, they were both, at heart, deeply passionate footballers and proud Hungarians. Both recognised the enormous talent the other possessed and the virtues he would bring to the national team's cause. Their rivalry never boiled over into anything acrimonious, but rather spurred the pair on to form what would be one of the most prolific international goal-scoring partnerships of all time from the inside-forward positions.

Alongside Kocsis and Puskás came Budai. While the lithe, athletic Hidegkuti was hardly an archetypical centre-forward, where he was now occasionally playing, the barrel-chested Budai looked little like anybody's definition of the typically fleet-footed winger. One of the many innovations adopted by Hungary was more athletic, streamlined kits, particularly compared to the ill-fitting, baggy shirts used by England. More than any of his teammates, Budai's kit hugged his torso like an impeccably tailored dress shirt.

However, while his physique may have given the impression of sluggish power, the quiet, reticent Budai was able to translate his physical prowess into deceptive speed and skill. He also possessed an excellent crossing ability, which made him an ideal foil for his Ferencváros teammate Kocsis and his outstanding aerial talents.

Budai made his international debut in Sebes' second game alongside Zoltán Czibor, who had been scouted by the same Ferencváros youth coach. It would be another few years before Czibor would establish himself in the team and make the other wing his own, in part because of often beguiling lack of discipline. 'Sometimes with Czibor,' remembered Puskás, 'none of us knew what he would do next, not even himself.'[3] This spontaneous unpredictability would bedevil Czibor off the pitch and give him a lifetime of problems, yet on the pitch it proved his greatest asset.

While Budai was a model of directness on one wing, Czibor was anything but on the other, a situation mirrored in the England team, where the brisk efficiency of Tom Finney on one side of the pitch was countered by the enigmatic style of Stan Matthews on the other. It wasn't until the national team's playing philosophy had evolved significantly that Czibor's weakness for wandering was transformed into yet another redoubtable weapon in the Hungarian armoury.

Politically, these selections gave Sebes a minor headache. Kocsis, Budai and Czibor all played for the traditionally right-leaning Ferencváros in 1949, but Sebes was already planning on putting his Honvéd conscription plan into action.

It would not be as simple in the case of two other players he brought into the fold, the inclusion of whom required some deft manoeuvring from the manager and some ideological compromise from those in charge. The first was towering centre-half Gyula Lóránt. He was commanding, a fine reader of the game and, with no shortage of skill, Lóránt was precisely the sort of player Sebes desired for his W-M, a pleasing combination of the classic creative Danubian centre-half and the more destructive British model.

There was, however, one major stumbling block to his selection. As Rákosi and the Hungarian Working People's Party had increased their stranglehold on the nation's political instruments in early 1949, Lóránt had attempted to defect and set up a travelling team of Hungarian émigrés. The scheme was detected and Lóránt and two fellow ringleaders were arrested and confined to a detention camp. Sebes' argument, made directly to Leader of the Interior Ministry János Kádár, was that by freeing Lóránt and allowing him to play for the national team, it might help persuade others of a similar disposition that Lóránt had undergone a change of heart and had seen the light of Rákosi's communist regime. Kádár demurred and Lóránt's gratitude towards Sebes convinced him to not make another attempt to flee the country.

It was a similar case for goalkeeper Gyula Grosics, one of the most fascinating figures in the Hungarian team. Of all the positions to play, goalkeeper – the most isolated role in the team, where blame and pressure are both most readily apportioned – was perhaps the least suited to the hypochondriacal (he regularly wore a red beret due to a conviction that it would protect him from brain tumours),[4] paranoid Grosics. This paranoia translated to a deep (and not unwarranted) distrust of the communist regime, and he too attempted to defect alongside Lóránt in 1949, despite all the inherent risks – risks that, as it transpired, became reality when he was arrested by the ÁVH, the Hungarian secret police. After a night of being interrogated and threatened, Grosics was placed under house arrest, his name destined to forever be treated with suspicion by the authorities.

The three-man management committee that Sebes had been a part of had discovered Grosics playing in the tiny mining town of Dorog. He had made his national debut in 1947, but had appeared only sporadically since then, in part due to frequent claims of injury. Still, Sebes sensed that Grosics possessed the requisite attributes, not least outstanding goalkeeping talent, to make him worth the risk and political wrangling. Following his arrest, the goalkeeper had been charged with treason and espionage, and though his case would never come to trial, he was banned from the national team for two years. Once again, Sebes' political instincts paid dividends, and Grosics' story is one of many of Soviet hypocrisy in the name of ideological success; had he not been one of the country's outstanding goalkeepers, it's impossible to imagine his intransigence being punished so leniently. On a personal level, the quality of Grosics' relationship with Sebes rarely progressed beyond functional, with the goalkeeper resenting his treatment at the hands of the authorities and equating them with the 'narrow-minded, iron-fisted communist' Sebes.[5]

In the cases of both Lóránt and Grosics, Sebes got his way, but not without knowingly increasing the pressure on him and his team once again. Squandering the ability of his talented team was one thing, but to do so with players who had attempted to defect would have created an even larger ideological stain. The faith that Sebes showed in his chosen players could not have failed to inspire a respect in him and his decisions throughout the team.

The secret police's net wasn't always so effective, and even as Sebes cast his eye over the embarrassment of riches he had at his disposal in 1950, he could look to Italy and wonder what might have been. There, playing for the unremarkable Pro Patria, was László Kubala, considered at the time to be perhaps the greatest footballing talent ever produced by Hungary, even as the redoubtable Puskás glided up the country's list of record goal scorers. A physical polymath, Kubala combined mesmeric dribbling skill, electrifying pace and sledgehammer power, a skillset that enabled him to play in any of the forward positions.

It hadn't taken long for his prodigious talent to be recognised. He spent his youth competing against players years older than him and made his debut for the Magyars aged only 20. Like Grosics and Lóránt (of whom Kubala was a teammate), he was spooked by the communist takeover in 1949 and fled the country. He too was captured but was the recipient of some serendipitous good fortune and was freed from a detention centre after being recognised, ultimately reaching Italy. His wife and young son would follow him, but only after swimming across the Danube to escape.

Kubala would spend the two years following his defection in legal purgatory, signing for clubs only to have his registration annulled by FIFA due to him having walked out on his club contract in Hungary. It wasn't until Barcelona flexed their legal muscles in 1951 that Kubala was declared a refugee and allowed to sign for the Catalan giants, where he would become one of their most beloved heroes. Kubala would eventually represent his adopted home country internationally. Some rifts were too vast even for the smooth-talking Sebes to bridge.

Not all who attempted to defect were as lucky as Kubala to escape or Grosics and Lóránt to receive clemency. By 1951, 30-year-old central defender Sándor Szűcs had faded from the first-team picture for Hungary but remained a reliable presence and back-up in the B and C teams, who Sebes always kept an eye on in case he needed a replacement for one of his stars. Enticed by word of a lucrative offer in Italian football, Szűcs attempted to defect alongside a singer with whom he was conducting an affair. However, the singer's fiancé was connected to the secret police, and the pair were caught.

Word reached Ferenc Szusza, Puskás and Bozsik, who rushed to speak with Minister of Defence and de facto Chairman of Honvéd Mihály Farkas in an attempt to diffuse the situation. By the time they met with Farkas, however, it was too late. Szűcs' execution served as a reminder to all players, including those in the national team, of the fragility of their current bargain – as soon as they were of no use to the regime, any transgression would be punished with brutal efficiency. Szusza was particularly devastated by the death of his close friend, and his grief and anger towards the regime played a substantial role in Sebes phasing him out of the team soon after.[6]

★ ★ ★

It had been decided that the national team would participate in the Olympics in Helsinki in 1952, giving Sebes a critical target to direct his team's energies towards. He set about bolstering his coaching staff, asking for Gyula Mándi and MTK manager Márton Bukovi to be appointed. Mándi was duly given a role and would prove to be the ideal partner for Sebes, bringing a degree of tactical nous and technical coaching knowledge that Sebes lacked. He also proved to be a much-needed mentor for the squad.

While Sebes was never less than acutely attuned to the needs of his players – he was even known to lecture their wives about ensuring they were never forced to play in a state of sexual frustration[7] – he was also aloof, in part by design, in part because of his personality. Mándi, however, was both a fantastic coach and a father figure. Mándi was also responsible for developing the Hungarian training programmes, which aimed to keep players mentally stimulated through a variety of games and exercises, almost always with a ball at their feet. This was in stark contrast to British training methods of the time, which consisted of brutal running drills without the ball in the surreal belief that starving players of the ball during the week would ensure they were hungrier for it come match day.

Bukovi, however, would not be granted a role, with Rákosi personally phoning Sebes to explain that he would be given Jenő Kalmár as a coach instead. Bukovi, never afraid to speak his mind and offer blunt assessments, did not fit the regime's idea of the sort of man they wanted looking after their prized piece of propaganda, unlike the ingratiating and authentically communist Sebes. Though it was a frustration for Sebes at the time, Rákosi's intervention was yet another example of the stars aligning for the Magyars. Bukovi would eventually join Sebes' staff in a semi-official capacity for the 1954 World Cup. In the interim, he would have an immeasurable impact on the national team via his work at MTK, which he may not have undertaken had he joined Sebes in 1950.

The decision to participate in the Olympics was a monumental one. The team had been barred from playing in the 1948 games due to rules about the professionalism of players, which ruled out the core of the Hungary team. After the decision was taken to play in 1952, many players were given what legendary Hungarian commentator György Szepesi called 'sham jobs' or officer roles in the Hungarian Army in order to establish their amateur credentials and make them eligible to play as Olympians.[8] Underlining the enormity of the Olympic decision was the fact that Hungary would not participate in the 1950 World Cup in Brazil, with the official line being that the government couldn't afford to send the large party on a trip to the other side of the globe. However, Rákosi was concerned with the possibility of his Golden Team being made to appear mortal in South America by attempting a major tournament too soon.

Just as Soviet regimes loved to leverage sporting success for their own nefarious means, so too did they do their utmost to minimise potential embarrassment. The Soviet Union themselves did not play at the 1954 World Cup in Switzerland after they had been humiliated in the first round of the 1952 Olympics by Yugoslavia. The loss would have been bad enough, had the Yugoslav nation not been led by Josip Broz Tito, whose well-publicised refusal to bow to the Kremlin and allow his country to become yet another satellite of the Soviet Union had created a tremendous and, for the Soviets, embarrassing rift between the two nations. Stalin was so enraged by the defeat at the Olympics that he ordered a media blackout on reporting the humiliation to the Russian people, and then disbanded the CDKA Moscow club side that had provided the bulk of the Soviet team.[9]

Rákosi granting permission for the Hungarian team to play in the Olympics was, in one respect, an enormous vote of confidence in Sebes' work and the performance of his players – Hungarian participation would never have been sanctioned had there been the slightest risk of the team not performing well. However, as was proving a common theme for the national team, every goal they scored, every triumph they enjoyed, every expectation they bettered was a double-edged sword when playing under a regime that was hellbent on exploiting their success for ideological purposes, as it raised the bar ever higher.

The proximity between the government and the team could have proved detrimental, were it not for Sebes' effective shielding of Rákosi's veiled threats about the team's performance from the players. Sebes' best efforts couldn't insulate the squad entirely from the perils involved in being so closely tied to the government's key piece of propaganda, however. For Lóránt and Grosics, in particular, there was the nagging sense that, even though they had been exonerated and freed, they were never absolved of suspicion and potential blame should a match end in defeat.

The rest of the team shared these same worries – all of them, that is, except Puskás. Although lacking a staunch political outlook and possessing an agricultural interpretation of social airs and graces, Puskás was no rube when it came to dealing with politicians. The dispute with the government official that led to his aborted ban in 1948 was demonstrative of an outspoken streak, though he wasn't so bold as to put voice to his more strident opinions, for example that the hobbling of Ferencváros was a 'disgrace'.[10] He did, however, view the team's close relationship with the communist regime as a situation to be manipulated and exploited, rather than something to fear. Puskás knew when to toe the party line, speaking publicly about the team's brand of socialist football, and when to remind those in the government that they needed his help as the undisputed star of the team more than he needed them.

On one particular occasion, the team were visited during training by Farkas, who, as well as being Honvéd's patron, was one of the most feared men in Rákosi's government, resplendent in an all-white suit. All the players were well aware of who Farkas was and his role in the secret police, and nobody wished to cross him. Puskás, however, found Farkas' outfit too ostentatious to resist. As his teammates stood in respectful silence, Puskás laughed and told Farkas that he had mistaken him for 'the ice-cream boy'.[11]

This remarkable exchange took place on Margaret Island. In the middle of the Danube, in the heart of Budapest, buttressed on both banks by sun-bleached architectural splendour, the island is an explosion of verdant green against the brown and grey of the city, a natural haven of almost impossible tranquillity amidst the hustle and bustle of one of the world's busiest metropoles. During the 1950s, the island had an army barracks, which was one of the national team's most frequented training grounds. The use of Margaret Island served not only as an indication of the relatively privileged position that the national team enjoyed in Hungarian society; it was also an apt metaphor for the protection and comfort they were afforded during the tumultuous late 1940s and early 1950s in Hungary. They existed in an oasis of calm, while all around them flowed the fast-moving, treacherous waters of the Danube.

★ ★ ★

With Honvéd now the team of the army, Sebes wasted little time in putting his plan to pool his resources into action. Sándor Kocsis and László Budai, both of National Service age, were conscripted. Both were heartbroken to be forced to leave their beloved Ferencváros, but quickly realised the futility of any attempts they could have made to remain. 'The choice,' recalled Budai, 'of playing for Honvéd or spending a few years on a distant border-post was no choice at all, really.'[12] Gyula Grosics was also brought into the fold, foreshadowing the role his rapid distribution would occupy in the national team's style of play.

The impact of this infusion of talent on Honvéd's fortunes was instantaneous. They won the first league title in their history in the 1949–50 season and would win another five before 1956. In 1952, they did so while going unbeaten, a testament to the alchemy the players had developed to extract the best from one another. At times, they operated on what appeared to be an almost psychic level.

The Honvéd project wasn't without some drawbacks, however. Initially, players were expected to complete three months of basic training, living in barracks while they did so. Puskás and Bozsik swiftly intervened, eventually securing preferential treatment for the players and the roles of sergeant major for themselves.[13]

The lack of organic competition in the league meant that those players who weren't playing for either Honvéd or Márton Bukovi's MTK, the only team capable of challenging the army team, found their chances with the national team extremely limited. It was a situation not lost on its beneficiaries, with Puskás noting, 'The system was also tough on some very good players in clubs other than Honvéd. They had no chance of forcing themselves into the national team, because we at Honvéd knew each other's game so well.'[14] Budai remembers the club became 'a bit of a hot-house with so many egos around. I mean, some of these guys were the best players in the world and they wanted things their own way.'[15] The results, however, spoke for themselves.

MTK's ability to keep pace with Honvéd was testament to a revolution of a different kind taking place at the club. In order to help move his team to the next level, Bukovi had begun to experiment with his nascent deep-lying centre-forward ploy, alternating between Péter Palotás and Nándor Hidegkuti in the role. The two men were sharing the same assignment for the national team, albeit with far less emphasis on dropping back. Palotás had grown up playing wing-half, giving him the ball-playing skills and positional awareness required to play in the midfield as the deep-lying forward.[16] Though not possessing the same goal-scoring instinct as Hidegkuti, the freedom afforded to Palotás enabled him to routinely score more than twenty goals a season. Hidegkuti was more prolific, but as Bukovi and the team continued to develop and refine the role, it was the younger Palotás who appeared to be destined for greater things. It wasn't long before Bukovi's team, who remarkably would outscore the Honvéd side featuring Kocsis and Puskás in 1951, 1952 and 1953, had caught the attention of the national team.

★ ★ ★

The national team played only nine times in 1950 and 1951, largely due to their non-participation in the World Cup and the resulting missed games in the Central European International Cup, a round-robin tournament that ran between 1948 and 1953. Their most notable result in these years was a 5-3 loss to Austria in Vienna in May 1950, not so much because of the match itself (a hard-fought contest in which Hungary battled back from behind three times before eventually succumbing), but because it would prove to be another watershed game against the Austrians. The defeat marked the end of the international careers of some of Hungary's veterans, including full-back and captain Sándor Balogh, and finally convinced Sebes the time had come to pass the baton to the next generation of players. It was also the last time that the Hungarians would lose an official match for more than four years.

1952 saw the resumption of a full-fixture schedule, and it would prove the year when Hungary truly announced themselves to the world. Prior to that summer's Olympic Games, the team faced an intimidating trip to Moscow, where they would twice play a Soviet Union XI in unofficial (by virtue of the Soviets insisting both matches be officiated by Russians, violating FIFA's rules), yet still highly touted matches. These games underscored another paradox of life in a Soviet satellite nation. The Kremlin held stringent beliefs about how leaders like Rákosi and their countries ought to behave and rewarded those who were seen to be going above and beyond in promoting communism and aiding the Soviets in the Cold War. There was, however, a line, which if crossed meant a country had gone beyond the beck and call of the Kremlin and were now risking making Russia appear weaker by comparison.

The matches against the Soviet Union were arranged ostensibly as Olympic warm-ups, but for the Soviets, they were also intended as a way of bringing the Hungarian team down a peg or two and demonstrating that no matter what success the Magyars had enjoyed thus far, and what glories they may go on to achieve, they were, at the very most, the equal of the Soviets and certainly not superior. Ironically, these matches did much to raise expectations for the Soviet team in the upcoming Olympics, where they would suffer their humiliating defeat to Yugoslavia.

Of course, the one hitch in the Kremlin's plan was the very real possibility that the capacity crowds of 80,000 Russians who filled Moscow's Dinamo Stadium on 24 and 27 May would watch as their team lost to Sebes' men. To help guard against this eventuality, the Soviets engaged in several underhand tactics designed to throw the Hungarians off their rhythm even more than the somewhat ominous trip to the Motherland to face the team of Hungary's de facto rulers. The players were escorted on long, draining walking tours of

Moscow's cultural sites and museums on match days, something that Sebes found unsporting enough that he was moved to remark upon it, despite the potential for diplomatic repercussions. Sure enough, upon his return to his hotel, he was called by Rákosi, who grilled the coach about his complaints. The implication, clearly, was that Sebes was not to make any further comments about what the Soviet officials were doing to disrupt Hungary's efforts to prepare.

Among the Hungarian populace, there was a persistent rumour that more serious orders came down from the Kremlin, demanding that the Hungarian players were not to try and win. This speculation only intensified when the Hungarians failed to beat the USSR in two subsequent meetings in 1954 and 1955. Sebes and the players maintained that this wasn't the case, but acknowledged that for the two matches in Moscow, the refereeing situation played into their hosts' hands. Both referees were Russians, and both operated outside the parameters that the Hungarians were accustomed to, particularly when it came to aggressive use of arms. Hungary drew the first match 1-1 and lost the second 2-1, but Sebes felt they were constructive exercises, nonetheless, revealing Grosics' tendency to 'dawdle about' (he would force the goalkeeper to play outfield in subsequent training sessions to help him develop a greater appreciation for the expediency of quick distribution), and the team's lacklustre performance at centre-forward.[17]

The team had begun to incorporate the deep-lying centre-forward role that was paying such rich dividends for Márton Bukovi at MTK, but were doing so gradually. In hindsight, the role appears to have few drawbacks in its capability of bamboozling defences that stuck rigidly to the W-M's 'three back' form of defending. However, despite the brilliant natural gifts of the Hungarian team, it also had the capacity to confuse matters. After all, the Hungarian players had also grown up knowing little other than the traditional front five found in both the classic 2-3-5 and the W-M. To suddenly be missing the attack's focal point could, if implemented in a slipshod manner, effectively rob the team of its most important member of the forward line. Matters weren't helped by the embarrassment of riches that Sebes had at his disposal in attacking positions, which tempted him into chopping and changing his team selections often. The first game in Moscow, for example, saw the team start with Hidegkuti and Ferenc Szusza, who was later substituted for Palotás, all of whom could play at centre-forward. It made for a remarkable show of attacking force, particularly alongside Puskás and Kocsis, but such transient team selection wasn't conducive to the chemistry and understanding required for a team in the 1950s to implement what was a truly radical change to their formation.

In the next warm-up match, against Poland, Sebes was unable to travel with the team, instead giving his coaches a letter to be opened just prior to kick-off with instructions. When the letter was opened, a chaotic reshuffle was required. Palotás, who was warmed up and wearing the No. 9 shirt, wasn't starting, and Hidegkuti, sitting up in the stands, was. It was a moment that underscored the fact that even on the eve of one of football's great tactical awakenings in one of its greatest-ever teams, there was still a degree of disorder and disarray. Crucially, however, it was also demonstrative of Sebes inching closer to figuring out his best team, as well as his excellent understanding of the psychological make-up of his individual players. Hidegkuti suffered ter-ribly from nerves before games, particularly when he would be playing out of his natural inside-right position. Sebes knew that by springing his involvement on Hidegkuti late, he would save him from expending an awful lot of nervous energy before a ball had been kicked in anger. Poland were crushed 5-1, and Hidegkuti continued at centre-forward in Hungary's next match, their final warm-up game before the Olympics, a 6-1 win over hosts Finland.

★ ★ ★

The Olympics undoubtedly represented the high point of the pressure on the Magyars to that point. They had demonstrated undeniable potential and were unbeaten (not including the unofficial matches in the USSR) for two years. The Olympics were the first opportunity to transform that success into silver-ware. At the same time, 1952 marked the pinnacle of Rákosi's time in power, when the Stalinist style on which he had modelled his dictatorship enjoyed the greatest degree of undiluted control. Inevitably, the greater the power wielded by the rotund, bald-headed Rákosi over the downtrodden Hungarian people, the more the players were aware of the acute mortality of the privileged posi-tions they enjoyed.

One example of their rarefied lifestyles was the smuggling they were able to get away with. Players brought back nylons, Wilkinson razor blades and even replacement parts for factory machinery from trips abroad, all of which could fetch a good price on the black market. The authorities knew what the players were up to, but generally turned a blind eye – after all, who wanted to be the customs guard responsible for disrupting the Golden Team?

As the gulf between the haves and the have-nots in Hungary widened, the players remained on the fortunate side, but with every passing day, it seemed they had further to fall. The Olympics promised to be all the more challenging as Sebes would be without his tactical doyen Mándi, who was denied permission to travel due to government officials deciding that his owning a shirt shop made him 'an agent of private enterprise'.[18]

Once the team stepped out onto the pitch for their first game in Finland, however, none of that seemed to matter. With a line-up that featured what would become recognised as the Golden Team's strongest forward line of Budai, Kocsis, Hidegkuti, Puskás and Czibor, plus new Honvéd recruits Grosics and Lóránt (who had joined in 1951, a year after the project had got underway), they defeated Romania 2-1, despite a late red card for Kocsis. The next game, against Italy's second-string Olympic squad, promised to offer a stiffer test of their credentials. Sebes, on the telephoned advice of Mándi, utilised the Italians' defensive dogmatism against them, opting to make more liberal use of the MTK-style deep-lying centre-forward. The Italian defenders simply couldn't cope with the constant movement of Palotás, who came into the forward line along with Lajos Csordás in place of Czibor and Budai. Unable to keep tabs on the striker, the Italians were made to pay dearly as Palotás found room to score twice in the opening 20 minutes in a 3-0 win. Italy's coach, the legendary former player Giuseppe Meazza, was quick to point out that Hungary had only beaten a watered-down Italy team, to which Sebes retorted that he was fully prepared to bring his team to Italy to face the full side.[19]

In the quarter-finals, Hungary met Turkey, who had received a bye in the preliminary round and had then narrowly scraped past a decidedly uncompetitive Netherland Antilles team 2-1. Their luck ran out when they faced Sebes' men, who, by now, had shaken off the rust accrued during their limited competitive action of the previous two years and were firmly in gear. Palotás, Kocsis, MTK defender Mihály Lantos, Puskás and Bozsik all scored in a devastating 7-1 display.

Four days later, in front of the second-largest crowd of the tournament at that stage, the Magyars won by the same margin against Sweden, buoyed by the support of a partisan Finnish crowd who had no interest in offering any neighbourly encouragement to the Swedes. Puskás described the performance as 'like a dream … It was one of those days. Once we'd hit our rhythm, we were virtually irresistible. Everything we did seemed to come off perfectly.' He even went so far as to express sympathy for the Swedish team, stating, 'Losing a semi is bad enough of itself, but 6-0 is a real battering and I felt quite sorry for them.'[20] The same compassion wasn't always extended to his teammates, who even when cruising towards victory were made aware of their captain's displeasure at any misplaced passes by his exasperated yells.

Hungary were now the talk of the Games, and while most waited excitedly to see what the team from beyond the Iron Curtain would do in the final, one man didn't need to wait for the gold medal match to make his judgement on the Magyars' merits. English FA Secretary Stanley Rous was, like the tens of thousands of others in attendance that day, enraptured by the flowing football and devastating finishing of the Hungarians as they battered Sweden, managed by the man Rous had recommended years before, George Raynor. Rous had done much to bring the English national team to at least a semblance of modernity, championing the appointment of Walter Winterbottom and recognising the gross inadequacy of placing the job of player selection into the hands of the FA Committee. However, he was now about to set in motion a series of events that would lay bare the inadequacies that ran to the very core of English football.

Amidst the hubbub of the post-match celebrations, the moustachioed Rous made a beeline for Sebes, telling him, according to Hungarian commentator György Szepesi, 'Mr Sebes, I think it's time we arranged a match between England and Hungary.' Sándor Barcs, President of the Hungarian FA, remembered Rous saying to him, 'Look, you'll have to come to London and play England soon. Let's shake hands on it.'[21]

Whichever man was the recipient of the original request (by all accounts of Rous' enthusiasm, he may well have attempted to persuade both men), it made little difference. Both Barcs and Sebes needed no convincing about the glamour of Rous' proposal – the prospect of facing the great England at perhaps the most famous stadium in the world spoke for itself. However, both men were well aware that it would be far more complicated than simply shaking Rous' hand, there and then. Such an event would inevitably require approval from the very highest levels of government. As Barcs would reflect later, 'I always say winning at Wembley wasn't as difficult as getting there.'[22]

Barcs and Sebes scarcely had time to digest Rous' request before their focus was wrenched back to the matter at hand – who Hungary would face in the final. The day after Hungary had confirmed their place, Yugoslavia came out on top of a far more even semi-final against Germany. After their defeat of the Soviets in the first round, the final being played between Yugoslavia and

Hungary had almost biblical undertones, with Sebes' team playing Abel to the Yugoslavians' Cain.

If Rákosi had been relatively restrained in his meddling up to this point, he now could no longer contain himself. Not only would a Hungarian victory be an enormous coup for his government, but defeating Yugoslavia, who had humiliated the Soviet Union politically and on the pitch in quick succession, would carry tremendous clout with Moscow. The Kremlin, for their part, cast aside the desire that they'd evinced in the two friendlies earlier that year to see Hungary's young star-studded team brought into line.

The opportunity to humble Tito's team was an absolutely irresistible prospect. On the eve of the match, Rákosi made his demands crystal clear, calling Sebes to tell him that 'failure would not be tolerated. It was not permitted to lose!'[23] Sebes wisely elected not to relay such a blunt message to his players, but the political subtext of the match couldn't fail to register with the young men, who had grown up watching their homeland pulled from pillar to post by foreign invaders.

The political intrigue extended onto the pitch, where the massed Hungarian attacking force found themselves thwarted repeatedly by one man, Vladimir Beara, who Lev Yashin would later call the greatest goalkeeper of all time. The most dramatic of these saves came from the penalty spot, when Beara denied Puskás, who was guilty of a rare moment of indecision and hit a tame penalty that the goalkeeper stopped down to his right. Puskás, never one to spare his teammates his unfiltered opinions of their performances, was livid with himself and 'spent the next few minutes diving around in the penalty box' in an attempt to earn a chance to atone for his error, according to Sebes.[24]

As the game wore on, however, Yugoslavia made fewer and fewer forays forward, and the Hungarian players began to relax, as they realised that if one team was to score, it was likely to be them. Sure enough, with 20 minutes remaining, Puskás was played through on goal. Despite having two defenders for company, he had the presence of mind to tap the ball past the onrushing Beara, before rolling it into the empty net. With 2 minutes to go and Yugoslavia unable to find a foothold to haul themselves back into contention, Czibor put the matter to bed, lashing a bouncing ball home on the half-volley.

Moments later, Puskás stood atop the Olympic podium. If Hungary's reputation had been confined to their corner of Eastern Europe, it certainly wasn't now (UK press coverage was limited, but even there, Hungary's reputation was growing, and *The Times* lamented that Hungary hadn't found their usual top gear for the record crowd in the final).

The Olympics had not only delivered Hungary the international recognition that both its citizens and its government craved (the country ultimately finished third in the overall medals table, a remarkable feat, given its size), but it represented the point where the football team truly came of age. In the words of Puskás, 'It was during the Olympics that our football first started to flow with real power ... When we attacked, everyone attacked; in defence, it was the same.'[25]

Sebes and Mándi, with tutelage from Márton Bukovi, would go down in the annals of football tactics history for what they would finally perfect over the coming months, but they deserved tremendous credit for what they had already achieved, much of it far ahead of its time. The pair were rigorous in their emphasis on dynamic, engaging training sessions, ensuring their players were in peak physical condition. They undertook advanced scouting and their team talks frequently focused on danger men in the opposition and how best to nullify them. Sebes' political sagacity extended to the relationship between him and his players, who he was able to keep motivated and focused, even after years of dominance.

But perhaps the pair's greatest achievement was enabling the players to have the freedom to play in the way that Puskás described. Sebes had tremendous power over the team and could have taken them in an entirely different direction. A stricter manager could have forced the players into a more dogmatic W-M, stifling the fluidity that had become the trademark of Hungary's attacks. It's impossible to conceive of so many goals being scored and shared across the five forwards if the W-M's traditionally rigid positions had been imposed.

Perhaps inevitably, the effervescent elan with which Hungary played was seized upon by the government and the supporters as 'socialist football', with a democratic approach to positions and roles, and skilled players who served as exemplars of the 'genius dormant in the proletariat'.[26] Equally, a less authoritative manager could have become overwhelmed by the attacking options he possessed and simply let the team run riot, losing the respect and discipline required to defend leads. Sebes and Mándi walked this tightrope in a masterful fashion, carefully cultivating a sense of freedom and fluidity allied with an overwhelming desire to win. It was this balance that meant that Bukovi's deep-lying centre-forward, when it was finally fully realised in Hungary's next match, had such a devastating impact.

★ ★ ★

In their first match as Olympic champions, Hungary travelled to Bern, one of the six cities that would play host to World Cup football in two years' time, to play Switzerland in the long-running fifth Central European International Cup. Puskás and his teammates were naturally confident, with the rapturous adulations of the 100,000-strong crowd who had welcomed them and their fellow Olympians back to Budapest still ringing in their ears. In addition, they were facing the team that would finish bottom of the International Cup without winning a match. Whether it was over-confidence, fatigue from the gruelling turn that their international schedule had suddenly taken during the Olympics, or a combination of the two, Hungary found themselves 2-0 down and reeling after just 11 minutes.

Worse was to come, when, after just 30 minutes, Sebes felt moved to substitute Péter Palotás, his centre-forward. Though still only 23, Palotás was already exhibiting surprisingly limited reserves of stamina, often featuring as a substitute or being substituted himself. Unbeknownst to all at the time, Palotás' struggles to play a full 90 minutes were likely the early manifestations of a heart condition that would eventually curtail his career when he was just 30 and result in his death, seven years later. Sebes elected to replace him with his MTK clubmate, Nándor Hidegkuti. Before Hidegkuti took the pitch, Sebes instructed him to work on linking the play between the attack and defence, as he did with MTK, instead of focusing on leading the line.

Hidegkuti's introduction proved to be a footballing eureka moment, the point where Bukovi's innovation of withdrawing the W-M's attacking focal point and instead having him turn provider finally clicked into place for the national team. Though still nominally the team's centre-forward, the most singular role in the W-M beyond the goalkeeper, the team was transformed by Hidegkuti's movement and positional sense. 'The Swiss were getting all their men behind the ball and drawing our defenders into risky attacks,' explained Sebes. 'Everyone in our team wanted to score, and we were exposed to counter-strikes.'[27]

Not only did Hidegkuti dropping deep shore up the team's defensive shape and help stifle the Swiss attempts to break out, but he was finding acres of space that Palotás, in his more advanced position, had been denied. In the 15 minutes between Hidegkuti's entrance and the half-time break, he assisted Puskás twice, drawing Hungary level.

The second half belonged entirely to the Hungarians, as they scored twice more to seal a 4-2 win. The MTK template of the deep-lying centre-forward had been available for some time, but nobody – not Sebes nor Mándi, perhaps not even Márton Bukovi – had truly fathomed quite what an impact it could have on the international stage. The chaos it created in the Swiss defensive ranks was a marked contrast to what had immediately preceded it when Palotás was on the field. 'It decided once and for all,' Sebes reflected, 'the player best suited to the deep-lying No. 9 role.'[28]

At the age of 30, Hidegkuti was about to finally enjoy an uncontested spell for his country. Hungary were already an exceptionally talented and well-coached team, but they now had the final piece of a highly intricate puzzle that would propel them to a new plane entirely.

ISLAND SUPREMACY

Even with England's disastrous expulsion from the World Cup in Brazil miti-gated by an indifferent press reaction, Stanley Rous, Walter Winterbottom and the England players knew it was imperative that they recovered quickly. A for-giving public may not have yet felt that England's role as football's great force had been relinquished, but any further defeats, particularly if they occurred closer to home, would have led to some probing questions about the team's quality and the FA's fitness to organise them.

The first match following the World Cup defeat to Spain, a 4-1 win away in Ireland, proved just the tonic. The selectors made wholesale changes, with five different players chosen from the last line-up in Brazil, two of whom, Jackie Lee and Allenby Chilton, made their debuts aged 29 and 32 respectively. England's next game was another routine win, 4-2 over Wales, with a fur-ther three players handed their first cap. One of those, replacing Chilton at centre-half, was Leslie Compton, who, at 38, was England's oldest ever outfield debutant and was almost three years Stanley Matthews' senior.

Chilton and Compton would each only appear once more for their country. Compton was, unsurprisingly, less than two years away from retirement. The advanced years of both players served to underline the enor-mous vacuum left at the critical position of centre-half by Neil Franklin's defection to the Colombian league and subsequent ostracism from the England team.

Though little had changed materially in terms of England's organisation in the immediate aftermath of the World Cup, they did, by accident, as much as by design, manage to give the impression that the disastrous showing against the USA and defeat to Spain had been anomalies. This fed the narrative that they simply had failed to perform in an unfamiliar tournament on a continent they'd never before visited, not that their footballing mastery was in any way under serious and sustained threat.

They rounded out 1950 with a close-fought draw with Yugoslavia at Highbury, where their unbeaten home record against Continental sides would have ended but for a brace from yet another debutant, Bolton centre-forward Nat Lofthouse. Next came a visit from Scotland, one that saw the selectors field England's most experienced post-war XI, featuring Alf Ramsey, Billy Wright, Matthews, Wilf Mannion, Tom Finney and, for only the third time at centre-forward, Stan Mortensen, to seek revenge on the old enemy for the defeat inflicted at Wembley in 1949.

No matter the best-laid plans of Winterbottom and the selectors, they were thrown into disarray when Mannion suffered a fractured jaw in an aerial clash just 10 minutes in. An injury to Mortensen later in the match would briefly reduce the home team to nine men. Despite a valiant effort by the wounded Lions, Scotland once again left Wembley victorious, yet England's apologists could again point to mitigating factors for their beloved team's failings. Nonetheless, there was no ignoring the fact that England's run of three defeats in six internationals was their worst since 1937.

Yet, just as it appeared that England were careening towards a nadir and a stark, long-overdue realisation that root and branch reform was desperately required, fortune suddenly seemed to smile on the team. The defeat to Scotland would prove to be England's last loss for two years. During this period, the World Cup fiasco would gradually fade from the country's collective footballing memory, as a new generation of players finally emerged.

Though plenty still departed the international stage almost as soon as they'd arrived, beneficiaries and then victims of the selection committee, a semblance of consistency was restored to the line-up after the loss of players who had played for their country both before and after the war, such as Tommy Lawton. Even the old warhorse, Stanley Matthews, was being quietly nudged out of the international picture. Having made his debut in 1934, the now 36-year-old seemed to have reached the culmination of his illustrious international career, appearing in the match with Scotland before injury forced him to withdraw from the squad for England's next two games, against Argentina and Portugal, after which he slipped from favour and appeared destined for an idyllic end to his career by the sea in Blackpool.

★ ★ ★

The first truly post-war England side was a remarkable group of young men, both on an individual level and a sporting one, several of whom still rank comfortably within the upper echelons as the greatest to ever represent their country. Though many of the players of this generation would discuss their experiences during the war with a shrug and a self-deprecating chuckle, many had undergone life-altering experiences, both physically and mentally. Forged in the crucible of war (or at the very least in the looming shadow of it) and invariably from working-class backgrounds, these England players, to a man, were acutely attuned to the social conditions the rest of the country found itself in and what privilege they enjoyed by virtue of their extraordinary ability to play football.

As the great goalkeeper Frank Swift faded from the international scene, two successors emerged in the form of Wolves' Bert Williams and Birmingham City's Gil Merrick. Williams, who served with the RAF, was nicknamed 'the Cat', due to his reflexes and agility. Merrick, meanwhile, had endured the unenviable task of replacing legendary Blues and England goalkeeper Harry Hibbs, but had proved himself a reliable successor at St Andrews. Merrick complemented his natural skills and imposing frame with fastidious study of opposing strikers, in order to try and gain an edge. Though Merrick would eventually secure the shirt for a string of caps and play in goal for all but one fixture between late 1951 and 1954, he may have wondered, at points, if it had been worth it. His England career could not be called a particularly happy one and ended on a sour note, as he became the victim of a cruel scapegoating campaign.

Though the era would be remembered as a golden age of high-scoring games and prolific strikers, there were several superb defensive figures who left their mark – both figuratively and literally – on the potent attacking forces of the 1950s. Right-half Billy Wright was a born leader, a fearsome competitor who exemplified the grit and steel of the archetypal British defender, and the 'supreme captain', in the words of Finney.[1]

Like many involved in football, Wright had not seen active duty during the war, instead serving as a physical training instructor after badly breaking his ankle, an injury which briefly threatened his career. Combative on the field, he was much the same off it, evinced by the fact he was one of the few players of the post-war generation willing to criticise what he perceived to be Stan Matthews' self-indulgent streak, once referring to England's maestro as 'a pain in the neck to his colleagues who waited in vain for the pass that never came'.[2]

However, he knew when and where to pick his battles. He would ingratiate himself with Walter Winterbottom, not only thanks to his consistency but by opening up to the cultivated manager in a way that few of his international teammates would. Winterbottom admired Wright due to 'his dependability, his solid experience, his sustained and reliable level of performance', characteristics shared by the manager, who preferred a captain of Wright's temperament to someone 'more flamboyant, more dramatic, faster with an opinion, a better talker, a dramatic leader of men'.[3] Such was their friendship that the two would co-author a book with writer Bob Ferrier in the early 1960s, divulging their shared belief in the virtues of coaching and views on how the game ought to be played. Like Winterbottom (and perhaps in deference to their friendship), Wright was also critical of the FA selection committee's meddling role, safe in the knowledge by the early 1950s that his name was as much a permanent fixture on the England team sheet as it was possible to be.

While Wright was destined to become the iconic defensive presence of the period, there were plenty of other outstanding stoppers, whose playing style ranged from the cerebral and measured to pure blood and thunder. Alf Ramsey unquestionably belonged to the former camp. He, too, served most of his time during the war on the Home Front, but owed more than most to the experience, as it gave him his first taste of organised football, leading him to sign as a professional after the cessation. Of equal importance, and the reason he would later refer to his time in the army as 'one of the greatest things to ever happen to me', was the fact that army life enabled the shy, retiring Ramsey to come out of his shell to the extent necessary to succeed in the rough and tumble world of English football.[4] His abilities were described by Finney as 'more functional than outstanding', but though he lacked the Herculean physique or fearless tackling of some he played alongside, he made up for it in meticulous observation of the game.[5]

In many respects, it's something of a surprise that Winterbottom ended up gravitating towards Wright as his on-field general and off-field confidant. While Wright was no luddite and was more open to the concept of coaching than many of his generation, Ramsey was the true philosopher of the early

1950s England team. Already playing in a Spurs team that would wow spectators and sweep all before them with their brand of 'push-and-run' football, Ramsey's mind had been awoken to the concept of testing the boundaries of the footballing orthodoxy and experiencing success as a result. For all his limitations, he rose to become an England regular, and did so thanks to careful analysis and exploiting weaknesses.

At the time, Ramsey's opportunities to put his nascent tactical theories to the test beyond his own play were non-existent. The same forces that hindered Winterbottom and forward-thinking coaches were magnified tenfold for any player who dared to think he might know better than the almost 30-year-old W-M system. It's fascinating to wonder whether the tactical innovations that Ramsey used to lead England to World Cup glory a decade and a half later could have appeared sooner and established England at the forefront of the burgeoning movement that would undermine the W-M, had he, and not Wright, captured Winterbottom's ear.

There were, of course, others for whom the war was considerably more taxing. Several future England internationals found themselves posted overseas and put in mortal danger. Harry Johnston, Blackpool's defensive stalwart, served in the Middle East, and returned to preside over the most successful spell of the club's history, becoming one of three regulars in the England team of the early 1950s supplied by the Tangerines. Closer to Wright than Ramsey in his style, yet still characterised as a 'cultured controller' by Winterbottom,[6] Johnston was perfectly satisfied with his lot as a centre-half in the W-M age, which meant every week going toe to toe – and often head to head – with an opposing centre-forward. Though certainly a defender of his time, he was not without a solid understanding of the finer points of the game. As Blackpool captain, he would frequently feign exasperation with his manager Joe Smith's lack of instruction, telling his teammates, 'We haven't got a bloody clue what we're doing, do we?' before taking it upon himself to outline a game plan.[7]

If the titanic contest between centre-half and centre-forward tended to be the decisive battle of the W-M era, it was the clash between the flying winger and the right or left full-back charged with stopping him that brought the fans through the turnstiles. Though Matthews remained the people's champion, there was little argument that his mantle as England's best winger had been taken up by Tom Finney. Less reliant on a menagerie of feints and tricks than his illustrious predecessor and more dependent on lightning pace, preternatural dribbling ability and whipped crosses that he could land on a sixpence, Finney was arguably the greatest England player of his generation. He, too, had experienced the sharp end of the Second World War, shortly after first breaking into Preston's successful wartime side, serving in North Africa under Montgomery.

Of the elite English footballers of the era, however, the player who had suffered the greatest horrors was one who rarely played without a boyish grin on his face. Stan Mortensen's career as a professional footballer had suffered an abortive start, as he failed to break into the Blackpool team he signed for in 1937 and narrowly avoided being released, before joining the RAF on the outbreak of the war. Still only 18 and nowhere near proven enough to qualify for the physical training roles that many of his future teammates received, Mortensen instead became a wireless operator and air gunner, flying in hulking bombers.

Though the most prevailing image of the RAF during the war was the darting and derring-do of the fighter pilots dogfighting their way over the Channel during the Battle of Britain, bomber crews were no less at risk. More than 8,000 bombers were brought down, despite the best efforts of air gunners like Mortensen, who sat at the very front and back of their aircraft with little but their turret between them and the Luftwaffe. Of the 125,000 who served under Bomber Command, over 57,000 were killed, while more than 8,000 were wounded and 9,000 taken as prisoners of war, a remarkable rate that testifies to the fact that, in most cases, once a bomber was successfully attacked or suffered a critical malfunction, its crew stood a vanishingly small chance of survival.

This exact scenario occurred for Mortensen when the Wellington bomber he was crewing came down. True to statistical form, the Wellington's pilot and bomb aimer were both killed, while the navigator suffered such severe injuries that his leg was amputated. Mortensen escaped with a head trauma severe enough that he had a metal plate inserted and was thereafter excluded from consideration for operational duty. He was also given the crushing news that he should curtail his short career as a footballer, due to the lasting effects of his head injury and the perils of heading leaden, leather balls.

It was a warning that he did not heed. While many others, having experienced such a traumatic incident and having made little headway professionally, would have begun the arduous search for a new career, hidden behind Mortensen's cheerful, impish exterior was a steely resolve. By the early 1950s, Mortensen was established as perhaps the best young inside-forward in the country, an expert at both supporting his winger and reading the intentions of his centre-forward, enabling him to plunder goals at a remarkable rate. The goal he scored against Argentina in May 1951, in the first game of what proved to be England's two-year unbeaten spell, took Mortensen's international record to an incredible twenty-one goals in twenty-three appearances.

★ ★ ★

The Argentina match, England's first-ever home game against South American opposition, was won 2-1, but played out in a similar vein to the Yugoslavia draw the previous November, with England coming perilously close to surrendering their famous unbeaten record against teams from beyond the British Isles. On this occasion, the first time a team other than Scotland had faced England at the Empire Stadium, England required two goals in the final 10 minutes from Mortensen and Newcastle's Jackie Milburn to emerge as 2-1 victors.

It was a similar story ten days later at Goodison Park, when Portugal pegged England back twice before wilting in the final 15 minutes and conceding three goals to lose 5-2. The Portugal match proved notable as the first time in Billy Wright's England career that he was dropped on the basis of form, even while Winterbottom's defence remained in a transitory state. The latest to audition for Franklin's vacated centre-half spot was 33-year-old Jim Taylor, who played both the Argentina and Portugal fixtures and was never subsequently recalled.

If the Argentina and Portugal matches had issued England a warning, their next match, against France at Highbury, was a full-blown shot across the bows. Though relatively prominent in football, thanks to the influence of Jules Rimet, who served for more than three decades as the President of FIFA, the French national team had lagged behind both the British and their Continental neighbours for decades. Aside from one aberration in 1932 – a 5-2 France victory in Paris over an England team with four debutants and only one player with more than eight caps – the French could have been forgiven for feeling that the game of association football had been invented by the British purely as an instrument with which to humiliate their old imperial foe. Of the eleven times they had met, England had won ten. On the two occasions that France had travelled across the Channel, England had beaten them by a cumulative score of 7-1. For two nations that had endured such a tumultuous relationship, football was a rare arena in which one dominated the other.

In 1951, however, with both France and England coming to terms with their diminished status in the world, their rapidly contracting empires and their war-torn states that had reduced them to relying on American aid, the French national team was on the rise. They would soon count among their ranks the mercurial Raymond Kopa and the prolific Just Fontaine as part of their team's first golden generation. Yet, even before these young stars had truly established themselves, the French team acquitted themselves admirably in north London, coming from behind to lead 2-1 before eventually settling for a 2-2 draw. Though England, who played the likes of Ramsey, Wright, Finney, Mannion and Milburn, enjoyed most of the play, they had Williams in goal to thank for the draw, as he pulled off several outstanding saves to preserve his team's precious record.

England's next major test came in November 1951, as they took on Austria. While France's footballing reputation remained relatively meagre, hence the shock they generated by producing such a polished performance, Austria were a brilliant technical side. Though few in England considered them the superiors of Winterbottom's men, there was at least an acknowledgement that the Austrians would provide a stiff test. *The Times* applied a typically imperial spin on the match, commenting, 'England today face what promises to be the most serious threat yet to their island supremacy against the challenge from oversea when they meet the vaunted Austrian side.'

Austria's coach, Walter Nausch, had played under Hugo Meisl in the 1930s *Wunderteam*, and had inherited his mentor's belief in the Danubian free-flowing, short-passing game, as well as his emphasis on the importance of utilising a familiar core of players. Nine of the Austrian starters were drawn from either SK Rapid or Austria Wien, and the squad had played together as a group virtually since the Austrian national team had been restored following the Second World War.

Winterbottom's pleas for a similar degree of consistency continued to fall on deaf ears. The team the selectors chose to face Austria featured players from eight different club sides and was characterised by a marked lack of experience; just three of the starting XI had more than six caps, compared to seven Austrian players who had at least twenty international appearances to their names. Even by the inconsistent standards of the post-war era, the Austria match saw something of a watershed selection, as 23-year-old Arsenal winger Arthur Milton was picked for his first and only cap to replace the injured Finney. A fine all-round sportsman, Milton nonetheless had just twelve league appearances to his name when he was selected. If his call-up appeared premature, it proved surprisingly prescient, given the brief nature of Milton's career. By 27, he had retired from football in order to focus on cricket, which would lead him to become the twelfth and, in all likelihood, last man to represent England in first-class internationals in both sports.

Austria had, the year before, become the first Continental team to triumph in Scotland, and had then thumped the Scots 4-0 in a return match in Vienna earlier in 1951. While still deploying a W-M, theirs was a probing, metronomic interpretation of the formation, with Ernst Ocwirk, at centre-half, a far more constructive than destructive presence. The Austrian style appeared to have the beating of the blood-and-thunder version practised by the British national teams.

All the ingredients were present for an England defeat. Instead, the home side rose to the occasion and produced their strongest performance in months, yielding a 2-2 result that, if anything, flattered the visitors, who had legendary shot-stopper Walter Zeman to thank for coming to their rescue on numerous occasions.

Better was to come. After triumphing over Scotland at Hampden Park in April 1952, England set out on their traditional end-of-season tour with three fixtures that looked as intimidating a run of games as they had faced in living memory. They would first take on Italy, one of the Continent's strongest teams, still smarting from England's stunning victory on their last visit in 1948. They would then travel north for a return match with Austria in Vienna, before rounding the tour off with an easier, yet still potentially tricky game versus Switzerland.

England did at least have the benefit of a slightly more settled team. Though still transient, the England squad was, for the moment, being selected in a slightly more consistent fashion, with a core of near-certain selections emerging. Gil Merrick had wrested the No. 1 shirt from Bert Williams. Alf Ramsey, Billy Wright and Jimmy Dickinson were firmly installed in the defensive and central positions. There even appeared to be a solution to the revolving door of debutants in the troublesome centre-half berth, since Neil Franklin's exile, in the form of Portsmouth's Jack Froggatt.

Tom Finney, despite a tendency to pick up injuries that may have done for lesser players' hopes with the selection committee, remained irrepressible and simply too good to ignore. Stan Mortensen, despite his phenomenal record, had, for the meantime, fallen foul of the vagaries of the selection committee, but the gulf in goals left by the Blackpool man's absence was being ably filled by another forward from a neighbouring Lancastrian club.

Bolton's Nat Lofthouse had served his time during the war as a Bevin Boy, helping to bolster the mining workforce that had been decimated by conscription. The work was dangerous and gruelling, particularly given Lofthouse's young age, and he would often finish an eight-hour shift and immediately get the bus to training or a War League match. However, it imbued him with both the raw physicality and relentless determination that would mark him out as the best exemplification of the classic English centre-forward of the 1950s.

The first match, in Florence, confirmed some of the worst prejudices the English media held about the Italians and their fans. Two men, Wright and Finney, remained from the famous Turin win, four years previously, but even they had cause to be taken aback by the brutal nature of the game, which descended into a physical battle, with both sides giving as good as they got. The result, 1-1 after England had led from the 4th minute, was tough but fair. The same could not be said of the treatment of the English players by the Italian fans, who pelted the field with glass bottles.

The reception at Vienna's Praterstadion promised to be somewhat less partisan. The Austrian crowd had a reputation as being objective lovers of good football, demanding of their own team and appreciative of play in the quick, fluid Danubian style. Though now playing second fiddle to their neighbours Hungary as the foremost exponents of this brand of play, their fans were eager to see their team's reputation restored following the ignominy of their annexation by Nazi Germany. It wasn't until the England party arrived in Austria, however, that the travellers came to appreciate the unique nature of the crowd that awaited them.

Thousands of British Tommies were stationed in the country, and the arrival of the England team sent them into a frenzy. Tickets to the match were traded on the black market for vast multiples of their face value. More alarmingly for the English players were reports that those soldiers who hadn't spent over the odds to get a ticket had staked huge sums – in some cases, weeks of pay – betting on an English victory. Despite being away from home and playing a match few would have been surprised if England had lost, the pressure on each player was immense. Even England's biggest stars of this battle-hardened generation would later recall the all-consuming trepidation they felt before each game for the national team as being some of the most nerve-wracking episodes of their lives. The idea of thousands of football-mad soldiers being left out of pocket while stationed in a foreign country was an added burden that none of the players needed. Rather than shirk this added challenge, however, Lofthouse summed up the collective attitude that, for better and for worse, exemplified the thinking of English football when he told Bill Eckersley, 'We'll simply have to win'.[8]

Austria had been, historically, an extremely happy hunting ground for the English national team. Three games in 1908 and 1909 had yielded three victories and an aggregate score of 23-3 in favour of the visitors. Vivian Woodward's mantle as his country's top goal scorer, which had been threatened by Tommy Lawton before his fall from favour and was in the sights of Stan Mortensen and Tom Finney, was indebted to these visits to the Continent; eight of his twenty-nine international goals had come in the three games with Austria (a further six resulted from three games against Hungary as part of the same two post-season tours).

Those days, unfortunately for England, were long gone, and the most recent meeting of the two teams in Austria, in 1936, had seen Meisl's team triumph 2-1 over an undistinguished Three Lions side. However, 25 May 1952 was to be England's day, as they turned in arguably their best performance since the 4-0 win in Turin. Winterbottom's men twice took the lead in the first half, only to be quickly pegged back on both occasions. As the second period wore on, Austria began to dominate and exerted huge pressure on the England defence. Then, with minutes to go, Finney and Lofthouse launched a lightning break, with the latter poking the ball home in heroic fashion as he was clattered by the Austrian goalkeeper.

Just as England's routs of Portugal and Italy in the late 1940s had sent their opponents into a spiral of existential consternation, so did their victory in Vienna seem to leave a lasting psychological effect on their opponents. Having lost just three games in the previous three years, following the Lofthouse-inspired defeat, Austria would go sixteen months without a win, during which time they were drubbed 4-0 by an inspired Republic of Ireland team in Dublin. The age of Austria as a force in world football, which briefly appeared to be continuing into the post-war years, was drawing to a close and, even as they finished third in the 1954 World Cup, they would never again truly reach the heights they had experienced in the 1930s and 1940s.

The English reaction, meanwhile, was one of understandable elation, laced with the imperially inspired condescension present whenever England vanquished a vaunted foe from the Continent. *The Times* wheeled out the well-worn British criticism of Continental teams, commenting that though the Austrians had posed a greater threat, their mistake had been 'trying to walk the ball into the net', whereas England had not hesitated. The most enduring piece of reportage from the game belonged to the *Daily Express*'s Desmond Hackett, who was effusive in his praise for the team and anointed Lofthouse the 'Lion of Vienna'.

As with many of England's best results of Winterbottom's early years, with the benefit of hindsight there were warning signs amid the glory of the smash and grab in Vienna. England had found themselves on the back foot for much of the game, out passed and outmanoeuvred by a more technically incisive and cohesive team unit. What's more, it had taken a Herculean individual effort from Lofthouse to heave England to victory. The battle scars he bore from his brutal clash with Austria's goalkeeper would pay for pints in pubs up and down the country for the rest of his life, but to expect such a stirring, sacrificial performance from him, or any other England player, each time the Three Lions took on a major opponent was folly, particularly with the selection committee wielding their scythe so remorselessly and indiscriminately.

England would see out the remainder of 1952 in the afterglow of the Vienna game. They rounded off their tour of the Continent with a thumping 3-0 win in Switzerland, before a hard-fought draw with Northern Ireland, a 5-2 win over Wales and a 5-0 defeat of Belgium rounded out the year. This string of satisfying results was helped by a sense of stability finally entering Winterbottom's teams, after years of flux following the loss of Lawton, Franklin and others of their generation.

★ ★ ★

If there had been any rumblings of discontent with the FA's running of the team, the apparent turnaround, if not in performances then at least in results, snuffed them out. The FA was to turn 90 in 1953, and after a near-century in which change and evolution had been resisted at almost every possible turn, they weren't about to rip up their rule book when the going appeared relatively good. Even Stanley Rous, who was almost congenitally predisposed to push back against the cushy status quo that ensconced the national team, was not going to propose a radical overhaul of how things were done. Instead, Rous was preoccupied with planning a footballing extravaganza to celebrate the FA's milestone birthday. Emboldened by the team's change in fortunes following the ignominy in Brazil two years before, he intended to mark the occasion by demonstrating England's prowess on the pitch for the whole world to see.

Firstly, England would have the opportunity to win the annual Home Championship when they faced Scotland for their opening match of 1953. After that, they would be conducting a tour of the Americas. Demonstrative of the world's broadening horizons, thanks to air travel as well as the gradual easing of the FA's long-standing isolationism, the tour had the added incentive of drawing a line once and for all under the debacle of the 1950 World Cup. Three games in three separate South American countries were intended to right the wrongs of the team's lacklustre displays on their first visit to the continent. The trip would be rounded off with a visit to New York City, where the Three Lions would hope to lay to rest the ghosts of their embarrassment against the USA in Belo Horizonte.

Every season since the end of the war, England had welcomed a foreign side to her shores to play the national team for a marquee match towards the end of the year, and 1953 would see the arrival of a star-studded Rest of the World team for the match officially designated to celebrate the FA's 90th anniversary. However, Rous still wasn't satisfied. After being enraptured by the performance of the Hungarians in their Olympic semi-final dismantling of Sweden, Rous had wasted little time in attempting to woo Gusztáv Sebes and Hungarian FA chief, Sándor Barcs.

However, his initial overtures for a visit of Hungary to England had been rebuffed, with Barcs later admitting he played for time in order to save face, as he 'didn't dare' let on just how limited his authority was.[9] Accustomed to a world of gentlemanly agreements and handshakes deciding such matters, and still blissfully ignorant of the political entanglements that would soon come to engulf the game at large, Rous had not appreciated the spiderweb of Soviet bureaucracy that would need to be untangled before the Hungarians could agree to a game, no matter how keen Sebes and Barcs were for it to happen.

Rous, though, was persistent. Several months after their meeting at the Olympics, Rous attended a summit of European Football Association leaders in Switzerland, at which Sebes was also present. This time, the forceful Englishman was determined to come away with an affirmative answer. After being cornered, Sebes, in a rare example of his enthusiasm for football eclipsing his political savvy, acquiesced to Rous' pleas and agreed to a game, to take place in late 1953.

Since Rous' original proposal, Sebes and Barcs had both been grilled by the Central Committee and Mátyás Rákosi himself about whether they could guarantee a Hungarian victory if the match was sanctioned. Though both men had expressed confidence that they could achieve the win over their Western foes that the Hungarian government and the Kremlin craved, they had yet to convince either that the result was set in stone. No matter how assured Sebes felt about eventually securing permission for the England fixture, he was not yet across the line, and so was quite alarmed when, several days later, Rous announced to the world what instantly became one of the most highly anticipated international fixtures in years.

Sebes' trepidation was warranted. He was promptly 'carpeted' by Rákosi for sanctioning the game without the General Secretary's say-so.[10] Eventually, Sebes was able to convince the menacing Rákosi 'that even if we lost, it would be a historic occasion. I told him that no foreign football team had ever left Wembley victorious, but in football nothing was for ever.'[11]

Privately, Sebes was delighted, even if he had received a stinging rebuke from one of the most feared men in the world. Once Rous had pre-emptively announced the fixture, there could be no backing down from the Hungarians without a significant loss of face. After so much foot-dragging and prevaricating from the Central Committee as to whether it was wise to risk the team's sterling reputation and, in turn, their effectiveness as an arm of the government's propaganda machine, their hand had been forced. Sebes would get his match.

Rous left the conference in Switzerland delighted to have secured what promised to be the cherry on top of a tremendous 1953 calendar with which to celebrate the FA's 90th anniversary. He could not possibly have countenanced the idea that he had just inadvertently sown the seeds for England's greatest-ever humiliation on the football field, at a time in the country's history when a show of global strength was desperately needed.

The four Tangerines. For the 'Match of the Century', the FA attempted to harness the magic of the Matthews Final by selecting four Blackpool players. From left to right: Stanley Matthews, Ernie Taylor, Harry Johnston and Stan Mortensen. (PA Images/Alamy Stock Photo)

The Hungarian team were known for the exuberance of their attack, and here centre-forward Nándor Hidegkuti demonstrates that flair while training at Fulham's Craven Cottage. (PA Images/Alamy Stock Photo)

Billy Wright (far right) and Ferenc Puskás (third from right) lead out the teams. The baggy-kitted, heavy-booted England players had just moments before joked among themselves that the Hungarians had the wrong kit. (PA Images/Alamy Stock Photo)

The Magical Magyars. From left to right: Ferenc Puskás, Gyula Grosics, Gyula Lóránt, Nándor Hidegkuti, Jenő Buzánszky, Mihály Lantos, József Zakariás, Zoltán Czibor, József Bozsik, László Budai and Sándor Kocsis. (Colorsport/Shutterstock)

Wright (left) and Puskás (right) exchange pennants beneath one of Wembley's famous towers. It would not be the last notable meeting the two would have before the day was through. (PA Images/Alamy Stock Photo)

The shot heard around the world. Nándor Hidegkuti's shot flies past Gil Merrick's desperate dive after less than a minute to give Hungary the lead, with England barely having touched the ball. (PA Images/Alamy Stock Photo)

Ferenc Puskás (centre, wearing No. 10) raises his arms aloft after scoring his famous drag-back goal, Hungary's third. Billy Wright (to the left of Puskás, facing the goal) was said by *The Times* writer Geoffrey Green to have missed Puskás in the manner of 'a fire engine going to the wrong fire'. (Photo by William Vanderson/Fox Photos/Getty Images)

Sándor Kocsis (third from left) is denied by a fine save by Gil Merrick while Zoltán Czibor (third from right) celebrates prematurely. The three watching England defenders are, left to right, Billy Wright, Jimmy Dickinson and Alf Ramsey, for whom the game would leave a lasting impression. (Photo by © Hulton-Deutsch Collection/CORBIS/Corbis via Getty Images)

Nándor Hidekguti (far left) scores his hat-trick goal, Hungary's sixth. In the process, he shattered the myth of England's supremacy, beneath the pseudo-Indian architecture of Wembley's Twin Towers. (Photo by Dennis Oulds/Central Press/Getty Images)

No hard feelings. England's indomitable captain Billy Wright (left) shares a drink with Nándor Hidegkuti (right), Hungary's hat-trick hero, at the post-match banquet. Both men knew they'd been involved in a changing of the guard. (PA Images/Alamy Stock Photo)

Gyula Grosics (left) and Nándor Hidegkuti (right) examine the film negatives of the match the day after their famous victory. Even in the hours immediately after the match, there was an inescapable sense of history having been written. (Trinity Mirror/Mirrorpix/Alamy Stock Photo)

8

BRAVE NEW WORLD

With the meeting of Hungary and England set and the footballing world collectively salivating at the prospect of the enthralling upstarts testing their mettle against the old masters, it was fitting that 1953 would prove to be an extended pathetic fallacy for the game's drama. In fact, in a century that was the most tumultuous and important thus far in human history, 1953 can stake a claim as the twentieth century's most eventful year outside of the two world wars, offering a tantalising snapshot of a moment caught between the modern world we know and an almost unrecognisable era.

No matter where one looked, change was occurring, often at breakneck speed. In science and technology, Jonas Salk successfully tested his ground-breaking polio vaccine that would all but eradicate the previously prevalent illness. Christine Jorgensen became the first American to undergo gender confirmation surgery, earning herself worldwide fame and becoming a trail-blazing advocate for transgender rights. REM sleep was discovered. In a Cambridge laboratory, scientists James Watson and Francis Crick and their team would ascertain the double helical structure of DNA, or what Crick would excitedly exclaim to the crowded pub he and Watson regularly visited, 'the secret of life'.[1] While Britain would debut her first roll-on, roll-off ferry, a rather more radical mode of transport debuted in the USA, as test pilot Scott Crossfield became the first to travel at more than double the speed of sound, a massive leap forward in the increasingly urgent quest for manned space flight. More ominously, the Soviet Union detonated a hydrogen bomb of around 1,000 times the energy of the atomic bombs dropped by the USA in the Second World War, in the process once again achieving nuclear parity with their Cold War foes and plunging the world at large into deeper fears of impending nuclear doom.

Culturally, 1953 would be the year that many in the West first experienced television in their homes. For Brits, the most hotly anticipated televised events of the year, the coronation of Queen Elizabeth II and the FA Cup Final, fell within a month of each other, enabling thousands to rent a set for both. Those who bought sets bore witness to the first-ever edition of what is now the UK's longest-running programme, *Panorama*, later in the year. Meanwhile, in the USA, record numbers would tune in to watch the trials and tribulations of Lucille Ball in *I Love Lucy*, and the multitudes would be rewarded for their faith in the upstart medium when the first colour sets and programming became available later in the year.

Popular music was continuing to morph into a more recognisably modern sound, as were its stars. Just hours into the new year, American country-and-western star Hank Williams was found dead in the back seat of a car on his way to his next show. At a time when most celebrities had their images carefully manicured and airbrushed to hide the slightest trace of imperfection, Williams had established enormous popularity and success with a string of often melancholic, maudlin hits about lost loves and broken hearts, the appeal of which had only been enhanced as his marriage publicly fell apart and he descended into a spiral of prescription drug and alcohol abuse to help numb a crippling back ailment. His death at the age of 29 only served to buff this veneer of authenticity and transformed him into a legend, one who would serve as the model for the flawed, tragic celebrity that would proliferate over the coming decades.

Fittingly, in the same year that Williams met his untimely end, two names who would become indelibly associated with the same tantalising dangers of celebrity got their first breaks. Marilyn Monroe appeared in the first edition of *Playboy* and starred in three films, most notably *Gentlemen Prefer Blondes*, establishing her as a Hollywood starlet. Meanwhile, in Memphis, a young man, his hair coiffed with rose oil and Vaseline, walked into the small, unassuming Sun Studio building in order to buy a short amount of studio time to record two songs. When asked who he sounded like by the receptionist, Elvis Presley replied, 'I don't sound like nobody.'[2]

While much of the creative, artistic output of the age offered a welcome distraction from the conspiratorial milieu of the Cold War and the looming threat of nuclear annihilation, some attempted to grapple with it head on. Monroe's future husband Arthur Miller debuted one of his most famous works, *The*

Crucible, a retelling of the Salem Witch Trials that served as a thinly veiled metaphor for the callousness and hysteria of McCarthyism, which had been inflamed by the growing spectre of the Soviet brand of communism.

Another pioneering piece of theatre to appear in 1953 was Samuel Beckett's *Waiting for Godot*, with the interminable anticipation for the arrival of its titular character interpreted by some as an allegory for the cloud of fear of nuclear destruction that hung over the world throughout the late 1940s and 1950s. Others, meanwhile, took a decidedly lighter approach to dealing with the prevailing obsession with spies and unexplained occurrences (the early 1950s represented the heyday of UFO sightings). Former Naval Intelligence officer Ian Fleming had his first novel, *Casino Royale*, published, telling the story of the suave, rakish spy, James Bond as he navigates a murky criminal underworld filled with twists and turns, subterfuge and deception. In the early 1950s, writers like Fleming were never short of inspiration for such tales.

Outside of football, the sporting world also enjoyed its fair share of landmark moments. Rocky Marciano, the heavy-hitting slugger, twice retained his World Heavyweight title. Ben Hogan achieved a historic Triple Crown of golf majors, despite having suffered life-threatening injuries in a car accident several years earlier. In baseball, Yankees star Mickey Mantle hit what was reputed to have been the longest home run in history, travelling a gargantuan 565ft and into the annals of legend.

However, none of these feats of athleticism were capable of matching what took place in the Himalayas during April and May. Ever since it had been established that it was the highest point on Earth in the mid-1850s, Mount Everest had held a significant sway over the climbing community. Located on the border between China and Nepal and standing 29,029ft above sea level, by 1953, dozens of attempts had been made to reach the mountain's summit.

For the British, Everest's peak was the subject of a particularly intense obsession. They had given the mountain its westernised name and had first ascertained that it was the tallest mountain in the world. More pressingly, having been beaten to both poles earlier in the twentieth century, most famously with Robert Falcon Scott's doomed race to the South Pole in 1912, Britain's pride in her heroic heritage of exploration had been grievously wounded. With blank spots on the globe now at a premium, there were few prizes greater than Everest, which had been dubbed the 'third pole'. In 1934, Sir Percy Cox declared that it would be a 'national humiliation were the final ascent to be allowed to pass to the nationals of any other country'.[3] The stark decline in Britain's Empire and the impoverished conditions many Brits now found themselves living in only served to intensify the desire of the country to see this most romantic of peaks surmounted.

The imagination of the British public at large was first truly captured in 1924 when an expedition featuring climbers George Mallory and Andrew Irvine came tantalisingly close to success. The two men were last seen by their team-mates within striking distance of the summit, which some continue to believe they may have reached, before disappearing, never to be seen alive again. The fate of Mallory and Irvine contributed another fateful chapter to the story of British exploration, and triggered Everest mania across the British Empire. Despite this, no expedition would come as close before the Second World War put a stop to attempts for several years.

The challenges to climbing Everest were legion. Aside from the requisite mountaineering skills, a team making a serious ascent would need to undertake a huge logistical operation, transporting weeks' worth of supplies up to Everest Base Camp. The sort of rations available in the 1950s pale in comparison to the luxuries developed for modern climbers. Towards the end of the 1953 expedition, several of the party members emotionally confessed to having secretly scoffed tins of sardines that they'd found, so desperate were they for any food with a modicum of taste.

After the days-long trek to Base Camp, hauling their supplies and their heavy, rudimentary oxygen apparatus with a team of native Sherpas, the climbers would set up their camp and begin exploratory sorties up through the various stages of the mountain. These climbs served both to gradually acclimatise the mountaineers to the high altitude and to plot a route up Everest, including through what is known as the 'death zone', above 26,000ft, where lack of oxygen leads to hypoxia, weakening the muscles and mental faculties.

If this work wasn't gruelling enough, it would all have to be done while racing against a ticking clock. The ferocious and vacillating weather atop Everest meant that any attempt to climb in the year before May was likely to be rebuffed by brutal winds and large amounts of snowfall. Between late May and early June, the monsoon arrives, bringing with it huge snow storms that can appear and engulf the mountain in a matter of minutes. This elemental capriciousness has been responsible for many of the climbing deaths on Everest's slopes.

Because of this window in the weather, lasting sometimes for less than a fortnight, any delays in the preparation or execution of the early stages of an expedition could prove fatal for its chances of reaching the peak. Before the Second World War, the mountain had always been attempted from Tibet, to the north, but China's annexation of the region meant that the 1953 attempt would be made from Nepal, to the south. Though it would prove a slightly easier route, it was still replete with issues. A 1951 British expedition, which intended to plot a route that the 1953 operation could take, had failed to complete the first major stage beyond Base Camp due to a huge, impassable crevasse in the Khumbu Icefall. This obstacle had been surmounted by a Swiss expedition in 1952 by stringing builders' ladders together to bridge the fearsome gap in the ice. The Swiss team had set a new record for climbing altitude but had fallen short of the summit, despite the best efforts of a team featuring a prodigious native climber, Nepalese Sherpa Tenzing Norgay.

As the Swiss team was mounting the most concerted attempt on the summit there had yet been, a British team were toiling away on an expedition intended as a trial run for their turn to try and stand atop Everest the following year. Unfortunately, the expedition proved so disastrous that the group was ultimately changed significantly for the 1953 expedition, with veteran climber Eric Shipton replaced as leader by Major George Hunt. The decision to try an untested team dynamic in the harshest of environs was made all the more precarious by the fact that, though Nepal had begun to permit climbers to enter from their side of the mountain, they were limiting this number to one team each year.

With the steady advances in oxygen apparatus technology and the growing knowledge of Everest's southern route, evinced by the Swiss record-breaking attempt the year before, it now seemed that it was no longer a matter of if Everest could be climbed, but when it would first happen. Nepal had already allocated the 1954 and 1955 permits to Swiss and French teams; if the 1953 expedition were to fail, it appeared likely that any hopes of the British reaching the summit first would die with it. This anxiety was reflected throughout the British press during the first half of the year, which covered everything from the boots the team would be wearing to their laborious movements across the globe to Kathmandu with fervour.

The hysteria ramped up considerably once it was known the team had arrived on Everest's slopes; daily weather updates oscillated from the doom laden to the hopeful, before the inevitable garbled reports of the attempts themselves began to filter back home. On the morning of Friday, 29 May, the country awoke to the news it had been dreading, with several newspapers running front-page headlines announcing that the expedition had failed.

The day these reports blared from the newsstands, however, the situation upon Everest could not have been more different. The second attempt on the summit by Tenzing Norgay and New Zealander Edmund Hillary, rather than being pushed back by the weather, was in uncharted territory, reaching higher than anyone – save for, perhaps, Mallory and Irvine – had before. At 11.30 a.m., the pair set foot on the summit.

The expedition had been far from easy, with illness and slower than expected progress up the mountain to establish the auxiliary camps, but through tremendous power of will and thanks to a relatively forgiving period of time before the monsoon arrived, the British expedition was a success. Equally miraculously, the news was spirited back to the United Kingdom via a series of coded messages, arriving in time to be broadcast to the crowds massing in London awaiting Elizabeth II's coronation on the morning of 2 June. Newspapers around the globe trumpeted this happy coincidence as a remarkable coronation gift, a sign from providence of the coming prosperity of this new Elizabethan age.

However, as the glittering monarchical splendour of the coronation and the awe-inspiring derring-do of the Everest expedition harked back to the glorious past of the British Empire's greatest triumphs, these were to prove exceptions, rather than the rule. In fact, by 1953, Britain and her empire were facing a reckoning the likes of which she had not encountered for centuries.

★ ★ ★

At home, the country was still coming to terms with the devastating effects of the Second World War. The Allies may have emerged victorious from the conflict, but it had wrought a terrible cost upon Britain. More than 380,000 British soldiers had died, along with 70,000 civilians, a huge increase in civilian casualties from the First World War, caused in large part by the Blitz. Those fortunate enough to return home were met with soaring rates of crime and divorce. Across the country, many city streets were in the same state of ruin that the Luftwaffe had left them in a decade before. Even Winston Churchill, the country's indomitable wartime leader, who had been restored to the position of prime minister in 1951, suddenly seemed faltering and fallible. He suffered a major stroke in 1953, leading to Operation Hope Not being put in place, planning for his death.

There were some green shoots of recovery, however. In 1953 Britain saw an end to rationing, putting thousands of 'spivs', who specialised in procuring rationed goods like bread, bacon and sweets, out of business. But there was no escaping the fact that Britain's maimed former soldiers and ruined city streets were a symptom of a dreadful malaise.

The same illness beset Britain's imperial standing. The loss of India to independence in 1947 had precipitated a rapid decline in the extent of its empire, some of it voluntary, some by force. Malaya had seen guerrilla warfare between British and pro-communist forces, escalating to the point where the British High Commander was killed in 1951, from which point Britain began to seek a de-escalation and a way out. This trend wasn't just limited to Britain's empire. The French began a bloody – and ultimately fruitless – final stand in Asia in 1953 and received further blows to their influence in Africa. Though it would take until 1956 and the Suez Crisis to truly make plain the extent to which Britain had fallen on the global stage, the wheels were very much in motion, three years earlier.

The political landscape reflected a changing of the guard in terms of the pre-eminent powers in the world. In 1945, the Yalta Conference had taken place between US President Franklin D. Roosevelt, Soviet premier Joseph Stalin and Churchill, in order to reorganise post-war Europe. Charles de Gaulle, Chair of France's provisional government, wasn't invited at all, and Churchill was outmanoeuvred at several points. It was a sign of things to come.

Both France and Britain were in such dire straits that they received billions of dollars in aid from the USA to survive the post-war years. Much of Britain's aid money was squandered with almost remarkable efficiency. Just decades before, the idea of relying on help from America would have been an affront to both British and French pride. However, in 1953, a new world order was taking shape, and the USA was one of the two major players.

America had experienced a huge wartime boom and in 1953 was riding an incredible economic wave, experiencing almost unprecedented peacetime growth. For Americans who had known nothing but crushing depression and war for two decades, many could scarcely believe how good they now had it. America, declared Churchill, was at 'the summit of the world', and they knew it.[4]

This gleaming city upon the hill was a further indication to Britons of the remarkable reversal of fortunes that they had been subjected to. The election of Republican President Dwight Eisenhower, who was inaugurated in March 1953, was a further blow to British prestige. Churchill and other British officials had been withering in their assessment of Eisenhower and his tactical acumen during the Second World War, and he responded in kind by frequently overruling or simply ignoring British advice.

Much of Britain's waning influence on the world can be linked to the loss of their exports' lustre. British steel, textiles and coal, three previously lucrative markets, had all lost their international competitiveness. No less important was the decline in British innovation. For centuries, Britons had led the way in exporting ideas and revolutionary inventions around the world, particularly during the Industrial Revolution, but by the 1950s, they were increasingly taking a backseat, as the likes of the USA and Japan emerged as leading lights in the new age of technological revolution. The sun, it appeared, was beginning to set on the British Empire.

There was, however, one British export that was continuing to thrive, and was thus assuming an ever-increasing importance in the English psyche: football. As Sir Richard Turnbull, a colonial governor, would summarise around the time, once the British Empire had 'finally sunk beneath the waves of history', it would leave behind just two lasting relics. The first was association football; the second was the expression 'fuck off'.[5]

★ ★ ★

As England was grappling with her new standing in the grand scheme of things, 1953 dawned with Hungary looking forward, rather than back. Mátyás Rákosi had continued to consolidate his power, officially adding the role of prime minister to his existing roster of titles that confirmed him as nothing short of Hungary's all-powerful ruler. In order to ensure his position remained absolute, he busily engaged in the worst totalitarian tactics, living up to his self-proclaimed billing as 'Stalin's best pupil' by following the example of the indomitable Soviet Union ruler. He conducted show trials, undertook sweeping political purges and did his level best to quash any and all dissent, all the while relentlessly promoting himself and his regime with propaganda.

One of the chief weapons in Rákosi's armoury was the suppression of Hungarian national pride, which he believed would help to douse any embers of rebellion. A small number of dedicated Hungarian socialists remained cautiously optimistic about a future wedded to communist ideology and the Soviet Union, regardless of how democratically the government had achieved its position. A larger proportion resented the strictures of life under the Rákosi regime and feared how far the bull-headed dictator would continue down the path of despotism. The situation was monitored with interest from the UK. On 24 May, for example, the *Observer* ran a front-page piece on the continued detention of a British businessman accused by the Hungarians of espionage, with an article later in the same edition detailing the desperate food shortages afflicting the country as a result of the hopelessly bungled agricultural collectivism policy.

Following the embarrassment of the Yugoslav–Soviet split, other satellite nations such as Hungary were even more wary of the potential reprisals from Moscow should any hint of dissent be detected. With Rákosi doing all he could to ape Stalin's methods, there was no question as to which side of the Iron Curtain Hungary lay on. They were firmly ensconced within the Soviet Union's orbit, and all that that ideologically entailed. At the very beginning of the Second World War, long before the Allied pact between Russia, Britain and the USA, Churchill had memorably described the Soviet Union as 'a riddle, wrapped in a mystery, inside an enigma'.[6]

By 1953, with the brief thaw during the war a distant memory, there was no question that the Cold War temperature had once again dropped precipitously. The year would see the execution of Julius and Ethel Rosenberg for allegedly spying on the American nuclear programme and helping to funnel secrets back to Russia, the case that truly underlined the degree of suspicion and paranoia with which the West and East viewed one another. Though the Korean War, a proxy conflict between the two superpowers that had dragged on interminably, in large part due to the Kremlin's intransigence when it came to sanctioning peace talks, would draw to a close later in 1953, there was little sign of a wider de-escalation between the USA and Russia.

If there was at least some semblance of stalemate between the two sides at the beginning of the year, it was shattered on 5 March with the news that Stalin had died, following a stroke. The Kremlin, without its indomitable leader of three decades, was thrown into disarray. Moscow's leading figures, among them Georgy Malenkov, the wily and scheming Nikita Khrushchev and the murderous Lavrentiy Beria, plunged headfirst into a murderous game of chess.

The group desperately hung on to the power Stalin had wielded, while at the same time they sized one another up and plotted their own routes to personally succeeding Stalin. By the time of his death, it was a shadowy game in which all in the Soviet leadership were well versed. Indeed, one reason Stalin had enjoyed such unadulterated power for so long was the merciless fashion in which he treated anyone, including friends and colleagues of decades, who he deemed to be capable of threatening his supremacy. Those who now found themselves vying for the leadership had long been accustomed to cloaking their true intentions and never showing their hand.

As they plotted against one another and formed clandestine alliances, the pre-eminent concern of Stalin's potential heirs was the immediate power vacuum and the effect it could have. Stalin had ruled with such force and power that there were fears that, with nobody who could realistically replace his cult of personality, there could be widespread uprisings, with thousands finally unafraid to challenge the conditions under which they toiled.

How likely this was, at least in Russia itself, is extremely difficult to say. The national newspaper *Pravda* had been in circulation for forty years, and the Soviet government had placed a special emphasis on increasing literacy, precisely to ensure that its state-controlled message was disseminated far and wide. By the 1950s, it was virtually impossible to delineate how many of the Russian people were aware of the untruths they were being fed by the Kremlin, and how many unknowingly swallowed them wholesale.

One such fabrication became known as 'the Doctor's Plot'. In the final years of his reign, Stalin had refused to mitigate the ruthlessness that had given him unadulterated power. Yet, despite his position of almost unassailable strength and control, Stalin's paranoia still ran rampant. He was only treated for serious medical conditions, due to his conviction that he would be poisoned by corrupt physicians. He regularly changed which room he slept in, and his motorcade was comprised of five identical limousines, in order to make it harder for potential assassins to reach him. In 1952, he reorganised the nine-man Politburo, replacing it with a twenty-five-member Presidium that diluted the influence of each individual member and enabled him to purge perceived enemies without causing as much of a stir.

But with the foes of the Second World War fading in the memory and the USA's opposition a distant one, Stalin decided he needed to conjure another bogeyman for the Soviet people that he, and he alone, could reliably keep them safe from. He settled on a centuries old scapegoat: the Jewish population.

In 1952, this dramatic shift towards anti-Semitism as yet another means of control had already, unbeknownst to the Russian people, taken its most insidious step, deep within the bowels of Lefortovo Prison, where nine prominent doctors had been imprisoned. Stalin charged that these men – all of them Jewish – had, for years, been conducting a nefarious scheme in which they would abuse their medical powers in order to assassinate high-ranking Soviet officials. Among them was Stalin's own personal physician. Naturally, he relied upon threats and torture to extract confessions for his fanciful plot, and in January of 1953, he released the news to the Russian people.

The Doctors' Plot was a perfect exemplar of the sort of indiscriminate terror that the Russian people lived under each and every day, a state of constant turmoil mirrored in satellites like Hungary. Just eight years earlier, the Red Army had played the leading role in liberating the Nazi concentration camps. Now, the Kremlin were resorting to the same baseless anti-Semitism that Hitler had used to whip up hatred in an attempt to unite support against a common enemy.

Nobody could consider themselves truly safe, not even Stalin's closest confidants. When Stalin died just weeks after the announcement of the Doctors' Plot and the government lost its tyrannical figurehead, the Kremlin dreaded what this sudden liberation from fear could unleash. As Khrushchev would later reflect, 'We were scared, really scared. We were afraid the thaw [caused by Stalin's death] might unleash a flood, which we wouldn't be able to control and which would drown us.'[7]

Quickly, and even as Malenkov, Khrushchev and Beria silently conspired against one another, a collective decision was reached that in order to stem a widespread backlash resulting from Stalin's death, the Kremlin needed to offer the people of the USSR an olive branch. What followed was a widespread campaign of what became known as 'de-Stalinisation'. Around 1 million political prisoners (out of approximately 2.5 million), who had been locked in the Gulag for years with no prospect of a trial, were freed. The prices for food and commodities were lowered in an attempt to improve living standards. Perhaps most tellingly, the Doctors' Plot, which had been introduced with such scandalised bombast mere months before, was disavowed as fiction, a proactive step that belied the fact that the story could quite easily have been allowed to fade from a public memory preoccupied with Stalin's death.

The Kremlin also declared a shift away from the absolute power of Stalin towards a collective leadership model. In the immediate aftermath of Stalin's death, Malenkov had appeared poised to inherit the vast majority of his power, as he assumed the premiership of the government as well as the roles of head of the Presidium and Party Secretary. However, after just nine days, he was forced to resign as secretary, which became a five-man committee that was, in effect, controlled by Khrushchev, establishing him and Malenkov as co-leaders. It would take Khrushchev several years to fully consolidate his power and emerge as the undisputed leader of the Soviet Union, after having denounced Stalin and his legacy of tyranny in his famous 1956 Secret Speech.

The repercussions for Rákosi and Hungary were almost instantaneous. Having previously subscribed to the exact image of singular, strong-man authority espoused by Stalin, Rákosi suddenly found his brand of iron-fist rule was no longer in vogue with his masters in Moscow. Before long, the de-Stalinisation changes taking place in Russia were sending ripples across Eastern Europe, and the people of the Soviet satellites were taking a marked interest in the changes being exhibited in Russia. Many, including the Hungarians, hadn't lived under the yoke of communist rule for anywhere near as long as those in Russia had, and they lacked the same degree of ideological indoctrination as their Russian cousins. Swiftly, those living under rulers who had modelled themselves on Stalin were asking why, as the Kremlin made overtures to greater freedom and an improved standard of living, they weren't receiving the same.

Rákosi's focus on industrialisation and economic nationalisation had proven catastrophic for the standard of living of the ordinary Hungarian, and even while he attempted to suppress the grumblings of his citizens, the Kremlin were more than aware that Rákosi enjoyed little in the way of support from many of his people, who lived under a cloud of fear, suspicion and plummeting levels of material comfort. In the cities, people had to make do with meagre wages and back-breaking work in the heavy industry factories that formed the cornerstone of Rákosi's economic plan. The workers even had to arrive early, in order to be read the latest state-sponsored propaganda from the newspapers.[8] In the countryside, farmers and agricultural workers found themselves forced into unwanted co-operatives that further ate into their incomes, a situation exacerbated further when this new socialist approach to farming led to the country's worst ever yield in 1952.

The profligacy and overtness of the Hungarian footballers' smuggling of goods back into the country, despite the fact that the team were already being paid wages for sham jobs or receiving an army officer's wage, could have been a source of significant resentment among the people. However, by 1953, Rákosi was becoming so unpopular that any form of subordination was celebrated.

It wasn't long before the situation began to unravel. In East Berlin, huge demonstrations took place in the most visible part of the Soviet Union in June. While the uprising was put down by Soviet tanks, it represented a huge Cold War propaganda victory for the West. Hungarians swiftly followed suit, when 20,000 downed tools at one of Rákosi's iron and steel works in protest at their pay and working conditions, sparking similar protests.

If the dictatorial Rákosi had been on thin ice with Moscow since Stalin's death, this proved to be the final straw. He was hauled to Russia for talks, where he was ordered to, in the words of the *Observer*, conduct 'a dignified self-liquidation'. Rákosi was stripped of his role as prime minister and replaced with his bitter rival, Imre Nagy, a more reform-minded member of the party. Crucially, however, Rákosi clung on to his position as First Party Secretary of the Hungarian communists and retained the support of the Hungarian Politburo.

What would follow over the coming years was little less than internecine warfare between Rákosi and Nagy. The drama was covered extensively in the British press, in some cases replacing the front-page slots that had been occupied by the final stages of the Everest expedition, days earlier. On 5 July, the *Observer* headline prematurely declared that Rákosi was 'out', following Moscow's intervention, only to report more soberly a week later that he was back in the fray. The blow to his position was, however, noted to be 'striking evidence that the process of relaxation in some of the satellite countries of Eastern Europe has acquired such momentum that its further development no longer depends exclusively, or even primarily, on the internal struggles within the Kremlin'.

It was an optimistic assessment that was shared by Rákosi's countrymen. As Nagy set about dismantling some of the more insidious aspects of his predecessor's regime, such as internment camps for political prisoners, the Hungarian people were able to feel some cautious hope about what lay ahead. There was no greater clarion call for that optimism than the beloved national team's impending visit to London.

9

UNCORKING THE STOPPER

Fittingly, for such an eventful year, it didn't take long for 1953 to prove to be one of the most dramatic years in English football's history. The First Division title was the subject of a titanic struggle between Arsenal, finally returned to the glory of the Herbert Chapman W-M era, and Tom Finney's Preston, whose early success in the first years of the Football League had set an impossibly high bar that the club had rarely come close to reaching since. In the 1952–53 season, however, anything seemed possible.

By March, with most teams having between eight and eleven games remaining, there were just five points separating Burnley at the top and Manchester United in ninth. Neither Preston nor Arsenal had marked themselves out as front runners at any point in the season, but they both hit form when it mattered most. Preston found themselves on top by the slimmest of margins at the beginning of April, before Arsenal constructed their best run of the season to overtake them.

The two then played each other at Deepdale, with Preston emerging victorious and then winning their last game, leaving them with nothing to do but wait for Arsenal to play their final fixture. The Gunners fell behind early on, but came roaring back to claim victory. Though tied on points, and despite having conceded four more than Preston, Arsenal won the title by virtue of their superior number of goals scored, which gave them a goal average just 0.099 better than their rival's. It was the narrowest margin that the First Division had ever been decided by.

Despite this incredible finish to the league season, by the time Arsenal clinched the title on 1 May, the minds of many fans up and down the country were already elsewhere. The FA Cup Final remained, alongside the matches played by the England national team, the high point of the season. Every year, close to 100,000 fans crammed themselves into the august surroundings of the Empire Stadium, Wembley, in the hopes of seeing their club lift the most famous piece of silverware in football. In 1953, the match had several added elements that enhanced its lustre to almost mythic proportions, even before the game took place.

In the weeks leading up to the final, Britain had been gripped by a patriotic fervour, the likes of which hadn't been felt since VE Day. The coronation of Queen Elizabeth II loomed, with the public understandably excited to see their charming young monarch formally crowned. As the empire waned and the Soviets and Americans vied for supremacy on the world stage, the British could take comfort in the continuity of their monarchical line, particularly as the youthful vitality of Elizabeth II seemed to symbolically usher in a new age for the country. In anticipation of the coronation, millions across the country either bought or rented television sets, still a considerable luxury at the time. This surge in the number of TVs in homes across the country coincided with the final, making it one of the first major sporting events to be broadcast to the masses.

At the same time, a sense of nervous anticipation swept across the nation, as millions eagerly opened their newspapers each morning anxious for news from the Himalayas. The prospect of the British expedition reaching Everest's summit magnified the already feverish patriotism sweeping the country. This milieu of nationalist pride enhanced the appeal of the final, but it took a back seat to one man as the chief cause in the game's unusually wide appeal.

The age of the great British hero may have passed, but for football in the 1950s, there was one player who stood head and shoulders above the rest in embodying that valorous archetype: Stanley Matthews. In 1953, Matthews was still the most famous footballer on the planet. Stanley Rous recalled that, even after her coronation, Queen Elizabeth II demonstrated a strong knowledge of Matthews' career and even knew the date of his birthday.[1] For more than two decades, he had dazzled fans with his vast array of tricks and his devastating bursts of acceleration. In an age when British football was pragmatic above all else, Matthews had shown that flair could be wedded to success.

Success, though, was relative. The fact that Matthews had never won either the First Division or the FA Cup owed much to his inability to swap to a more successful club. The retain and transfer system, which had existed since the

1890s, still effectively wedded players to their clubs permanently, with no freedom of contract. Players signed on a year-by-year basis but were barred from looking elsewhere when their contracts expired. Clubs, meanwhile, could (and very often did) sell player registration rights to other teams with little to no consideration for the player's feelings on the transfer – after all, if the player in question refused to move, his existing club could effectively blacklist him from the game. For players of the time, particularly those like Matthews who had earned a not undeserved reputation for being outspoken and stubborn in his dealings with managers and owners, there was almost no hope of engineering a move from one club to another.

This unscrupulous status quo was exacerbated as the owners colluded to keep wages artificially low (the maximum wage in the English leagues increased by £1 a week in 1953, to the princely sum of £15, at a time when the average earnings of a manual labourer were more than £9). The fact that a player couldn't hope to earn more elsewhere meant that there was less incentive to seek a move. From the perspective of the clubs themselves, no matter how much they might have wanted a particular player, none were willing to induce a player to go on strike for fear of their own players doing the same, and few owners would indulge footballers who had.

By 1953, Neil Franklin, despite still being just 30, was now an outcast, languishing in the lower reaches of the Second Division with Hull City. Wilf Mannion had served a long suspension for striking in protest against Middlesbrough's refusal to sell him in 1948, with his manager, legendary former player David Jack, at one point threatening that 'if Mannion won't play for us, he will never play in League football again'.[2] Remarkably, Mannion, who would spend much of his career crusading (or agitating, in the view of club owners and the FA) for improved wages and a fairer transfer system, had first been alerted to the rank unjustness of the system by a meeting with, of all people, baseball legend Babe Ruth. Ruth had been stunned when Mannion told him his paltry wages as the pair gazed out at a capacity Highbury crowd and asked why the players had simply never organised and gone on strike.

These conditions were the reason that so many players featured for only one or two clubs in their entire career during the 1950s. In Matthews' case, it was Stoke City and Blackpool, who he was allowed to join after years of simmering resentment between Matthews, Stoke manager Bob McGrory and the club's board. Despite being beloved at both teams, neither side had been able to reciprocate by providing the great man with silverware. He had inspired

Stoke to become a solid mid-table First Division side, but the closest they came to the title was fourth in 1935–36. They reached the FA Cup Quarter-Final round twice, the second of which, at Bolton's Burnden Park, ended in disaster as a crush of people desperate to catch a glimpse of Matthews in the first season since the end of the Second World War resulted in thirty-three people being killed.

After his move to the coast, Blackpool reached the 1951 FA Cup Final, where they faced Newcastle. As soon as their berth in the final was confirmed by a victory over Birmingham City, national attention turned to Matthews, who now had a golden opportunity to earn the winner's medal that had eluded him for so long. Despite the 'Wizard of Dribble' playing superbly, getting the better of the Newcastle back line time and again, Matthews' teammates were unable to capitalise, and Newcastle won 2-0. Matthews was now 36 and the likelihood of having another opportunity to cap a glittering career with silverware appeared remote.

In 1953, however, Matthews returned to Wembley, determined to make amends. Prospects appeared grim when, with a little over 20 minutes remaining, Matthews' Tangerines found themselves 3-1 down to Nat Lofthouse's Bolton Wanderers, despite Bolton effectively playing with ten men after Eric Bell tore his hamstring. Matthews had been unusually quiet, and Bolton appeared to have the match under complete control. As the Wanderers' defence began to flag, however, Matthews gradually found himself with more time on the ball and began to work his magic, tormenting full-back Ralph Banks repeatedly. Unlike two years before, Matthews' teammates were now far more receptive to his offerings, with Stan Mortensen scoring a hat-trick, his third being the equaliser in the 89th minute. In injury time, and with Bolton doggedly clinging on to the draw, Matthews once again danced his way to the touchline and fired in a low cross, which was slammed home by Bill Perry. Matthews had his medal, and England had what they thought was a fairy-tale ending to a modern-day Arthurian legend, with venerable BBC commentator Kenneth Wolstenholme eulogising 'a great end to a great career'.

Matthews, however, wasn't finished by a long shot. Almost as soon as referee Sandy Griffiths had blown the final whistle, a national clamour to see Matthews restored to the England national team began. Despite his reputation, his England career at that point had consisted of just thirty-three caps; a respectable total in those days, but a far cry from the haul that would have been expected for a man of Matthews' standing within the game. Tom Finney, the man with whom Matthews had to endure constant comparison by virtue of their subtly different approaches to the same position, had at that stage accrued forty-four caps, despite being seven years Matthews' junior.

Certainly, the hiatus caused by the Second World War had halted Matthews' international progress. He had appeared in thirteen of the fourteen internationals before the outbreak of war. However, he had found his opportunities limited following the war, thanks in part to his renown for being something of a maverick and whispers of teammates' smouldering resentments over what they perceived as Matthews' selfish playing style. However, as keen as they were to wield their power, the selection committee were far from immune to public calls for a certain player to receive a call-up, particularly when they were so unanimously vociferous. If nothing else, giving a player of Matthews' repute an international swansong would help provide a useful smokescreen should the national team stumble.

★ ★ ★

Not that the FA had particular reason to fear failure at the precise moment that Blackpool captain Harry Johnston was climbing Wembley's famous steps and lifting the FA Cup. After the disastrous 1950 World Cup campaign and subsequent hangover, the team, under the guidance of Walter Winterbottom, had found its footing again, embarking on an unbeaten run that had begun in May 1951. While the performances and finer details of the matches had often fallen short of the results achieved, as far as the FA were concerned, England were winning and nothing more needed to be said on the matter.

During the 1952 end-of-season tour, the team appeared to have found another gear, powered by the first settled team consisting almost entirely of post-war players, fighting their way to a draw with Italy before scoring their famous victory in Vienna and cruising to a comfortable win over Switzerland. Their triumphant sortie across the Continent was followed by a brief stumble, a 2-2 draw against Northern Ireland away in Belfast, but this had been put right by the Three Lions attack scoring five in successive games against Wales and Belgium.

Winterbottom's side had then survived their first test of 1953, halting Scotland's run of successive wins at Wembley with a 2-2 draw, in yet another game where the result perhaps flattered England, even as the Scots required an

89th-minute equaliser. The draw meant that the 1952–53 Home Championship title was shared between the two teams.

While games against the old enemy inevitably got the blood pumping, for England the visit of Scotland had been but a curtain raiser to what promised to be one of the most exciting – and testing – calendar years of football in the national team's long history. FA Secretary Stanley Rous had worked tirelessly to ensure that the FA's celebrations of their 90th birthday would be greeted by a glittering set of games that would give the national team the opportunity to put to rest any doubts that they remained the foremost power in the footballing world.

A month after the Scotland match, during which time the First Division reached its dramatic conclusion and the nation basked in the fairy-tale of the Matthews final, England set their sights on South America for what was their first tour of the continent (not including the Brazilian World Cup, three years prior). As was the case whenever the England team played abroad, the red carpet was rolled out for the most feted side in international football. On their first stop, in Argentina, the country's President Juan Perón personally hosted an audience with the players when they arrived in Buenos Aires (the players would also attend a service held in the memory of Perón's wife, Eva).[3] For all the ceremony and excitement surrounding the game – an estimated 125,000 packed the Estadio Monumental for a warm-up game between a Buenos Aires XI and FA XI three days beforehand – the full fixture proved a damp squib, scuppered when a storm of biblical proportions left the referee Arthur Ellis with no option but to abandon the match midway through the first half.

From there, England travelled to Chile for a rematch with the only team they'd managed to beat in Brazil three years earlier. They repeated the trick again, by virtue of yet another goal from Nat Lofthouse, who maintained his record of more than a goal a game on his fourteenth appearance, and a fluke from Manchester United starlet Tommy Taylor, whose cross inadvertently lobbed Chilean goalkeeper Sergio Livingstone, the son of a Scot who had done for Chilean football what figures like Jimmy Hogan had done for the game in Continental Europe.

As with so many of England's matches in recent years, the performance was far from convincing, but given the alien climes they were playing in and a frenzied crowd of more than 55,000 in attendance, Winterbottom's team could feel justifiably pleased to have seen off the challenge. Unfortunately, Chile was to have the last laugh, with several of England's players picking up illnesses, described as 'Chile tummy'. They arrived at their next stop, the Uruguayan capital of Montevideo, severely depleted and late after the tempestuous weather that had curtailed the fixture with Argentina caught up to the party again. With the situation dire, Stanley Rous stepped in, persuading the Uruguayan FA to postpone the match for twenty-four hours to give the England players some time to recover. The South American authorities, wanting to put on a spectacle and test their players against the very best England had to offer, eventually acquiesced.

Rous' intervention was timely, to say the least. While both Argentina and Chile boasted relatively strong teams, Uruguay were a different proposition altogether. Two-time winners and current holders of the World Cup, they were inarguably South America's primary footballing force in the decades before Brazil emerged as an all-conquering power at the end of the 1950s. Their team embodied both quintessential Latin American skill with an uncompromising physicality that made them more than a match for the robust English, and they boasted mercurial talents such as attacking midfielder Juan Alberto Schiaffino, who would soon become the world's most expensive player after signing for AC Milan.

Despite England raising their game valiantly, as they had done for the matches against Austria in Vienna, they finally relinquished their two-year-long unbeaten record. Uruguay struck midway through each half, with England registering a late consolation from Taylor after striking the woodwork twice. Uruguay, though, were excellent value for the win, at points rendering their opponents dumbstruck with their rapid passing and inventive moments of skilful trickery. As was typical following any defeat, England's advocates could point (not without justification) to a gruelling travel schedule unlike anything the players had experienced before coupled with the illness that had swept through the party as mitigating factors in their defeat.

For all the miles they'd clocked up on their invidious schedule, and for all the illness and injury they'd had to contend with, the England party had one last stop, one which promised to be more profitable than the tough games in South America. If the tour's first three games had been sporting tests of the English players, their final match, against the USA, was purely psychological. Though only Billy Wright, Alf Ramsey and Jimmy Dickinson had survived from the humiliation in Belo Horizonte in 1950, the mental scars were still evident, and England's determination to achieve a degree of retribution wasn't dampened in the slightest, even after torrential rain saw the game pushed back twenty-four hours. Watched by a meagre crowd of fewer than 8,000 (many who had intended to watch the game were put off by the delay), in the cavernous surroundings of Yankee Stadium, the match began in a fashion that soon had the three World Cup veterans in England's team experiencing a worrying case of déjà vu, as the Three Lions created, and spurned, several gilt-edged chances.

It took until 2 minutes before half-time for Ivor Broadis to put England ahead, and his goal uncorked the dam. Goals from Finney and Lofthouse in the first 10 minutes of the second period appeared to put England completely out of sight, before a chaotic 12-minute spell, inspired in large part by English complacency, saw the USA carve an unlikely route back into the game. Otto Decker (a German-born player, who had grown up in England as part of the *Kindertransport*) got a goal back, only for Lofthouse's run and shot within 1 minute to restore the three-goal cushion. The USA then scored a penalty and, 1 minute later, Decker got his second to put England on the ropes.

It wasn't until another goal from Finney made the score 5-3 that England could breathe more easily, before Redfern Froggatt put the game to bed with England's sixth. It was a satisfying, if unconvincing, end to the tour, one which laid to rest some of the demons that had bedevilled the England team's psyche since the World Cup. The win over the USA was just the second game in the country's 280-match history to have ended 6-3 to either team. Few would have predicted that such a lopsided scoreline would occur in any of the national team's fixtures on the horizon.

★ ★ ★

Even with the attention of the country and government fixed on the national team, Mátyás Rákosi's regime could not have failed to be pleased with the ongoing developments in the domestic Nemzeti Bajnokság I competition. In 1952 the army-run Honvéd had won their third title in four seasons, inspired by the core of national team players who, by now, were reaching the peak of their collective powers. Teams were simply powerless to resist their free-flowing, elastic forward line. Effectively putting an end to one of Zoltán Czibor's balletic runs meant leaving room for the charging powerhouse Ferenc Puskás, while marking both of them left the arch marksman Sándor Kocsis unmolested to plunder goals at will, which he did in 1952 more effectively than any other year of his career, with thirty-six strikes in the twenty-six-game season. Though this record was a significant drop from the goal-scoring exploits that the now *persona non grata* Ferenc Deák had achieved in the immediate post-war years, it was nonetheless a testament to Honvéd's goal-scoring prowess. Teams were now so utterly petrified of playing them that many set up in an extremely defensive fashion from the first whistle, with no more lofty ambition than damage limitation.

The only team to come close to Honvéd was Márton Bukovi's MTK, who were by now benefiting regularly from their coach's daring use of the deep-lying centre-forward and their symbiotic relationship with the national team. In 1953, following Nándor Hidegkuti's revelatory performance against the Swiss for Hungary, MTK (playing under the name Vörös Lobogó, 'Red Banner', reflecting the continuing encroachment of Soviet propaganda into the sport) would win the title, with Honvéd a close second and the rest of the league trailing far behind.

The fact that the league's competitiveness was now hopelessly lopsided in favour of the state-controlled teams was a moot one for Rákosi's government. As far as they were concerned, they had thrown their weight behind Honvéd and MTK, and now they were indisputably the strongest two sides in Hungary. That they had redistributed some of the league's best players away from certain clubs and towards their favourites, a decidedly non-socialist approach, was quietly ignored. Of equal importance to the government was the fact that Ferencváros, once the powerhouse of Hungarian football, were now nothing more than a shadow of their former selves, having been decimated for their supposed right-wing sensibilities and harbouring political dissidents in the stands at games. In 1952, after they had been stripped of even their traditional club name, Ferencváros finished a dismal ninth, losing half their matches and conceding twice as many as they scored. The message, even as Stalin's death sent ructions throughout Eastern Europe, was clear – Rákosi's government was not to be meddled with.

The Hungarian government's principal piece of sporting propaganda remained, however, the national team. The huge success of 1952 meant Gusztáv Sebes and his team entered 1953 faced with greater levels of pressure than ever before. From the moment the England fixture was set, it became Sebes' unequivocal focus, but he was well aware that while the showpiece game carried, by far, the greatest sporting and political cachet, he simply couldn't afford for his men to take their foot off the gas in the meantime. Any signs of a drop-off in performance, even if it was as a direct result of him preparing for the England encounter with experimental tweaks to tactics or player selection, would be seized upon by the authorities, who were already wary after Sebes' presumptive approval of the match without their say-so.

If the atmosphere surrounding Rákosi's government and its ever-increasing fixation on the *Aranycsapat*'s utility as its most potent propaganda tool had been controlling before, by mid-March, after Stalin's death had thrown the entire Soviet Union into a convulsion of almost hysterical paranoia, it became megalomaniacal. Though Sebes had been blessed with a truly remarkable generation of players at his disposal and a collection of superb coaches, from MTK's Márton Bukovi through to national team assistant Gyula Mándi, who had brought together a remarkable tactical system, his job was never less than treacherous. By 1953, he had become a lightning rod for the now immense political scrutiny the team were under, providing them with the protection and insulation needed for them to play with the exuberant freedom they were so joyously associated with.

After recording their thirteenth consecutive win (not including the unofficial pair of matches in Russia) in their last match of 1952, a 5-0 rout of Czechoslovakia, Hungary began 1953 with a disappointing draw with Austria. The match, as games between the two neighbours always did, carried a symbolic significance, and the Hungarians were relieved to have escaped with their unbeaten record intact after having initially fallen behind. Hungary were well aware that their next game would require a significant improvement. For their last match of the Central European Championships, Hungary faced their greatest test of the tournament, a trip to Rome to face Italy.

Playing a high-profile game against the tournament's most historically successful team was reason enough for Hungary to have their guard up, but to add further fuel to the fire, the Magyars sat atop the standings, level on points with Austria, who had played all their games. Italy, meanwhile, had only played four of their fixtures and knew that even just a draw would give them the opportunity to catch Sebes' team in the standings. For Hungary, the equation was simple: win in Rome and return home as champions. The political mathematics were equally straightforward: now they had proven themselves capable of winning silverware, they were expected to win everything available to them. Anything less would be considered a failure.

Though there was no question of the Central European Championship carrying the prestige of the previous year's Olympics, the upcoming World Cup or the much-anticipated meeting with England, it was still an opportunity that

Sebes and his players were desperate to seize upon. To win in the Italian capital was an even greater incentive. No side had enjoyed such a comprehensive and sustained history of success over the Magyars as Italy.

While Hungary had swatted the second-string *Azzurri* aside en route to the Olympic gold the previous summer, that had been their first triumph over the Italians in seventeen games, a run that stretched all the way back to 1925. However, the pre-match prognostications had rarely been so good for Hungary. Italy were still struggling to emerge from the long shadow cast by the famous *Il Grande Torino* players, who had filled every outfield position when the two nations met on Hungary's last visit to Italy in 1947 and who had later perished in the Superga air disaster. The tragedy meant that the Hungarian team was more star-studded than the Italian side, a rare occurrence indeed.

For the worldly Italian fans, who were known for their appreciation of foreign players, far more so than the insular British supporters, the prospect of seeing the cerebral József Bozsik, the goal poacher extraordinaire Kocsis and, above all else, the magisterial Puskás was an enormously exciting one. If the Hungarian team had had any doubts as to their newfound status as European sporting celebrities following their success in Helsinki, they were set straight before they'd even reached Rome. As soon as Italian railway workers got wind of the guests of honour rolling down the tracks, they held the Hungarian train up in the hopes of merely catching a glimpse of some of the team's stars. When they found the travelling party were obliging enough to greet them, they insisted upon showing Puskás a brand-new engine they had nearby. Before Sebes and the rest of the Hungarian officials knew what was happening, Puskás was in charge of a moving train, and it required a frantic intervention to halt the team's captain from disappearing down the line.

The fanatical reaction of the railway workers to the Hungarians was mirrored in Rome. If the sense of occasion surrounding the match and its import for the Central European Championship hadn't been enough, the game would inaugurate the redesigned Stadio dei Centomila. A sweeping bowl structure, the stadium was named thus as it could now seat 100,000 spectators, ensuring a veritable cauldron of noise capable of rivalling the Colosseum in ancient times. If there was one team in 1953 adept at coping with hysteria, however, it was Hungary.

Given the pivotal nature of the match, Sebes wanted to emulate as closely as possible the revelatory formula he had stumbled across in Bern in Hungary's last away game, when his team had turned the match against the Swiss around in stunning fashion after the introduction of Nándor Hidegkuti and the full implementation of the deep-lying centre-forward gambit. His plans threatened to be scuppered as the game drew close and it became apparent that the MTK striker would be little more than half fit. While the gamble of playing a compromised Hidegkuti was one Sebes was willing to take, he made concessions in his team's attacking verve to compensate.

So prolific had they been at the Olympics that they had gone into the game with Switzerland with a reckless abandon, with every outfield player surging forward when the team won possession. In Rome, Sebes made it clear to his three backs, Mihály Lantos, Jenő Buzánszky and Gyula Lóránt, all of whom had played in Bern, that their primary role was to defend, and to trust that the team's attack would be capable of overwhelming the makeshift Italian defence unaided.

From the first whistle to the last, the match in Rome proved a masterclass. Fittingly, in the capital of the country known more than any other for their methodical, dogmatic approach to football tactics, it felt as though everything Hungary had planned and developed over the previous months and years came to fruition in a single game, even allowing for the fact that Hidegkuti's fragile fitness saw him substituted for clubmate Péter Palotás at half-time. Hungary triumphed 3-0, with the defence stubbornly shutting down every Italian attack.

The Hungarian front line, meanwhile, led the Italian defence on a merry dance, repeatedly making their blue-shirted opponents appear leaden footed or simply bamboozled as they interchanged positions with one another and alternated passing styles, drawing the Italians towards them with series of short passes before cleaving the defence apart with decisive through balls. Hungary had spurned a number of good opportunities before Hidegkuti fired them into the lead just before the break. From that point on, with Italy forced to chase the game, there was destined to be only one winner.

Puskás, who had been unusually profligate for the first hour of the match, made amends by scoring twice in 5 minutes. Both goals demonstrated his remarkable close control, as he hoodwinked the Italian defenders with his ability to halt his momentum and turn on a sixpence before slotting the ball home. In typical Puskásian fashion, he spent the brief moments when he wasn't at the heart of Hungary's play demanding the ball from everyone, including goalkeeper Gyula Grosics, and voicing his displeasure when he was overlooked for a pass.

It was yet another signal victory in the Sebes era for his team. So comprehensive was the Hungarian win that they were applauded from the field by the Italian fans, and the local press were similarly eulogistic. England's rout in Turin five years previously had been seen as an impressive – yet not shocking – example of an extremely strong team playing the classic British style. Hungary's success was a different matter entirely. The Italian newspapers found much to applaud in not only the margin of the Hungarian victory, but in the manner in which they went about winning. It wasn't simply that they had the superior players. Hungary had tactically outmanoeuvred Italy, making the usually stoic *Azzurri* defence appear chronically sluggish and rigid, and brought into question the fundamental wisdom of the entire Italian approach to the game.

Hungary left the country engulfed in an even more rampant fervour than when they'd entered, but they had little time to bask in the glory of one of the most spectacular results in the nation's history. With Italy dealt with, attention turned firmly towards the England match, now six months – and six fixtures – away.

★ ★ ★

After the historic victory over Italy, Hungary had a relatively sedate summer before their schedule ramped up in preparation for the trip to Wembley. In July, Hungary's next jaunt abroad saw them return to Scandinavia, the scene of their Olympic triumph a year before, where they overcame George Raynor's Sweden in a hard-fought game 4-2, needing late goals from Kocsis and Hidegkuti to break the Swedish resolve. The game was significant for taking Puskás to a remarkable fifty-nine goals in forty-eight games, eclipsing the fifty-eight-goal record of Imre Schlosser and granting him both the standing as Hungary's all-time top goal scorer and the title of international football's most prolific player. What made this feat all the more remarkable was that Puskás was still just 26, a fact that was easy to forget, given his occasionally domineering personality, undimmable confidence and his unequivocal status as his country's talisman.

With two successive victories away to strong teams, the Magyars' next match, against Czechoslovakia in Prague, ought to have been a simple exercise in consistency. Sebes was now reaping the rewards of his carefully constructed plan of centralising his players at Honvéd and MTK and sticking with a small talent pool in order to engender the players' relationships and synergy with one another. In the four matches since the comeback win against Switzerland, the team had remained largely unchanged, with full-backs Buzánszky and Lantos, midfield pair Bozsik and József Zakariás, and forwards Kocsis, Hidegkuti, Puskás and Czibor starting every game, with winger László Budai, centre-half Lóránt and goalkeeper Grosics missing just one.

Sebes had every intention of maintaining this line-up into the team's five-match autumn schedule, particularly as the Hungarian league season, now following the Soviet example, was almost finished by the time the national team met the Czechs, meaning his players would be fresher. However, his carefully laid plans were thrown into disarray by a rare moment of ill-discipline within the squad. In September, following national team training, Budai, Czibor and Kocsis enjoyed an unsanctioned night of drinking, the extent of which was described by a livid Sebes as 'a bender'.[4]

Though innocuous when compared to the protests and strikes that had exploded across Hungary over the summer, it was another incident that laid bare the growing divisions at the heart of Hungarian society. The make-up of the national team squad had shifted dramatically from the years immediately following the war to the players Sebes now had at his disposal. There was no question that the new generation of Hungarian players were technically superior to those they had replaced, but that came with its own set of challenges. The team that Sebes had managed, first as assistant to Tibor Gallowich, then as part of the three-man committee, had consisted of players coming towards the ends of their careers, men who had lost their prime years to the war and were determined to make up for lost time, having been afforded what they recognised as an extraordinary opportunity to do so in the service of their country.

The flame of the previous generation's torch was still carried by the likes of Bozsik, Grosics and Puskás, among several others, who were never less than acutely aware of the honour that was being afforded them in playing so regularly for the national team. Bozsik had had to endure a long wait before he truly secured his national team place, watching from the wings while his best friend Puskás was feted as the next great star. Puskás, though more than happy to play the joker in the team and bring a degree of levity to the camp amid an increasingly stormy political backdrop, was deadly serious when it came to playing football. His bullish response to the 1948 accusations from the Hungarian FA of disrespect was characteristic of his attitude whenever his desire and motivations were questioned, and his occasional on-pitch tantrums when a Honvéd or Hungary teammate elected not to pass to him were borne of his relentless quest to win as much as his supreme self-confidence.

Crucially, Bozsik, Grosics, Puskás and the other senior members of the squad could all also recall with clarity the war and its horrors, cowering in fear in cellars and attics as the Red Army fought the Nazis from street to Budapest street, the country feeling at times that it would simply rip apart as it was battled over by two great powers. It was little coincidence that the three players involved in the drunken antics were among the youngest members of the core squad – Budai was 24, Czibor 23 and Kocsis 22. The three were of an age where they could only dimly recollect what life had been like in Hungary before 1939 and were less aware of just what freedoms and privileges their status as national team footballers meant, as the rest of the population grappled with the privations and scrutiny of life under Rákosi's government (even after Imre Nagy had been installed as prime minister).

The temptation to merely ignore the drunken transgression of the three players in order to keep the team at full power must have been immense for Sebes (indeed, the press criticised the decision to meddle with a winning formula),[5] but he felt the need for discipline trumped all else. He could not risk setting a precedent when a repeat incident could spur government intervention into his running of the team.

Beyond his adroit reading of the possible political ramifications of the situation, Sebes' own beliefs and morals played a role in his decision. He was always seeking to impress upon his players the prerogative that their unique positions within Hungarian society bestowed upon them, and the fact that three of his players were flaunting their status and taking their relative freedom for granted was a grave affront to Sebes' socialist sensibilities. All three players were dropped by their furious manager for what proved to be a straightforward 5-1 victory over the Czechs. Remarkably, such was Hungary's reputation for team synergy that the news penetrated the Iron Curtain and reached Fleet Street: Bob Ferrier, in the *Daily Mirror*, boldly announced to his readers that 'now England can win easily' following the three expulsions.

Budai was restored to the starting XI two matches later after Sebes learned he had not stayed out all night as the other two players had. Ultimately, Sebes chose to appeal to Czibor's and Kocsis' patriotism, as well as their self-interests, in order to reintegrate them into the team. He visited them both individually and explained that in exchange for their professionalism, they would have the opportunity to write their names into Hungarian legend by defeating England.[6]

★ ★ ★

After the glamour of their jet-setting trip around the Americas, the England national team's four remaining fixtures in 1953 could be split into two distinct groups. Two were the team's bread and butter – pulsating matches against Wales in Cardiff and Northern Ireland in Liverpool. Both games formed part of the 1953–54 Home Championship, and the competition had been given added impetus by virtue of being used to determine Britain's two entrants to the following year's World Cup. The other two fixtures were decidedly more exotic – the visits of a Rest of the World select XI and Hungary.

While England's summer tour had enabled them to play teams of a style they would not have met in Continental Europe, crucial experience with the World Cup less than twelve months away, it had done little to shift perceptions of the team's best line-up. Billy Wright remained an indomitable presence at right-half, with Portsmouth's Jimmy Dickinson (the only player in the line-up against Wales based at a club south of Birmingham) almost equally as indispensable. The reticent Alf Ramsey, though now 33, remained a firm choice for England's biggest games and thus had played in every match of the tour of the Americas.

The same was true of Blackburn's Bill Eckersley, whose performances on the other side of the Atlantic had secured him the left full-back berth. However, the critical centre-half position between Ramsey and Eckersley was proving a continuing source of vexation for Walter Winterbottom and the selectors.

Blackpool captain Harry Johnston had been called up to his first squad in two years after the Tangerines had confirmed their place in the FA Cup Final and had then started each of the four summer tour games. In many respects, Johnston was the ideal centre-half. As well as his physical attributes and adroit reading of the game, he was also a commanding presence in the dressing room. The reason that it had taken the selectors so long to land upon Johnston as a successor for the exiled Neil Franklin was largely down to the fact that when the Blackpool man had first been tested as Franklin's replacement, it had come in Scotland's 1951 victory at Wembley. Despite Johnston delivering a solid performance, to have been involved in such a grave aberration was not something the selectors looked upon lightly. Now he was back in the fold, but time was against him. Johnston would be 34 by the time he donned the white No. 5 jersey against Wales, an age that lent him tremendous experience, but had diminished his pace, stamina and reflexes.

The situation with the forwards remained turbulent. Not since the late 1940s and the famous win in Turin had the FA turned to the same combination of players with any degree of regularity. The haphazard manner in which players were selected was exacerbated by the ease with which a selector who had not travelled to physically watch the players he was judging could weigh up the relative merits of one forward compared to another, purely on the basis of recent goal-scoring records. Winterbottom, normally diplomatic when it came to the restrictions that the selection committee process imposed upon him, did occasionally vent his frustrations:

> One bad game and the selectors would throw a man out … even if he did well he wasn't safe … Towards the end [of my time as manager] I would present my team and then let them try to argue me out of it. The trick of it was to stick to the men who were most important, and to make concessions to the committee where it didn't matter so much.[7]

One man who enjoyed an unusual degree of safety was Tom Finney. Now 31, Finney had lost none of the relentless drive and dribbling prowess that made him the most feared winger of the 1950s. Critically, he was no longer as susceptible to the injuries that had marred much of his earlier career and his ability to dodge and ride crude tackles was now a crucial part of his arsenal. By the autumn of 1953, he had missed just two national team matches in two years.

Perhaps the most coveted and hotly debated position in the entire team, centre-forward, also finally appeared settled. Just as Franklin's sudden move to Colombia left a gaping void at centre-half, so too had the FA been left scrambling for a long-term solution to Tommy Lawton at No. 9, who had effectively vacated the shirt when he had dropped down to the Third Division.

At long last, one of the many pretenders to Lawton's crown had proven himself capable of coping with the pressure of expectation and given the selectors no reason to look elsewhere. Nat Lofthouse's two goals against the USA had taken his record to seventeen goals in sixteen caps. The Bolton Wanderers man was more nuanced than the crude bulldozer critics made him out to be, but it was unquestionably the British centre-forward brief, which he fulfilled so completely, that made him so lethal in internationals. The combination of

Lofthouse and Finney, close friends off the field and in possession of an intangible chemistry on it, was simply too much for many opposing teams to repel.

The potent combination of a pinpoint Finney cross being met with a thundering Lofthouse header may have become de rigueur for England, but it did nothing to stop the selection committee's continuous meddling with the rest of the forward line. There was no position more prone to flavours of the month than the two inside-forward roles, where a single eye-catching performance in the league could win a player a cap. Since the beginning of the 1952–53 season, England's inside-forwards had included Eddie Baily, John Sewell, Redfern Froggatt, Ivor Broadis and Manchester United starlet Tommy Taylor, nominally a centre-forward whose abilities were such that he could not be overlooked for the national team but were not yet strong enough to dislodge Lofthouse.

True to form for the selection committee, none of these five would play the first match of the 1953–54 campaign against Wales. Instead, two debutants, Albert Quixall and Dennis Wilshaw, received the call, Wilshaw coming in to replace yet another inside-forward, Bolton's Harold Hassall, who withdrew through injury.

The most generous of FA apologists would be tempted to argue that the selectors were doing their due diligence in leaving no stone unturned. To everybody else, it was just a continuation of the antiquated, occasionally nepotistic, inconsistent method of picking players that made England the very antithesis of teams like Hungary, with their small, rarely disturbed pool of players. As Stanley Rous would wryly note, 'They say of the camel that it looks so weird it could only have been designed by a committee, and some of our international teams were just as ill-balanced as a result of the system.'[8]

The same morass and confusion that beset the inside-forward roles was true of the left wing. Billy Elliott, Jack Froggatt (cousin of Redfern) and Johnny Berry had all been trialled since October 1952, yet the selectors ushered in the new season by returning to Jimmy Mullen, the Wolves winger, who had won his first cap back in 1947 but had only been picked five times since. However, the FA now found themselves faced with a vociferous campaign that stymied their ability to select wingers uninterrupted. With his stirring display in the last knockings of the FA Cup Final, Stanley Matthews had dragged Blackpool to victory from the jaws of defeat and defied his 38 years of age with his stamina and undimmed ability. Football fans up and down the country were now of the opinion that Matthews deserved the opportunity to try and perform the same heroics for his country on the right once more, with Finney moved to the left to compensate.

Following the final, Matthews had been swiftly added to the roster for England's summer tour of the Americas, but he had understandably withdrawn through fatigue. His last appearance for the national team had been in 1951, yet his stature remained unblemished and, in the immediate afterglow of his finest hour, the selectors, themselves no strangers to nostalgia and certainly not disinclined from currying public favour, saw an opportunity they could not resist.

However, while the clamour for Matthews to don the white shirt of England once again continued through the summer, within the secretive walls of the FA headquarters at Lancaster Gate, the mood towards the man himself and his recall was significantly cooler. Walter Winterbottom, for all his limited influence over player selections, appreciated Matthews' undoubted talents but was exasperated by the winger's individualist streak that too often came at the detriment of the team, a frustration shared (but rarely voiced) by many Matthews played alongside.[9]

These precise mechanical reasons were less of an issue to the selectors. As evidenced by their constant chopping and changing of the team, they cared little for Winterbottom's desire for consistency and regarded the idea of coaching a team unit to be greater than the sum of its parts with a deep suspicion, but they still harboured their doubts about bringing Matthews back into the fold. In an age when the club chairmen and owners (who made up almost all of the selection committee) were kings and the players little more than pawns, Matthews was a rare example of a player who had got his way and forced a move, something that no club owner wished to see rewarded, lest it give other stars similar ideas.

For Matthews' part, he harboured resentments that meant while he would never deign to turn his nose up at an England recall, it was equally not something he hungered insatiably for. He was well aware that Winterbottom, a man less than two years his senior and with scant professional experience as a player, regarded him as a luxury. It was an accusation Matthews had encountered time and again during his career and which, as a player utterly fanatical about his personal fitness, he felt keenly.

As for the FA, there was little love lost. Matthews was, above all else, a footballing man, one who loved the game and who shared Winterbottom's belief in the virtues of coaching, even if he felt they didn't apply to a player of his ability. The FA, and the group of club powerbrokers who formed the selection committee in particular, represented to Matthews the worst aspects of the sport: the relentless back-biting and grubbing for power; the stranglehold a small monopoly had over the game; and the men who had got rich by exploiting *his* natural gifts, all the while denying him what should have been the going rate for his services. The parsimoniousness of the FA was, for Matthews, no better exemplified than when they had docked a sixpence from an expense claim he had filed for a cup of tea he'd bought at a train station on a trip up to play against Scotland.[10] As far as he was concerned, the less he had to do with them, the better.

Unlike the rest of the England squad, Matthews was also less in need of the £30 appearance fee that accompanied every national team cap. Despite the prohibitive maximum wage failing to match inflation, Matthews had played long enough to put some away and had combined his marketability as England's foremost player with canny investments. Unlike others, he was not in thrall to the FA and the hope of a long, prosperous international career.

Ostensibly, England's first game of the 1953–54 calendar demonstrated they needed little help from Matthews, with the 4-1 win in Cardiff suggesting near supremacy. As so often with England since the war, however, the match itself told quite a different story. Midway through the first half, Wales took the lead through the great inside-forward Ivor Allchurch, ably assisted by 21-year-old centre-half/centre-forward John Charles, whose star, already in the ascendancy, gained a considerable boost after his stirring performance. Charles proved more than a physical match for Bill Eckersley, Tom Garrett (receiving his third and what proved to be last cap) and Harry Johnston, repeatedly winning his battles with them and buying his inside-forward time and space to perform. All Charles didn't do was score, but it wasn't for lack of trying. Gil Merrick, back in the team having been rested against the USA, was in inspired form, delivering what was perhaps his best performance in the England goal in order to keep the Welsh at bay.

★ ★ ★

Though important from a World Cup qualification stance, the Wales match had little of the lustre of England's next fixture. Officially billed as the FA's 90th Anniversary Celebration Match (though, since the confirmation of the Hungary game, arguably no longer *the* stand-out fixture of England's season), Winterbottom's team would be entertaining a Rest of the World XI at Wembley. Not since 1938 and the FA's 75th birthday had England played a representative side in peacetime, when they had enjoyed a 3-0 triumph over a Rest of Europe team at Highbury, inspired by a 23-year-old Stan Matthews. Fittingly, the Rest of the World match was the fixture that finally saw Matthews brought in from the cold and reinstated in the team for the first time in over two years. Given the two teams' remit to entertain, there was no more appropriate stage on which to unleash Matthews and his menagerie of leg-buckling tricks.

Although the match against the Rest of the World would eventually be expunged from the FIFA records as an unofficial fixture, at the time it was treated by both sides with the utmost seriousness. The FIFA selectors wasted no time on the sentimentality of the occasion and made no concessions for inclusivity. While the team bore the moniker the Rest of the World, it offered a damning opinion of players beyond Europe's borders. Of the twelve players who took the field, there was a Spaniard, a Swede, a German, an Italian, an exiled Hungarian, three Austrians and four Yugoslavians.

To underline the gravity with which FIFA viewed the fixture, they even deemed it necessary to set aside the sterling reputations of many of the stars and conduct a trial match against Barcelona before the main event. If such rigmarole had put off some, however, there was little evidence in the quality of the team that met England. Walter Zeman and Vladimir Beara, regarded as two of the best goalkeepers of the era, each played a half. Ahead of them was an intimidating defence consisting of Josef Posipal, Gerhard Hanappi, and Joaquín Navarro, arguably the least decorated of the FIFA side (he was subsequently given the nickname *El Fifo*, thanks to his somewhat surprising inclusion in the team). The half-backs consisted of Zlatko Čajkovski and Ernst Ocwirk, the man who had been singled out by England before their famous games against Austria in 1951 and 1952, thanks to his reputation as his team's metronome.

Of the forwards, two stood out for the Rest of the World, both in terms of renown and in significance to England and their upcoming fixture against the Hungarians. At centre-forward was AC Milan's Swedish star, Gunnar Nordahl. With British football still dominated by the bulldozing centre-forward archetype, Nordahl represented the future. Though his 6ft 1in frame meant he was more than capable of battling with defenders in a physical sense, his real skill was as a penalty box poacher, and by 1953 he was well on his way to writing his name into Milan and Serie A's record books. Despite his preternatural goal-scoring feats, the Rest of the World team represented a rare opportunity for Nordahl to display his talents on the international stage. He had been a lynchpin of George Raynor's first Sweden team, leading Raynor's relentlessly drilled unit to their historic victory at the 1948 Olympics, where he was top scorer. However, his move to Milan had put paid to his international career because the Sweden team was resolutely amateur and Nordahl's professional status in Italy made him ineligible to play for his country. His international career, in which he scored forty-three times in thirty-three games, was over at the age of 27. Nordahl was of special interest to England because of Raynor's influence on his style of play and early development.

However, for the 97,000 who crammed into Wembley on the day of the match, an overcast, autumnal Wednesday in mid-October, the Rest of the World's inside-right would have been of even greater interest than Nordahl, had his nationality in the match programme not been listed as Spanish. By that point in 1953, László Kubala had become a cipher for the Cold War. Following his daring defection from Hungary as Rákosi took over in 1949, Kubala had endured a year of professional and personal limbo. He had been reduced to guesting for a team made up of Eastern European refugees, while the Hungarian authorities accused him of breaching his contract and defecting in order to avoid military service, a charge that FIFA upheld as they banned Kubala from professional football.

Kubala's eventual salvation would come in an unlikely form. After impressing Real Madrid and Barcelona, both tried to sign him. The latter got their wish, but only after appealing to Spain's military dictator, Francisco Franco. Franco, a committed anti-communist who engaged in widespread repression of anyone who dared to espouse socialist doctrines, recognised the propaganda potential of conferring Spanish citizenship on a highly promising footballer fleeing from a totalitarian Soviet satellite. Kubala would eventually star in a film to hammer the message home, but by that point, his value as a piece of anti-communist agitprop had already been enshrined by his stellar performances in Catalonia.

If any of the Wembley crowd were on the look-out for hints as to how Hungary might approach the England match, they would have to have been clued up enough to know of Kubala's long, twisting backstory (no major newspaper mentioned his Hungarian roots, and *The Times* misidentified him as being Czechoslovakian), as no other Hungarian would feature for the Rest of the World side. The Hungarian government would certainly have refused permission for one of their star players to line up alongside the dissident Kubala, but Sebes himself had no interest in even raising the question. He knew he had already prepared his men for the upcoming fixture far better than the FA and Walter Winterbottom had. Why give the English a helping hand by offering a preview of what they could expect from his players in November? Beyond purely tactical reasons, Sebes viewed the entire ethos behind the FA's birthday celebrations and the match against a representative team with utter contempt, deriding it as nothing more than an exercise in appeasing 'English idiots', as he and his team poured their efforts into their preparations for the trip to Wembley.[11]

Kubala may have been billed as Spanish, but his style was still couched in the energetic, effervescent street football of Budapest, as he played with sparkling enterprise and the supreme confidence found only in players of the highest order. While Kubala was displaying his prototypical Hungarian flair and ebullience, Nordahl was giving the unwitting England defence a preview of the tactics that would be deployed against them by Gusztáv Sebes. The Rest of the World team was being managed by the legendary Austrian coach, Hugo Meisl, one of the great exponents of the Danubian variations on the W-M, and he had no issues with giving his players, particularly the forwards, free rein within the general confines of the formation. The net result was Nordahl repeatedly dropping deep to collect the ball, acting as a water carrier between the half-back pairing and the inside-forwards.

For England centre-half Derek Ufton, yet another change from the selection committee who was receiving his first and only cap, it was a baptism of fire. Here was one of Europe's most feared strikers, and yet he was showing a marked indifference towards positioning himself near the goal. Ufton, who combined his football with a first-class cricketing career, was torn between shadowing Nordahl as he dropped deep and remaining in his familiar defensive position. In the end, he was caught between the two options and achieved neither, leading 'a purposeless life', in the words of Meisl.[12] Nordahl was left free to pull the strings, while Kubala and inside-left Bernard Vukas had the space vacated by Ufton in which to run rampant. Kubala and winger Giampiero Boniperti both netted twice as the Rest of the World took the lead on three separate occasions, only to be foiled at the last by an Alf Ramsey penalty in the final minute of normal time, securing England an entertaining, yet fortuitous 4-4 draw against Meisl's talented but previously untested team.

England's defence being breached on four occasions by a set of players, talented though they were, who had no experience of playing with one another should have set alarm bells ringing, particularly given the ease with which Nordahl had teased Ufton out of position. Instead, the English remained blithely oblivious. The papers bemoaned the draw and lacklustre performance, but failed to identify the underlying tactical cause. In the words of Jonathan Wilson, the press 'seemed not even to recognise' the role Nordahl had played, instead equating the fact that he himself had failed to score with an ageing player whose best years were behind him.[13] Geoffrey Green in *The Times* summed up the collective stupefaction of the English when faced with any sort of attacking dynamism when he wrote, '[to] describe the continental methods acutely is difficult. Penetrating thoughts on the subject tumble over in confusion, and the white sheet of paper remains a reproach matching the confusion and emptiness of the English defence at times yesterday.' Meisl conceded that Nordahl 'really did not look impressive', before qualifying that by explaining, 'decoys rarely do. Gunnar's task was to hang back, to switch into any vacuum, in short, to uncork the English stopper.'[14]

One writer who did buck the trend (but also failed to specifically identify the movement of Nordahl as the principal reason for England's defensive undoing) was Clifford Webb, the *Daily Herald*'s football correspondent and frequently one of the England team's most vocal critics. He used the game as an opportunity to lambast the derision with which the likes of Jimmy Hogan had been treated, raging, 'The game in this country has become grim and desperate ... it all goes back to the inventor of that crushing phrase, "Get stuck in." No three words ever had so shattering an effect on any sport.' He concluded ominously, 'The boys from Budapest will skin us alive unless there is a sensational improvement in England's performance.'

The analysis of the game from within the England set-up was no more discerning than that of the press. Ufton played the role of implied scapegoat and was summarily dropped, never to play for his country again (thus earning the curious accolade of being the only player to have played for England but never *against* a specific country). Had Ufton retained his place, or if Harry Johnston had featured in his stead, the experience of playing against the roaming Nordahl could have proved invaluable in helping the England centre-half identify a glaring flaw in his game and the system in which he operated. As it was, the selection committee's incessant meddling had once again scuppered a golden opportunity for England to glean a shred of information about dealing with the Hungarians and their brand of football.

The Three Lions were now a month away from facing Hungary, with only a game against fellow W-M zealots Northern Ireland beforehand. The time for learning and preparation had come and gone. Whatever England's fate proved to be, they were now consigned to it.

10

THE SILENCE BEFORE THE STORM

In a year in which the Cold War took on a new significance and paranoia over infiltration attempts, real and imagined, on both sides of the Iron Curtain reached fever pitch, the image of Gusztáv Sebes conducting his last scouting trip before he took his men to Wembley is an irresistible one. Like a character from a John le Carré novel, Sebes took in England's performance against the Rest of the World team from the stands, watching with keen interest and a sense of growing excitement, as Gunnar Nordahl strayed from his nominal position of centre-forward and continually left England's defence in disarray.

At first glance, there was little to distinguish Sebes from the tens of thousands of punters present in Wembley Stadium that day, garbed against the British autumnal chill and clustered beneath a cloud of tobacco smoke. However, taking a closer look at Sebes' thick, woollen overcoat, his dark eyes, widow's peak and his frequently Rhadamanthine expression, one could detect an air of clinical detachment, an inscrutability about his demeanour that set him apart from the rest of the enraptured, enthusiastic punters. Though the reasons behind his mission were nothing more nefarious than getting a gauge on his team's upcoming opponents, the slight edge Sebes must have felt as he stood behind enemy lines was emblematic of a point in time when Cold War suspicions were at their most rampant.

A day after the frenetic scenes of the Rest of the World match, Sebes returned to Wembley, now in the role of nascent sports scientist. With boots on, Sebes wasted no time with sentimentality as he stepped onto Wembley's hallowed turf and began to put the pitch through its paces. He found the British drizzle had rendered even the best-tended football pitch in the country relatively sluggish. He struggled to get a ball to bounce higher than a metre off the grass, hinting that his players would need to put some extra zip behind their intricate passes if they were to reach their intended target. Next, he measured the pitch's very dimensions, numbers he considered to be of critical importance to the approach his team would take. A smaller pitch meant a more concentrated space, and a greater emphasis on the sort of rapid interchanging of passes and positions that the Hungarian attack was famous for. A larger pitch, meanwhile, would make the role of Hidegkuti even more critical, as he would either find himself with more space to roam in front of the England defence, or, if the Three Lions' centre-half elected to shadow the striker, leave England's two remaining backs even more exposed. It was this latter scenario that Sebes found to be more likely, given Wembley's larger than normal playing surface.

Sebes' activities, watched only by a couple of puzzled groundsmen clearing up the detritus left by the previous day's spectators, would have been far more befitting of an underhand Cold War spying case had they not been sanctioned by Stanley Rous himself. Sebes, emboldened by the English FA chief's willingness to give an upcoming opponent the run of the national stadium, decided to try his luck with another venturesome request, asking Rous if he'd be willing to let him travel back to Hungary in possession of one of the regulation English leather footballs that would be used in the game. The English ball had a reputation for reflecting the sort of football it was typically used for – hardwearing, heavy and, when wet, more reminiscent of a piece of medieval weaponry than elite sporting equipment. For decades, England's players had grumbled about being made to play with light, unfamiliar balls when abroad, and foreign teams had experienced the reverse, learning of the British ball's robust attributes by virtue of their players almost knocking themselves unconscious on attempting to head it in the first knockings of a match.

The match ball was recognised by Sebes as yet another piece of the puzzle that would help him to topple England, another marginal gain he could achieve when no advantage was too small or piece of knowledge too inconsequential. Quite whether out of arrogance, naivety, a sense of gentlemanly valour or a combination of all three, Rous readily agreed, giving Sebes not one but three balls to take home.

It's entirely possible, given the hysterical speculation about the impoverished standards of living behind the Iron Curtain in some quarters of the English press, that Rous mistakenly thought that the Hungarian national team that had been sweeping all before them were simply desperate for equipment that met English standards. As would become apparent in Hungary's upcoming match with Sweden, the acclimatisation of the Hungarians towards the ball proved to be more important than anyone could have anticipated. Rous handing it over, no questions asked, was akin to Germany wiring the Allies a chunk of deciphered Enigma code to help them along. The entirely above-board nature of Sebes' trip and the warm welcome he received from the English may have been banal in comparison to the Cold War yarns woven by Ian Fleming in his newly published novel *Casino Royale*, but as he returned home with a mental map of the Wembley pitch and the very ball his team would be playing with, even the phlegmatic Sebes must have felt as though he had pulled off an act of espionage befitting the most devious double agent.

★ ★ ★

Sebes had departed for London having watched his team continue their imperious run of form. Since beating Sweden in July, the national team had endured a three-month gap between matches, an interminable length of time for a team that relied so heavily on their connection with one another. Finally reunited in October, bar Zoltán Czibor, Sándor Kocsis and László Budai after their disciplinary indiscretions, the team swatted Czechoslovakia aside 5-1 and then, a week later, beat Austria 3-2 in Vienna, a result which cemented the Magyars' supremacy over their old rivals. The coach returned from his mission with three weeks before Hungary's last warm-up fixture, a return match in Budapest against George Raynor's Sweden.

It was no coincidence that the Hungarians would be playing their last game before England against a team coached by an Englishman and who owed much of their recent success to their loyal adherence to the W-M. Sebes had arranged the fixture specifically because he felt the Swedes would provide Hungary with a close approximation of the approach that England would take. Since Sebes' visit to London, Hungary had been training at Honvéd and in Népliget public park[1] on pitches that roughly resembled the dimensions of Wembley, with training matches against teams playing the English style, and had been practising with the precious English balls, something the fleet-footed Hungarian players loathed. Jenő Buzánszky spoke for the entire squad when he likened the experience of playing with the thick, leather spheres to 'kicking something made of wood'.[2] Sebes even went so far as to utilise smoke machines around the training pitch in an attempt to recreate the London smog in case his team were forced to contend with reduced visibility when they walked out at Wembley.[3]

The Sweden match was intended as a dry run, putting Sebes' theories into action. In fact, so preparational was the fixture for the trip to Wembley that the manager freely admitted his mind was elsewhere, already racing ahead. 'I nearly forgot about the match with Sweden, and didn't prepare for it properly at all,' remembered the coach, an oversight which goes some way to explaining the events that followed.[4]

A crowd of 80,000 expectant Hungarians were present for the national team's first match in the new Népstadion, which was still under construction after five years of building by a large but somewhat ramshackle force of volunteers and soldiers, all eager to demonstrate their nationalistic pride (with most of the Hungarian players still officially enlisted in the armed forces, they themselves were routinely wheeled out for photo opportunities showing them mucking in and helping to build the very stadium in which they would soon play). Determined to ensure that their team travelled west with the wind in their sails, the crowd roared their heroes on through the early stages of the game, as they settled into the familiar pattern of attacking while their opponents aspired to nothing more than holding them at bay.

It wasn't long, however, before the enthusiastic cheers of the crowd abated, making way for disgruntled murmurs. Hungary had had little trouble slicing through the Swedish defence four months earlier, and the 6-0 mauling the Magyars had subjected the Swedes to in the Olympic semi-final the year before was still fresh in the memory. Today, however, things seemed different. The crowd had expected their team to be brimming with confidence, enthused about the prospect of travelling to England to prove their greatness, once and for all, and enjoying the dramatic (if still incomplete) surroundings of the Népstadion. Instead, Hungary appeared laboured and uncomfortable with the English-style ball, their attack missing its usual fluidity, with the inviting gaps the front five always seemed to find simply not appearing. If this performance against an English-coached team, playing in a close facsimile of the English style, was a portent for what was to come at Wembley, then it was a grave one indeed.

Of course, George Raynor was no ordinary Englishman. He had been forced to look for opportunities abroad because he had little hope of infiltrating the insular world of the English leagues. He hadn't served a notable apprenticeship as a player. Furthermore, he dared question the strict, dogmatic orthodoxy of the W-M (even as he used it as the foundation for his success with Sweden), and he believed that the key to winning matches was not held by the twenty-two men on the pitch alone. In these latter two beliefs, he shared a kinship with Sebes, and in this particular battle, despite having travelled hundreds of miles to Budapest and having been forced to rebuild his team after losing his star players to professional leagues, Raynor would very nearly get the better of his opposite number.

Just as Márton Bukovi, Sebes and coach Gyula Mándi had identified the centre-half and his susceptibility to be pulled out of position as the key to unlocking the W-M, so too had Raynor. Thanks to two games against the Hungarians in just over a year, Raynor had pinpointed the Hungarian use of the deep-lying centre-forward as the focal point of *their* system and hatched a plan to subvert his opponent's greatest tactical strength. If they could somehow stop Hidegkuti, the Swedish team would cut the key supply line to the other Hungarian forwards. Raynor achieved this by issuing a strict set of instructions to his players which essentially amounted to a prototypical version of zonal marking. Different players were given responsibility for closing Hidegkuti down, depending on where on the field he popped up, negating the danger of the centre-half alone shadowing him and thereby finding himself marooned far out of position.[5]

All of Hungary's success, their Olympic gold medals and the fifteen-match unbeaten run the team were on, suddenly seemed to count for little. Something that makes Hungary's success at the start of the 1950s all the more impressive is the relative lack of home fixtures they took part in. In the three years before the Sweden match, they had only played in Hungary five times. Far from weakening the team's appeal, however, this had merely served to bolster their mythology among the Hungarian people, as stories of their heroics abroad filtered back in the state-run press and via the radio with the commentaries of György Szepesi, who himself became a huge celebrity, thanks to his chronicles of the team's adventures.

The lore surrounding the team's abilities made their flat performance against the Swedish all the more difficult to fathom for the thousands of spectators. By half-time, with the score deadlocked at 0-0 and Hungary looking limp, the murmurs of the crowd were turning to groans, the disappointment of many seeing the Golden Team in the flesh for the very first time palpable. No excuses could be found in the Hungarian line-up, which featured all the usual suspects, as well as Czibor, Budai and Kocsis after their disciplinary-enforced absences. To make matters worse, even the team's indomitable captain, the one player everyone looked to to haul them through tough spots and bawl out anyone not giving his all for the cause, Ferenc Puskás, had missed a penalty.

Into the second half, the continued obstinance of Sweden's defence transformed into a growing belief that they could do more than just stifle Hungary. On the hour mark, Raynor's team took the lead, only for their stoic defence to falter shortly after, allowing first Péter Palotás (who had replaced Kocsis at half-time) and then Czibor to score and put Hungary ahead. Sweden, however, would enjoy the final say, netting a richly deserved equaliser with 4 minutes remaining to leave Hungary in no doubt as to the enormity of the task awaiting them in England.

Just as the Hungarian newspapers were always the first to heap praise upon their footballing superheroes after they won, so too did they waste little time in disavowing and lambasting them after their failures. It had been so long since the team's performance had been anything other than exemplary that the inability to defeat the amateur Sweden team was seized upon with the same vitriol as if they had been heavily defeated. Puskás recalled:

We got well and truly sorted out by the fans and the press after this draw. They were saying, 'It's not worth you going over to Wembley if you can't do better than that. The English are a serious football team, unbeaten for ninety years at home, they'll murder you.'[6]

It was an opinion echoed in the British press, who reported on the game of an upcoming opponent with unprecedented interest. In the *Daily Herald*, Clifford Webb wrote, 'Nobody would have wagered a forint … on that possibility [of Hungary beating England] after watching today's performance.' In the same piece, Webb quoted Raynor, who said that if 'England cannot beat the Hungarians now that we have shown how to slow them down I shall be greatly disappointed'. Given Raynor's personal experience of English football's obstinance when it came to accepting lessons from abroad, it was a highly optimistic assessment.

★ ★ ★

The Hungarians, of course, hadn't needed a primer on the British game. It was, after all, the form of the sport from which all others, including their own inimitable brand, sprang. The personnel may have changed, the style fluctuated between finesse and physical, depending on what each situation called for, but fundamentally, the Hungarians could anticipate an almost identical English approach as when the two sides had last met in 1936.

The same could not be said for England, who would be coming up against a team the likes of which they had never played before, deploying an alien formation and underlying philosophy. Had the England team or a club in the Football League attempted something so radical, they would have been met with ridicule and derision in equal measure. The notion that a *foreign* team could have developed the game and found a way of playing that undercut the venerated W-M merely added to the farce. Not even a cursory glance at Hungary's glittering recent run of results or the whispers coming from the Continent about the Magyars' prowess could convince the FA to prepare more diligently for the coming fixture.

To their credit, a delegation including Winterbottom did travel to Budapest to take in the preparatory game with Sweden, but the timing of this fact-finding mission, a mere ten days before the Hungarians set foot on the Wembley turf, was indicative of the laissez-faire attitude towards England's opponents. The FA were playing the role of a spoiled, overindulged, naturally gifted yet lazy public schoolboy, content to coast along, accustomed to succeeding despite applying only the bare minimum of effort, suffering the occasional embarrassing result but highly adept at convincing others (and themselves) that any setbacks were mere aberrations, even as the evidence to the contrary continued to mount. Raynor advised one FA delegate that a key to his plan had been having his wingers drop back to help defend, to which the man scoffed that he wasn't about to ask Stanley Matthews to undertake the drudgery of tracking Zoltán Czibor.[7]

As always, Winterbottom was an outlier. Even after witnessing Hungary toil, he was under no illusions of their qualities, telling *The Times*' Geoffrey Green that they were 'quite the finest team he had ever seen'.

In yet another serendipitous twist of fate for the Hungarians, the FA presence at the Sweden match confirmed many of the Englishmen's worst long-held biases about football on the Continent. For decades, there had been rumblings of new strains of football coming from Europe, of exciting variations on the staid British formula, of mighty new forces rising ready to challenge the British hegemony. As far as the FA were concerned, all had proved to be damp squibs. The laboured, ponderous play of Hungary against Sweden came in stark contrast to their billing as a lightning-quick attacking unit, their inability to slice through Raynor's well-organised defence appearing to defy their system's apparent deconstruction of the W-M.

It was, by all accounts, a poor showing from Hungary, one that heaped pressure on the team and Sebes, but it's debatable whether or not the game ultimately aided Hungary more than it hindered them. True, the English were hardly likely to upset the apple cart, even if they'd witnessed a breathtaking show of attacking prowess from Hungary, eviscerating the W-M in the process. To diverge from their decades-old tactics scarcely a week before the match would have been unthinkable.

It would, however, at least have served as a shot across the bows, an exigent warning that the England team must keep their guard up. As it was, the FA delegation returned from their one and only in-person scouting trip of Hungary since Rous had seen them at the Olympics the year before with a spring in their step, anticipating not a threat, but a grand opportunity for the England team to stamp their superiority over the rest of Europe once more.

★ ★ ★

Four days before Hungary played Sweden, England had contested the last fixture, against Northern Ireland, before they met the pretenders to their throne. In stark contrast to the Sweden game for the Hungarians, the fixture against the Irish could not have been less instructive of what England could expect from their coming foes. Northern Ireland were, to all intents and purposes, a mirror image of the England team, but with inferior players. They were beholden to the W-M and ardent believers in the traditional British player archetypes; eight of their players plied their trade for English clubs. To expound matters, they provided little gauge on how ready England might be to face a truly exceptional opponent. The two teams had met nineteen times since 1928, resulting in two draws and seventeen wins for England (it had been the Republic of Ireland team that had inflicted England's first home defeat by a non-British team in 1949).

True to form, England won 3-1, a scoreline that masked a laboured performance that did nothing to quell the grumblings in the press and on the terraces that, for all their recent solid results, England were far from the powerhouse that many assumed they still had every right to be. Nonetheless, the win, as part of the Home Championship, confirmed England's place at the next summer's World Cup. Equally significant, meanwhile, was the insight it gave into the minds of the selectors about who had made the grade to face Hungary.

For once, England's players couldn't blame the incessant meddling of the selection committee as the chief reason for their failure to find top gear. Gil Merrick, Bill Eckersley, Billy Wright, Jimmy Dickinson, Stan Matthews, Nat Lofthouse, Albert Quixall and Jimmy Mullen had all retained their spots in the team following the Rest of the World match, with Tom Finney and Alf Ramsey out with injuries. However, with the crucial contest with Hungary looming, there remained a complete lack of consensus on what England's defence should look like.

Having been dropped for the Rest of the World match in favour of Derek Ufton, Harry Johnston was brought back in at centre-half to face Northern Ireland. To his right, despite Ramsey's injuries becoming increasingly common, there was little contingency planning in place for when his ageing legs inevitably caused him to miss games. For the trip to Goodison to face the Ireland team, he was replaced by debutant Stan Rickaby (who, like Ufton in the match before, would make only one appearance for his country, with his career ended by injury in 1954). Up front, Lofthouse's club teammate, the injury-prone Harold Hassall, who had last featured for the Three Lions in 1951, had replaced Stan Mortensen.

As was so often the case with the selection committee's continuous tinkering, Hassall's call-up raised more questions than it answered. The diminutive forward offered a seemingly faultless audition and scored twice, taking his international record to a highly respectable four goals in five matches, yet, like Rickaby, Hassall never again donned an England shirt before having his career cut short by a devastating knee injury a little over a year later.

Predictably, it was Hassall's clubmate, Lofthouse, who netted England's other goal. The strike took Lofthouse's tally to a superlative twenty goals in nineteen international appearances, a number which left him, still aged just 28, sixth on the all-time list for England, three behind his childhood idol Lawton (as well as Mortensen) and two behind his best friend, Finney. Setting to one side his incredible goal record, the desire and commitment Lofthouse had exhibited when playing for England alone were enough to have made any of his detractors think twice. The game with Ireland once again showcased the sacrifices he was willing to make, as he split his head open scoring the winner, subsequently missing the last 15 minutes of the game to have stitches. As he was helped down the touchline by a policeman, with a towel draped over his bloody head, few in Goodison Park, least of all Lofthouse himself, would have assumed the place he had held for eighteen consecutive internationals was under any sort of threat.

★ ★ ★

With Northern Ireland seen off, England's attentions blithely turned to Hungary, who they would face exactly two weeks later. In Hungary, meanwhile, Gusztáv Sebes' and his team's preparations were anything but lackadaisical. The response to their failure to comprehensively trounce Sweden had been a mixture of alarm and brutal condemnation. After such a long and sustained period of success, the swift and vitriolic response to what was, after all, nothing more than a lacklustre performance in a relatively inconsequential fixture, came as a shock to the team.

If the press and government had hoped to sting their players into a spirited response against England, however, the gambit backfired, as self-doubt swept through the squad. In a matter of days, Sebes watched helplessly as years of momentum and self-belief evaporated on the eve of the team's most high-profile game in their history.

Taking his players beyond the Iron Curtain and into the West was always a source of some anxiety for Sebes. He dedicated hours to ensuring his players were content and extolling his genuine belief in communism, yet the fear of a László Kubala-style defection (particularly given the past failed attempts of squad lynchpins Gyula Lóránt and Gyula Grosics) was never far from his mind. Though the players enjoyed the best of life in Soviet Hungary, living outside the crippling poverty and constant fear that much of the population was subjected to, Sebes was always mindful of the distracting, disorienting effect that exposure to the world outside of the Kremlin's sphere of influence could have on them.

He, along with the Hungarian sports officials and Mihály Farkas, the head of the armed forces (who had a direct line to a phone on Sebes' desk), aimed to organise the team's trips abroad with military precision in order to mitigate the chance of any of the players having their heads turned. Ever since the execution of Sándor Szűcs, officers from the secret police had travelled with the team, which was enough to keep most of the players toeing the line. An inevitable exception was Puskás, who would delight in giving his minders the slip before casually returning to the team hours later and remarking, 'Go, on, admit it, you thought I'd fucked off for good, didn't you?'[8]

The situation following the Sweden draw, however, was such that Sebes now took drastic action. Instead of flying directly to London, he decided at the very last minute that his team would take the train across the Continent instead, stopping en route in Paris, where Sebes had lived during the 1920s, and where, while working for Renault as a fitter and union representative, he had experienced his awakening as a socialist. He scarcely could have imagined, as a young man supplementing the meagre income earned from his itinerant football career as a fitter in a car factory, that he would one day return to a hero's welcome, in charge of the most feared footballing side on the planet. But return he would – and in need of a favour.

Given how accustomed the Hungarian team had become to dealing with crowds thronging at Budapest's Keleti Station to see them off or welcome them triumphantly back home, it was an eerie, disquieting atmosphere as they were bade farewell by a sparse assembly of family and friends, the usual mob still smarting from the team's showing against Sweden. Sebes hoped that the extra time spent together on the ride across Europe would give his players the opportunity to come to terms with the Sweden match before their arrival in England.

This, however, was of secondary importance to what he had planned in Paris, where he had contacted old friends from his Renault days and arranged for a practice match against the works team that he himself had once played for, Olympique Billancourt. It was a wager that wasn't without jeopardy. Any hint of Hungary struggling to overcome their amateur opponents would compound the doubts and worries that had been created by the Sweden game. Nonetheless, it was a risk that Sebes was willing to take.

The team's train rolled into Paris, greeted by the sort of reception they'd become familiar with, something which Sebes felt 'boosted the team's spirits a bit'.[9] The Parisian clamour to catch a glimpse of these soccer heroes at the station was, however, nothing compared to the Billancourt match. An estimated 15,000 people turned up, hoping to witness a moment of *Magyar* magic, and they weren't disappointed. An 18-0 scoreline underlined the fact that Hungary weren't just there for a gentle warm-up, but to rediscover their mojo. Regardless of the limitations of their opponents, the gambit worked. Puskás remembered the result 'really did help to get the taste of that bad match with Sweden out of our mouths. Our whole attitude had changed before we arrived in London.'[10]

Reaching London a few days before the match, the Hungarian squad checked in at the Cumberland Hotel in the upmarket district of Marylebone. Though the area's red-brick, Victorian and art deco architecture would not have drawn much attention from the Hungarian boys who were accustomed to the grandeur of Budapest (even in its somewhat diminished post-war state), the pace and style of London life was dazzling. London in 1953 was still closer to its wartime hue than the vibrancy of the swinging sixties, but it was nonetheless a shock to the system after living in Soviet-inspired Hungary. The evening before the match, Sebes would even treat his players to a trip to the Prince of Wales Theatre to see *Pardon My French*, a show advertised with a poster emblazoned with the tagline 'Ze smash 'it with Londoners', alongside several scantily clad women. This foray into Western decadence was deemed necessary by Sebes in order to help quell his players' own pre-show nerves.

Having been recklessly accommodating when Gusztáv Sebes had made the trip to watch England take on the Rest of the World several weeks before, the FA performed an about-turn when it came to the Hungarian team themselves and refused them permission for even one training session on the Wembley pitch. The one test of the surface's zip and spring that the visitors were permitted came while wearing dress shoes as they visited the ground in the run-up to the match. Instead, they had the use of Fulham's Craven Cottage ground. If Hungary had felt hard done by, they could console themselves with the fact that England were also barred from training at Wembley and were having to endure dog-racing trials taking place on the track surrounding the playing area at Chelsea's Stamford Bridge as they were put through their pre-match paces.

Other than not being able to train at Wembley and acclimatise themselves to football's most famous environs, the Hungary team's preparations could not have gone more smoothly. There were no injuries to contend with, save for Grosics complaining of a cold, something which Sebes bluntly attributed to his goalkeeper's tendency towards hypochondria rather than anything more serious.[11] The party avoided the issues suffered by England when they had visited Chile and had been laid low by illness because they chanced upon a Czech restaurant with a Hungarian chef, who was all too pleased to help his illustrious patrons avoid any unintended dietary surprises.[12]

Even though the concept of celebrity footballers was still some years off – fans in the 1950s could expect to run into their First Division heroes catching the bus to the ground for matches, or stumble across them while they worked their part-time jobs during the week – London, nonetheless, had a buzz of excitement about their exotic visitors, even celebrating their guests with an exhibition focusing on the football team entitled 'Sport in Hungary' and organised by the British Hungarian Friendship Society. The frosty response at home to the team's game with Sweden, meanwhile, had thawed, and hundreds of well-wishing telegrams began to arrive at the hotel. Ever attuned to his team's individual personalities and recognising any and all opportunities to improve morale or provide extra motivation, Sebes stuffed a suitcase full of these missives to take with him on the coach to the game.

★ ★ ★

The day of the match dawned grey and cool, a thick, oppressive mist blanketing the capital after a pounding rain storm overnight had left the roads slick and treacherous. At their team hotel in Hendon, the England players awoke with a familiar mixture of pride and anxiety. The former stemmed from the prospect of representing their country; the latter from what failure to defend the nation's record of never having lost at home to a team from the Continent would mean for them, their careers and their reputations. The newspapers had carried articles anticipating the fixture for months, including reports from Hungary's games against Sweden and the Renault team, a compliment rarely afforded to foreign sides.

Fans lucky enough to have a ticket travelled from all over the country. On the day of the match, the *Daily Mirror* reported that a schoolboy who had been caught playing truant had, as a form of ultimate punishment, been banned from watching the BBC's coverage of the match.

Behind all the nationalist bravado that had enveloped the fixture, most England fans with a passing awareness of Hungary's pedigree would have settled for a draw and the preservation of their proud record. It was a stance echoed by the sportswriters, who predicted a grave threat to England's unbeaten status, with little cause for comfort other than the good old-fashioned British knack of being able to extricate themselves from even the most hopeless of scrapes. Bob Ferrier, in the *Daily Mirror*, had a 'hunch' that England would escape with their record unscathed, even as he postulated that to lose the record to a team that owed so much to Jimmy Hogan would be particularly galling. The influential French scribe Gabriel Hanot, who would go on to be instrumental in the creation of both the European Cup and Ballon d'Or, was similarly persuaded by England's peculiar *je ne sais quoi* when it came to snatching results, arguing that their '*bravoure*' could be enough to quell the Hungarians.

With any English optimism tempered with a heavy dose of caution, logic dictated that the most sensible team selection would place an emphasis on solidity and consistency. The FA, though, had other ideas, instead continuing with their quixotic quest, swapping and rotating players with complete abandon in the search for some ineffable chemistry or result. After at least maintaining a semblance of consistency in the team in recent months, the selection committee saw the Hungary test not as a cause for caution but as a reason to indulge in their most vacillating tendencies.

Though the team would technically be the most experienced of the post-war era in terms of the number of caps accrued, this was largely due to the presence of several veteran players rather than a testament to any grand design. Gil Merrick maintained his position in goal, with the stalwarts Bill Eckersley and Alf Ramsey directly ahead of him. Try as they might, the FA had yet to find a satisfactory understudy for the ageing Ramsey, whose dwindling pace and physical attributes made it patently clear that his days as an international, and even as a First Division player, were numbered. In a claim that would prove ill-fated to say the least, Geoffrey Green in *The Times* declared that Ramsey's key weakness – 'slowness on the turn' – would be 'heavily counterbalanced by his tactical mastery'.

The critical role of centre-half, the defensive fulcrum, was given to Harry Johnston. It was an arrangement that the FA were far from happy with, attested to by the sporadic use of Johnston since his debut all the way back in 1946, just weeks after international football had resumed following the end of the war. The selection of debutant Derek Ufton to face the Rest of the World had represented the FA's last throw of the dice in finding a true successor to Neil Franklin, but the four goals conceded against the all-star forward line had forced the selection committee's hand. Even for those in the FA who felt Hungary's supposed strength to be nothing more than hot air emanating from the Continent were not willing to throw in another untested player at the heart of the defence to try and stop the likes of Ferenc Puskás, Sándor Kocsis, Nándor Hidegkuti and company. Instead, the task would fall to the 34-year-old Johnston in just his tenth cap.

Further up the pitch, Billy Wright, easily identified from the stands by his shock of blond hair, won his record fifty-fifth cap, the fortieth in the role as the team's indomitable captain. Alongside him came Jimmy Dickinson, making the half-back duo the only truly established pairing for England.

The same could not be said for the forwards, where the selectors took several decisions that bordered on the astonishing. Some were enforced. Tom Finney, having missed the Rest of the World and Northern Ireland games, was slated to return to the team at outside left, but injured his groin while training with the England squad at Stamford Bridge and was forced to withdraw. In his stead came one of England's two debutants, George Robb.

Robb is a fascinating relic of a bygone era in British football, and indeed even in 1953 was something of an anachronism. The 27-year-old had only turned professional earlier that year, having carved out a successful amateur career as a teammate of Ramsey's with Tottenham, training on his own in the evenings while teaching full-time at Christ's College in Finchley during the day. There was a time when amateurs and professionals mixed regularly in the First Division (Bernard Joy had been the last amateur to appear for England in 1936), but by the 1950s they were an endangered species, as money and crowds flocked to the game like never before and the need to safeguard top talent from the prying clutches of other clubs made it imperative that clubs secured players on professional terms. Having become professional mere months before and only being drafted in as Finney's replacement with two days to go, it's not a stretch to imagine Robb's emotions leading up to the match being akin to those endured when suffering the familiar nightmare in which one finds oneself before thousands, expected to complete a task with little or no preparation (he would at least be wearing clothes).

On the opposite wing, there was no such issue. Stanley Matthews had looked spritely and effective in the two games since he'd returned to the team, and there was little question of his involvement once it became apparent that the Hungary game would represent the first time an England match at Wembley would draw more than 100,000 spectators, many of whom were just as excited to see the old maestro as they were the footballing supermen from the East. Matthews was the only player who could genuinely approach the Hungary game in a sanguine fashion. He had won his second cap in 1934 when World Champions Italy visited Highbury in one of the first matches between England and a foreign interloper billed as an unofficial world championship match, and since then had faced Germany, Czechoslovakia, France, Portugal and Spain in similarly high-stakes circumstances.

In an attempt to harness some of the magic from Matthews' glorious triumph in the FA Cup earlier in the year, a debut was handed to Ernie Taylor, Matthews' teammate at club level, at inside-forward. Blackpool had endured an indifferent start to the season following their FA Cup heroics, lying in eleventh in early October after three straight losses and having scored fewer goals than rock-bottom Sunderland. Four wins on the trot, however, catapulted them up the table just as the selectors were finalising their squad to face Hungary.

Though Matthews had won the plaudits following the Cup Final, it was agreed among the Bolton and Blackpool players that it had been Taylor's marauding presence at inside-right that had been the key to unlocking the full force of Matthews' potential. Taylor's selection to face the Mighty Magyars was undoubtedly made in the hopes of achieving the same effect again, although quite why the FA had elected to wait until the team's sternest test in years to put the theory into practice was anybody's guess.

Jackie Sewell, whose transfer in 1951 from Notts County to Sheffield Wednesday had briefly made him the world's most expensive player, was named as the other inside-forward. Though more experienced than Taylor – the Hungary game would be his fifth cap – Sewell had not played internationally for more than a year, during which time no fewer than eight different players had been tried in the inside-forward role.

It was at centre-forward, however, that the biggest shock came. Nat Lofthouse had last been seen in an England shirt being helped from the pitch with a bloodied towel draped around his head, having just put the game beyond Northern Ireland's reach with a header, maintaining his ratio of more goals than appearances for his country on his nineteenth cap. He had well over 100 league goals to his name and had earlier that year been named Football Writers' Footballer of the Year and joined an exclusive club of players to score in every round of the FA Cup in a single season. Indeed, his play since his heroics in Vienna just over a year before had proved his blood-and-thunder performance on that day to be the rule, not the exception. Though he was nursing an injury, to omit Lofthouse from the team, even by the FA's dubious standards, was a remarkable decision.

Instead, his place was taken by Stan Mortensen, completing a triumvirate of Blackpool players in the forward line. Mortensen, at 32, four years Lofthouse's senior, had a similarly impressive record for the Three Lions, having netted twenty-two times in twenty-four games, a ratio helped substantially by the four he scored on his debut in the famous 10-0 destruction of Portugal in 1947. However, by 1953, his considerable powers were beginning to wane. His previous cap, against the Rest of the World team, had been his first in more than two years. In less than two years he'd be playing for lowly Hull City in the Second Division and his England career would draw to a close much sooner than that.

There was at least some logic to his selection at centre-forward for only the third time for his country. Though far from bereft of power – Matthews recalled Mortensen's 'monstrous and explosive shot with either foot'[13] – Mortensen was less of what Brian Glanville would term a 'brainless bull at the gate' and more a predator.[14] Ordinarily, this dichotomy would have worked against him; the selectors had historically looked to the centre-forward to imbue the role with power and physicality. However, against the fleet-footed Hungarians, Mortensen's agility, plus the pre-existing relationship between him, Taylor and Matthews, was the reason he was given the nod over Lofthouse. Even in their faltering draw with Sweden, the FA delegation had registered the speed with which Hungary aimed to move the ball and the natural pace of many of their players, and likely saw Mortensen as a more obvious fit for what they expected to be a match played at a breakneck speed. Nonetheless, to replace Lofthouse after he had proven himself as the man capable of filling Tommy Lawton's boots was a tremendous risk, one which epitomised the constant meddling of the selection committee.

★ ★ ★

For Hungary, despite the esprit de corps garnered from crushing the Renault factory team and the smooth running of their pre-match preparations, there wasn't a single man in the party who didn't feel some degree of trepidation. The word Grosics went so far as to use was 'afraid'.[15] Even the cool-headed Sebes, who rarely betrayed his emotions, good or bad, inadvertently laid his cards on the table when his last pre-match tactical talk to the team ran to more than two hours in length.

Normally concise and crystal clear, Sebes gabbled and went over concepts and ideas that were, by now, second nature to his players. Sándor Barcs, head of the Hungarian FA, recalled Sebes speaking 'for ages ... He was so excited, he wasn't making much sense.'[16] When Barcs confided in Puskás that he hadn't understood a word of Sebes' presentation, Puskás gave an impish grin and replied, 'Neither did I.'[17]

Central to Sebes' instruction was that, unlike the game in Rome where Hungary had focused on remaining defensively resolute and hitting the Italians on the break, they were to treat England with no such respect. First and foremost, the plan was to attack. Hidegkuti was to bide his time, beginning the match as an orthodox centre-forward with the intention of lulling

Harry Johnston into a false sense of security, before picking his moment to drop into the deep-lying role. The efficacy of this ploy hinged upon the degree that Johnston was expecting Hidegkuti to roam. England had made no special arrangements for handling Gunnar Nordahl in the match with the Rest of the World, and few of the English writers had predicted Hidegkuti would play a significant role, instead focusing on Puskás, Kocsis and Czibor as the danger men. *The Times* did declare that 'Hidegkuti is a centre-forward who lies back to provide openings', but even this undersold just how pivotal he had become to the *Magyar* gameplan. Sebes also ordered that special attention be paid to the one player in England's ranks he felt could have commanded a place in his team, telling Lantos, Bozsik and Czibor that they were not to let Matthews out of their sight.

The entire episode, however, did more harm than good, as Sebes' nervous excitement transmitted itself to his players, who were long accustomed to their manager's taciturn, unflappable demeanour and were unsettled by his sudden volte-face. The team had achieved an astonishing amount together, repeat-edly reaching what felt like a pinnacle – the 6-1 win over Austria when Sebes first chose his desired team, the gold medal at the Olympics, the consummate defeat of Italy in Rome to win the Central European Championship – only to then surpass it. Yet, as their bus wound its way through the labyrinthine streets of London towards the imposing edifice of Wembley and the stadium's twin towers, no one on board could help but question, however briefly, if everything up to that point had been a fluke, if they were about to be brought back down to earth in the most humiliating, high-profile fashion imaginable. Everything felt like it was in place, no stone had been left unturned – but surely it couldn't be that simple against England?

One element that did help settle the jangling Hungarian nerves was the team selection. The squad arrived in London with a confidence in their line-up that Winterbottom would have given a limb for during his tenure in the England job. A distinct line could be traced through all of Hungary's recent success to the team that would take the field against England. Of the XI selected to start at Wembley, nine had started the Olympic Final against Yugoslavia, fifteen months earlier (with just Kocsis and Budai absent), and ten had begun the piv-otal match against Switzerland. The only player who hadn't started that match was Hidegkuti, whose introduction and unusually deep positioning in Bern had ushered in the team's brave new tactical era. The high of 1953 so far – the comprehensive win in Rome against Italy – as well as the low – the recent match with Sweden – had both featured the exact same starting side as would play at Wembley.

It was a testament to Sebes and Gyula Mándi's remarkable foresight that they'd been able to achieve such a degree of consistency in the team. Though the unit had truly come together over the eighteen months before the game with England, it had been gestating for years. Sebes had pooled players at Honvéd and collaborated with Márton Bukovi's MTK to form the nucleus of the team and introduce the tactical imprint that was as ingrained as a seam in stone by the time they reached Wembley. As Puskás attested to, this approach had perhaps closed the door on players from other clubs who otherwise would have warranted a place, but by late 1953, evidence that an alternative approach or different set of players could have improved the Magyars was scant. The disciplinary issues of Kocsis, Budai and Czibor now seemed an eon ago; by the time they reached London, the players were united in their hopes of success, dreams of glory, and belief in themselves.

Of course, certain players felt the exact emotional balance differently. Puskás, as always, was nothing less than ebullient at the opportunity to show the world, once again, what he was capable of. The player who, even at the very start of his career, had never been anything less than exacting in terms of what he demanded from his teammates and coaches was relishing the prospect of proving himself against England. The same was true of his boyhood best friend Bozsik.

Unlike Puskás, whose precocious natural talent had carried him almost straight into the national team following the war, Bozsik had had to bide his time, watching as his friend was showered with plaudits in the press while the same writers cast aspersions on his languid, calculating style of play, which some derided as ponderous and demonstrative of a dim-witted player. He had proved them wrong and become the team's undeniable lynchpin in the centre of the field.

As well as Hidegkuti dropping deep, so too had Bozsik's partner, half-back József Zakariás, begun to drop further back to aid the defence as an auxiliary centre-half, often leaving Bozsik to his own devices in a prototypical 4-2-4 midfield, where he acted as a crucial pivot, deciding whether to feed the ball to Hidegkuti or to use him as a decoy. Whereas many players would have wilted upon being handed such responsibility, Bozsik had thrived, and understood better than anyone the critical role that the withdrawn Hidegkuti in front of him now played.

Bozsik, Puskás and several of the others in the team could vividly remember their childhood in war-torn Hungary, as the country lurched from Nazi occupation to life under the Soviets. These memories couched everything on the football field in a comforting perspective. More pertinently, they had grown with the team, witnessed the rise from a solid side to world-beaters, and knew it was their job to see the work through. Zakariás and the right-back, Jenő Buzánszky, the only player in the side still playing for a club other than Honvéd or Bukovi's MTK, both also fit this description.

For others, even the worst horrors of the war weren't always enough to distract them from the political spectre that lurked malevolently over the team. Lóránt knew it was only his effective combining of the physical 'stopper' and the more elegant, Danubian interpretation of the centre-half role that had separated him from an unimaginable fate in a grim detention camp after his failed attempt to defect when Rákosi took power. Though he knew that he would never be free from scrutiny as long as the communist forces remained in charge, it had been Sebes' intervention alone that was responsible for the life of relative luxury he now enjoyed. These circumstances were more than enough motivation for the defender to quietly deliver month after month, an under-appreciated cog in the Hungarian machine.

With such a redoubtable example alongside him, it was no surprise that Mihály Lantos, though five years Lóránt's junior, had already developed into a similarly dependable presence. Hungary's reputation for free-flowing football preceded them, yet Lantos had developed into a secret weapon as the team's set-piece specialist, the *Magyar* answer to Alf Ramsey in the England team, his skill in dead-ball situations yet another potent weapon in an already well-stocked arsenal.

For Grosics, the threat of the government loomed larger than perhaps for any other player. Always prone to hypochondria, Grosics' paranoia could never be put entirely to rest while he lived a high-profile life under such a repressive and image-conscious regime. Nonetheless, by 1953, he was an elite goalkeeper in an era when the fearless, domineering style pioneered by Eastern European and Soviet goalkeepers such as Grosics, Russia's Lev Yashin, Yugoslavia's Vladimir Beara and Austria's Walter Zeman made them the best in the world.

As the disciplinary indiscretion earlier in the year had proven, not all those in the Hungary team necessarily played with such awareness of their country's recent history or laboured apprehensively under the yoke of Hungary's political situation. Sebes had transmuted the drinking binge of his three young attacking stars, Kocsis, Budai and Czibor, from a shameful incident into a powerful reminder of just what an incredible opportunity they had before them, if only they would accept the responsibility and seize it. The short-term exile of the players from the team had become a long-term advantage, as the three returned to the fold with renewed hunger and purpose, a boon considering that Kocsis had, like Lofthouse and Puskás, scored more goals than he had appearances for his country (a remarkable record of thirty-five in thirty-two caps). Czibor and Budai, meanwhile, both offered devastating, Finney-esque directness from the wing, as well as the innate understanding of when to cut inside and interchange with their inside-forwards.

★ ★ ★

For all of the patronising airs and condescension that emanated from the rooms of the FA's Lancaster Gate headquarters towards nations from beyond Britain's borders, the match programme of the day was remarkably even-handed. In his introduction, John Graydon lavished praise on England's opponents, celebrating their dedication to attractive, passing football, Hungary's countrywide passion for the sport and the application the squad demonstrated in coaching the younger generations. Graydon even allowed that their recent draw with Sweden had been caused in part by the use of the 'larger-sized English ball' loaned by Rous. Most portentously of all, Graydon declared that 'for co-ordinating quickness of thought and movement they are the best Continental football team I have ever seen'. While the England matchday programmes were never less than gentlemanly in their discussion of their opponents, no matter how mismatched in ability they were with England, it was rare that superlatives were so readily dished out.

Away from Graydon's gushing write-up of the *Magyar* team, however, there was plenty to give the England-supporting punters in the stands reasons to be confident. An undercurrent of superiority ran through much of the programme. The FA sincerely wished 'that our visitors will carry back home pleasant memories of their visit' to Britain and to Wembley, a statement that placed Hungary in the role of souvenir-gathering tourists rather than serious opponents.

The player profile section of the programme tapped into the classic David vs Goliath cup tie trope of mentioning almost every Hungarian player's day job.

Grosics, Budai, Hidegkuti and Károly Sándor were all listed as clerks; Lóránt, Czibor and Mihály Tóth (Czibor's understudy) as civil servants; Buzánszky as an accountant; Lantos and back-up goalkeeper Sándor Gellér as working on the railway; Bozsik as a Member of Parliament for a Budapest district (a position he'd been forced into by Rákosi shortly after the Olympic victory as the government sought to capitalise upon the players' popularity); Zakariás as a machine toolmaker; forward Lajos Csordás as a university student; midfielder Imre Kovács as a carpenter; and both Kocsis and Puskás were described as being enlisted in the Hungarian Army, Kocsis as a captain and Puskás as a major. Whether intentional or not, the effect, when compared to the profiles of the fully professional England players, drew a telling distinction between the home team and their technically amateur opponents in the minds of the reader. Of course, in reality, these jobs were little more than a show for the Hungarian proletariat, with the exception of Bozsik's political career, with certain Hungarian players showing far greater levels of dedication to maintaining the charade than others. Any English fan expecting to see a set of scrawny civil servants, more accustomed to dark, dusty offices than a football pitch, would soon be set straight.

As was standard for programmes of the day, the teams were shown in a formation that even by English standards was woefully out of date. Both sides were depicted in a rigid, pre-Chapman 2-3-5 set-up, with the centre-half advanced alongside the left- and right-half. This practice would continue well into even the late 1960s, in spite of Alf Ramsey's England spelling the downfall of the W-M and its antecedents. Even in 1953, there were certainly more than a few fans who, flipping to this page in the programme, gave their neighbour in the stands a friendly nudge and shared a chuckle over such outdated notions as only playing two backs. The match would not be 20 minutes old before those same fans would be scratching their heads, wondering how on earth they could square everything they thought they knew about football and its tactics with what Hungary were effortlessly demonstrating before them.

★ ★ ★

As the crowds began to filter into the stadium, they were treated to a full performance from the Royal Air Force's Central Band. In the knowledge that their audience that day was likely to be somewhat less discerning than the usual classical crowd, the band largely stuck to orchestral arrangements of songs from

Frank Loesser smash musical hit *Guys and Dolls*, which just months earlier had reached the West End after becoming a sensation on Broadway. They did, however, perform an ode to the day's guests of honour, playing 'Hungariana'.

The strains of the band filtered into the bowels of the stadium but did not register with either set of players as they went through their pre-match rituals. The two dressing rooms were charged with the energy that permeates the ring before a heavyweight title fight. For England, the reigning champs (at least in the eyes of their countrymen), the weight of expectation was enormous. Theirs was an onerous task, the pressure of upholding their reputation and swatting aside yet another pretender to their crown, effectively meaning victory would be greeted not with joy, but mere relief, while defeat would be a complete catastrophe. They were already at the top; there was nowhere to go but down.

For Hungary, the young upstarts attempting to steal the belt, the reality was setting in, transforming their belief, unshakeable in the days and months before, into rampant self-doubt. This was their one shot to prove to the world what they were truly made of. Yes, a reverse fixture in Budapest appeared likely (and would be confirmed in the aftermath of the Wembley game), but England had been defeated abroad many times before. Beating them on home soil, at Wembley, would be the only way of making a truly definitive statement, and Hungary knew that if they missed their chance, in all likelihood they would not get another. They needed to achieve a decisive knockout.

The tension was only broken when, having spotted Ernie Taylor in the tunnel, the 5ft 6in Puskás returned to the dressing room to gleefully tell his teammates that England would be fielding a player even more diminutive than him.[18] To maintain the suddenly less inhibited atmosphere, Puskás then bet Kocsis that he couldn't manage 100 consecutive keepy-uppies. Kocsis duly took him up on the wager, reaching ninety-nine before being unceremoniously tackled by Czibor. Puskás paid up regardless.[19]

As the RAF band made their way through their last number before the national anthems, the two sets of players finally came face to face in Wembley's tunnel. It was here that a moment occurred that would enter footballing folklore and, in many ways, served as the perfect metaphor for the events that were about to unfold.

As the players sized one another up in their full battle regalia, the English players were surprised – and amused – to see the Hungarians wearing low-cut, flimsy looking boots, in stark contrast to the standard-order thick, leather, ankle-high boots of the English players. England's players knew they had a reputation for a tough, uncompromising brand of football, but seeing players emerge from behind the Iron Curtain, with its supposedly hardscrabble lifestyle and manufacturing prowess, wearing shoes that looked more appropriate for an upper-class dandy than a football team, they couldn't help but scoff. So taken aback was Billy Wright that he turned to Stan Mortensen and uttered the 'immortal' words, in Wright's own self-aggrandising assessment, 'We should be all right here, Stan, they haven't got the proper kit.'[20]

It was a moment of shameful hubris, yet it goes some way to absolving the English players, who were, more than anyone else, about to become sacrificial victims of decades of institutional and technical complacency. The Hungarians, meanwhile, oblivious to English snickering, were mentally sizing up their opponents. The Western media blackout in Hungary meant that they had only fleeting knowledge of England's stars like Matthews and Wright, some of which had been gleaned from cultural attachés surreptitiously ferrying information back to Hungary. Irregular England players like Sewell and Johnston were an almost completely unknown quantity, let alone debutants like Taylor and Robb. For the most part, the Hungarians would have to rely on their wits and get a gauge of their opponents as the match unfolded.

And then, all of the anticipation, the expectations, the hopes, fears, the political intrigue and everything else tied up in the game beforehand was over. There was nothing left to do but play. The pitch cleared of dignitaries. Billy Wright and Ferenc Puskás, the two captains, met in the centre circle for the coin toss, which Wright duly won. The England man decided to let Hungary kick off, to give them their first test of whether in the knee-knocking atmosphere of Wembley they would be able to pull off their usual slick passing.

Wright retreated and, as Puskás waited for a teammate to join him in the centre circle and for the referee to give an introductory toot on his whistle, he nonchalantly flicked the ball skywards and began to effortlessly juggle it with his left foot. To his teammates, it was an act of insouciance they'd come to expect from their imperturbable leader. To the watching England players, accustomed to foreign opponents quaking in their boots in the moments before a game at Wembley, it was ominous.

11

THE MATCH OF
THE CENTURY

Even before the first kick, Hungary appeared to be scheming. As Ferenc Puskás prepared to take the kick-off, Sándor Kocsis and Nándor Hidegkuti huddled in close to him, as if plotting a clandestine raid on the England defence. As soon as Dutchman Leo Horn blew his whistle, the Hungarians launched into what appeared to be a scripted routine. Puskás and Hidegkuti remained standing, while Kocsis seized the ball and passed it to József Bozsik, who nonchalantly chipped the ball forward to László Budai, bursting out of the blocks and charging down the right wing. Budai took one touch to pluck the ball out of the air and another to begin a one-two with Kocsis, who summarily sent the stocky winger on his way with a long ball down the line.

So meticulously orchestrated did Hungary's play appear from the very first second that it was a slight surprise that the fluid, one-touch passing move that had opened the match didn't end with the ball nestling in Gil Merrick's net. However, Kocsis' pass was overhit and Jimmy Dickinson, who'd spotted Budai's rapid foray forward, was able to knock the ball out into touch. An over-eager Budai then committed a foul throw and England could breathe for a moment.

Almost immediately, they wasted their throw and gifted Hungary possession deep within their half, with Budai again looking to maraud his way through the now-massed ranks of England defenders. This time, the England defence did a more comprehensive job of clearing their lines, with Stan Mortensen managing to get a foot on the thumped clearance, the first time an England forward had touched the ball.

The respite, once again, didn't last. Before Mortensen could truly bring the ball under control, Bozsik had poked it away to his fellow half-back, József Zakariás, who became yet another Hungarian to shun a controlling touch before picking his pass, returning the ball to Bozsik, now in several yards of space.

If one moment from the match could be used to encapsulate everything one needed to know about the teams, the months and years of fate, destiny and design that had led the two nations to this point, it was what followed. The collective talent of the Hungarians was, even with the match still in its first minute, evident for all to see. The manner in which they seemed subconsciously aware of where each of their teammates would be at any given moment was a testament to the coherence of Gusztáv Sebes and Gyula Mándi's punctilious coaching.

England's abilities were considerable, but they were rendered inert, almost invisible, by Hungary's movement. In this opening minute of the match, it was as though the RAF band that had performed before the match had transposed their music to the two teams. The England national team, like the country itself, was that of Elgar – brimming with pomp, blessed by circumstance, grand and imperious but inescapably staid and set in its ways, held in higher regard by its own countrymen than outsiders. Hungary, meanwhile, were taking their cues from the same spirit that had inspired Liszt and foreign composers like Brahms and Strauss when they'd ecstatically rhapsodised about the country, the aquamarine waters of the Danube, and the Hungarian people. With less than 60 seconds on the clock, the Hungarian attack was diametrically opposed to the static, three-decades-old formation that the English were dogmatically sticking to. Instead, players were changing and moving with almost mesmeric rapidity, a veritable Wurlitzer of world-class talent twisting the blood of their opponents.

As Bozsik received the ball, his head was already up, scanning the ground in front of him for the most opportune pass, or failing that, where Puskás was, in the knowledge that childhood best friends or not, there would be hell to pay if his captain was indeed open and he failed to pick him out. Even the bull-headed Puskás, however, couldn't argue with the option that presented itself to Bozsik – Hidegkuti, with his back to goal, entirely unmarked, roughly 30 yards out. Bozsik duly found him with yet another first touch pass.

The arrangement had been that Hidegkuti would begin the game acting as a typical centre-forward, sitting on the shoulder of the centre-half, aiming to lure Harry Johnston into a false sense of security before suddenly dropping deep. However, it had taken less than a minute for Hidegkuti to sense that there was little point in hanging around. He received the ball completely free of the attentions of any defender, a statement that would be verging on sacrilege for the England backs had Hidegkuti been stood where they expected him to be.

Hidegkuti controlled Bozsik's gentle pass with his left foot and knocked it forward with his right, turning towards goal as he did so. Ten yards ahead of him, the sheer brilliance of the tactical tweak to the W-M that Hungary had implemented was plain for all to see. Harry Johnston, a decorated and highly respected central defender, was crouched on the edge of the box. Though his body language suggested poise and anticipation, his positioning was the complete opposite. As Hidegkuti began his advance, Johnston lurched forward, then back, then, with Hidegkuti now just a couple of yards away and presented with a smorgasbord of options, Johnston simply stood up, paralysed by indecision and powerless to defend against the Hungarian when he had no idea which course of action Hidegkuti might take.

As it transpired, Hidegkuti was in no mood to indulge the English's decades-long love affair with the inertia of the W-M for a second longer than he needed to. Sensing that Johnston was hopelessly stranded, a hapless vessel surrounded by a tempestuous sea of charging crimson shirts, Hidegkuti took him on, selling Johnston a dummy that had the defender lunging to his right while the striker glided past him on his left. Hidegkuti's touch took him just inside the England area. Bozsik was on his right, awaiting a lay-off. Kocsis was on his left, trailed by a frantic Jimmy Dickinson. Budai was on the right wing, ready to swing in a cross should Hidegkuti pick him out.

But Hidegkuti didn't need any of his teammates. Instead, with Johnston and Alf Ramsey still out of reach, the forward unleashed a shot which rocketed past the despairing dive of Gil Merrick and into the top corner of the net. There were still less than 50 seconds on the clock. The Hungarian players huddled around Hidegkuti in celebration, scarcely believing how simple their opening goal had been.

★ ★ ★

From the kick-off, England broke quickly, hoping to enjoy some possession of their own and to demonstrate that Hungary's goal was nothing more than a minor setback. Jackie Sewell attempted to seize the initiative with a forward charge followed by a neat back-heel, before continuing his run into the box and being dispossessed just as he shaped to shoot. That, however, was as threatening as England looked in the opening exchanges. As befitted their preparation, England's attacks had little rhythm or evidence of an underlying philosophy, instead simply responding to each situation as it developed. This amorphous, reactive approach wasn't without some merit, as it allowed England to adapt to games, but compared to the incisive passing and hypnotic movement of the Hungarian attack, such as moments later when Hidegkuti played a perfectly weighted through-ball to Czibor only for the winger to stumble on the edge of the area, England's off-the-cuff style looked woefully languorous.

After the frenetic opening, the game settled into a pattern, with England attempting to launch rapid attacks and being frustrated time and again, while Hungary aimed to pick their opponents apart with intricate passes. The record 100,000-strong crowd, for their part, had not allowed Hungary's early lead to diminish their enthusiasm for the contest. Both a crunching tackle by George Robb and Stanley Matthews' first touch of the ball were greeted with roars of encouragement, something that was far from a given at Wembley – the Empire Stadium crowd was notorious for its often-indifferent support for the home team. Bob Ferrier, in the book he co-authored with Winterbottom, noted that, in his opinion, England had only once truly enjoyed a fully supportive Wembley crowd (against Argentina in 1951) and Winterbottom's team would have stood a far better chance against the Hungarians had the crowd been more interested in getting behind the home side.[1] Both left wingers were drawing attention, Robb for his lively contribution in his first cap; Czibor, as excitedly noted by the BBC commentator Kenneth Wolstenholme, because he was popping up in every attacking position *except* on the left touchline.

With nearly a quarter of an hour on the clock, neither side could feel too disheartened. England had fallen behind but could reasonably claim to have stymied Hungary's early assault. Hungary, meanwhile, had the lead but could have been forgiven for wondering if they'd squandered their chance to put the game to bed. Kocsis, the man nicknamed 'Golden Head' for his superlative aerial ability, missed a glorious headed chance from a raking Czibor cross. A short time later, a fabulous interchange between Puskás and Hidegkuti saw the latter slot home, only for a truly baffling offside call – Hidegkuti was on the edge of the D as Puskás played the ball, while Johnston was a yard inside the penalty area and Ramsey stood on the edge of the box – to rule the goal out. Both teams could also point to the fact that their most potent attacking forces

– Kocsis and Puskás for Hungary, Mortensen and Matthews for England – had yet to make a telling contribution.

Just as the ebb and flow of the match appeared to be established – England rushing forward, Hungary probing – all hell broke loose. There had been 14 minutes of goalless football since Hidegkuti's lightning opener; there wouldn't be as lengthy a break between goals until a subsequent eight strikes had found the back of the net.

★ ★ ★

First, England found an equaliser. Surprisingly, given the role of maligned dupe that posterity has given him, it was Johnston who was the instigator, robbing Puskás on the edge of the England area and seizing the initiative by advancing unchecked to the halfway line, before finding Mortensen who, after virtually no involvement in the opening quarter of an hour, found himself in some space. Aware of the Blackpool striker's pace, Mihály Lantos attempted to block his path, fearing that any attempt to tackle him directly would enable the swift Mortensen to simply knock the ball clear and charge past. Given such freedom, Mortensen opted to pass, finding the onrushing Sewell as he charged into the centre of the area.

With only the imposing frame of Grosics to beat, the Sheffield Wednesday star made no mistake, taking a touch before deftly sliding the ball into the corner of the net. After a brief celebratory embrace with Robb, Sewell headed straight back to his own half for the kick-off. England, evidently, scented blood.

In a match with countless, almost imperceptible, shifts in momentum and emphasis, how Hungary reacted to Sewell's goal may well have been the pivotal one. They had taken the lead so early, and with such ease, that it might have stunned even their own players into thinking it something of a fluke. They had then spurned several inviting openings and seen a perfectly good goal ruled out for offside. Now, with their lead gone, the home crowd roaring their support and their opponents with their tails up, Hungary could have been forgiven for wilting.

So accustomed were they to simply steamrollering opponents after they'd scored early, it was something of an alien experience to find themselves pegged back by a truly spirited opponent. The Olympic Final against Yugoslavia and the win earlier in the year against Italy had both been so perfectly executed that they'd never really experienced a setback. The Swiss game, which had shown Sebes and the players the light in regard to the pivotal, meta-breaking role that Hidegkuti could play, had started badly, but once Hungary found the solution, they'd breezed through the rest of the match. This felt different.

Plenty of teams had arrived in England with designs on their host's throne, only to be thwarted in a variety of ways. In recent memory, France, Argentina and Austria in 1951 and the Rest of the World team the month before had all taken the lead in England, only for the Three Lions to fight back. As these sudden Hungarian doubts swirled, they were underpinned by the knowledge that in order to secure the opportunity to play England in the first place, Sebes had promised Mátyás Rákosi success. The consequences of denying him in such a public manner did not bear thinking about.

Faced with an instinctive fight or flight situation, Hungary chose the former option. Almost immediately, they fashioned another chance for Hidegkuti, whose close-range shot was blocked by Johnston. A hopeful looping ball from Budai then deceived the England defence and was brought down effortlessly by Kocsis, with Johnston again managing a heroic block. Hidegkuti was now dropping deeper frequently, at one point collecting the ball inside the Hungarian half directly from a Grosics throw. The uncharacteristically profligate Kocsis was guilty of missing yet another gilt-edged chance, receiving Budai's pinpoint pull back (via a preternatural dummy for Puskás, perhaps the most redoubtable example yet of the synergy between the Hungarian forwards) on the penalty spot but allowing his touch to get away from him and enabling Merrick to smother the ball, leaving Kocsis prostrate on the pitch, pounding the turf with his fist.

When Hungary did make their chances pay and retook the lead, almost exactly 5 minutes after Sewell's equaliser, it came not in the swashbuckling style with which they were synonymous but in decidedly scruffier fashion. A poor kick from Merrick gifted the Hungarians possession and they worked the ball to Czibor in his nominal left-wing position. The No. 11 raced to the by-line and cut the ball back for Puskás, who was brought down by Johnston. Lying prone on the floor with Johnston, Ramsey, Wright and Dickinson surrounding him, Puskás somehow hacked the ball from the melee and it bobbled to Hidegkuti, whose touch was composed and whose finish, though close enough to Merrick for him to get something on it, had the power to find the net. The Hungarians once again celebrated in a leisurely manner, so much so that referee Horn felt moved to gee Hidegkuti back to the halfway line so he could restart the game.

Having relinquished their lead once, the Magyars weren't about to do so again. With 20 minutes of the game gone, they knew that England had the ability to make the most of their limited opportunities, but that defensively they were there for the taking, in no small part due to Hidegkuti's almost completely unencumbered access to the ball in the England half. Within seconds of England's kick-off, Hungary had won the ball and launched an attack that ended in Budai screwing a shot wide. Budai then turned creator, passing for Kocsis, whose shot was inadvertently blocked by Hidegkuti.

There was a strong sense of inevitability about the trajectory of the match, aggravated by England's total inability to hold on to the ball for more than a few panic-stricken seconds. No moment better encapsulated England's deer in the headlights act than when Matthews, by a distance the most experienced man on the pitch (including the referee), was caught offside receiving the ball back after taking a throw-in.

If Hungary had regained the lead in an atypically ragged fashion, they then extended it in beautiful, quintessential Golden Team style. An eight-pass move saw all five of the Hungarian forwards touch the ball, including Hidegkuti in the centre circle, which he was by now, in the words of Jonathan Wilson, 'dominating … as a squash player looks to dominate the T'.[2] Budai chipped a ball into space on the right flank for Czibor, who was once again busy making a mockery of the England players' dogmatic interpretation of shirt numbers and positions. Puskás had started the move's forward thrust from inside his own half and, determined to make up for a quiet opening by his stratospheric standards, he charged into the area to receive Czibor's pull-back.

What happened next would become one of the most iconic goals in football history, the entire match in an incredible split-second microcosm. Czibor's pass was struck hard, but Puskás just about brought the ball under control on the corner of the 6-yard area. Even so, he was in a cul-de-sac. Gil Merrick's formidable 6ft 1in, 13-stone frame guarded the left side of his goal, his arm braced against the post.

The one teammate close to Puskás was Czibor, who was offside. The only options seemingly open to Puskás were to trap the ball and hope reinforcements arrived in time or attempt to thread the needle and squeeze the ball across the face of goal and inside the far post. Given his character and the limited opportunities he'd had so far to impose himself on the game, nobody who knew Puskás doubted that he would shoot. However, in that moment, everybody but Puskás could see a significant impediment – the unmistakable figure of Billy Wright, England's defensive stalwart, blond hair bouncing, tearing into the box.

Seasoned pro Wright, on that day extending his record as the most-capped England player in history, knew it would be folly to attempt to tackle Puskás directly. The Hungarian captain's stocky frame was between Wright and the ball, and it appeared impossible for the charging Wright to win the ball without first clattering into Puskás and conceding a penalty. Instead, Wright sprinted towards the 6-yard area, in between the goal and his opponent. Arriving with Puskás still with the ball at his feet, Wright lunged, anticipating that Puskás would cut inside and take a shot.

'He was expecting me to turn inside,' remembered Puskás, 'and if I had done he would have taken me and the ball off the pitch and into the stands.'[3] To every onlooker, and to Wright himself, the odds were stacked in his favour: 'Nine times out of ten that tackle would have won possession. But this was the tenth time, and my opponent was Puskás.'[4] At the precise moment that Wright should have met the ball, Puskás, in possession of that innate sense of football's ceaseless geometry only found in elite players, impudently dragged the ball back with his left foot, nipping it off Wright's toe, just as he appeared certain to poke it out for a corner.

There was an audible gasp from the crowd. Wright slid past Puskás completely and lay in a heap on the turf, watching helplessly as Puskás, having barely moved from the spot on which he had received Czibor's pass, spun to face the goal. Johnston had raced back in step with Wright and was now stationed at the far post. Puskás, however, had no interest in the England centre-half. Instead, he planted his right foot in the turf and, with a mighty swing of his trusty left, rocketed a shot through the ostensibly non-existent gap at Merrick's near post and into the roof of the net.

Even for a man of such remarkable pedigree, it was a goal that stood alone as a thing of sheer, undeniable brilliance. Puskás celebrated with both arms aloft, his back arched, like a gymnast crowning the final flourish on a triumphant routine. He would later remember it as his favourite among the legions of goals he would score throughout his career.[5]

If there was one definitive moment of the game, this was it. The interchanging and speed of the Hungarians had made fools of the English and their stuffy, staid approach, shattering everything that England thought they knew about how winning football must be played. On an artistic level, the goal was a beautiful, heady mix of balletic poise and devastating power, again in stark contrast to the muddled, disordered, haphazard play of the English. Above all else, it put a decisive two-goal gap between the two teams, one which would not be bridged.

As befitting a goal of such magnificence, it spawned an equally memorable piece of reportage. In his match report, the following day, *The Times'* Geoffrey Green described Wright's failed intervention on Puskás as 'like a fire engine going to the wrong fire'. No other line, save for perhaps Desmond Hackett's dubbing of Nat Lofthouse as 'The Lion of Vienna', the year before, would stick in the collective English memory with such tenacity between the war and Wolstenholme's immortal lines of commentary that accompanied Geoff Hurst's hat-trick goal in the World Cup Final, thirteen years later.

★ ★ ★

England were still punch drunk when Hungary put the result beyond doubt, just 3 minutes later. A foul on Budai gave Hungary a free kick on the left. With the white shirts sluggishly preparing for the Hungarian players to filter into the box and a high ball to be swung in, Bozsik seized upon the dallying and attempted an audacious effort from the best part of 25 yards out. His shot lacked power and was so unexpected that even Puskás hadn't anticipated it, with the captain trying too late to get out of the way of the ball. The inadvertent touch proved telling. Merrick appeared to be content to watch Bozsik's original shot drift wide, but the deflection from Puskás sent it spinning into the corner of the goal, leaving the England goalkeeper gazing helplessly without so much as a cursory dive. The body language of the England players ranged from disbelief to grim resignation.

England were now 4-1 down, having still only played 27 minutes. Since the advent of professionalism in the English game in 1885, England had only conceded four at home on four previous occasions: the Rest of the World match that had immediately preceded the Hungary game at Wembley; the 1928 match with the Scotland side immortalised as the Wembley Wizards; and in two remarkable games (neither of which took place at Wembley) in 1920 and 1937, when England had won 5-4 against the Scots and Czechoslovakia, respectively. Any prospect of a repeat of those latter two victories appeared vanishingly remote. Instead, after what Bob Ferrier in the *Mirror* referred to as 'a seven-minute atomic spell of sheer exalted soccer', in which Hungary had scored three times, England now dared not set their ambitions any higher than damage limitation.

The 10 minutes following Puskás' deflected second goal were largely uneventful, aside from Merrick making a couple of straightforward saves. Hungary appeared to have dropped down a gear, conserving energy and no doubt taking stock of a situation that, in their wildest dreams before the match, they could not have imagined. Even having reduced the breakneck speed of their play, Hungary still appeared to be by far the superior team, keeping the England players in a constant state of nervous paranoia that any second yet another devastating attack could be launched.

Winterbottom's best-laid plans of aiming to play the Hungarians at their own game, with a pacy attack and Mortensen at centre-forward, were in tatters. Intimidated by the pressing of the Hungarians, particularly the forwards, few of the England players dared dally on the ball for long, and instead were reduced to launching hopeful balls towards Grosics' goal, the sort of approach that a Lofthouse figure could perhaps have capitalised upon. Mortensen, however, was barely 5ft 7in and was far more comfortable with the ball at his feet than he was in aerial duels, particularly with the long scar on his head still bearing witness to his gruesome brush with death during the war.

Hungary, for all intents and purposes, seemed to be toying with England in the manner of a vindictive cat taunting a badly injured mouse. Then, seemingly out of nowhere, England conjured up some belief in their own abilities and produced their best moments since Sewell's equaliser. Wright found Matthews who, for the first time in the match, had the opportunity to take Lantos on. Perhaps in the knowledge that the full-back had depleted almost none of his energy reserves in the 35 minutes they'd played, Matthews elected to skip inside, then swerved past Czibor, who had dropped back to help defend.

Now free of Hungarian attentions, Matthews swung a sumptuous cross into the box, the sort he had made his glittering reputation with. George Robb fulfilled his end of the bargain, meeting the ball firmly and sending it back across goal towards Grosics' back post. As Robb and the England players followed the flight of the ball in every expectation that it would end up nestling in the net, Grosics took his first opportunity to prove to the capacity crowd that the class of the Hungarian footballer wasn't restricted to just outfield panache, diving to his left and clawing the ball away when it looked for all the world like it had already passed him.

Buoyed by Matthews' moment of invention, England, as they had on so many occasions in recent memory, found a way back into contention when all the odds seemed against them. Matthews' composure to play his inimitable natural game seemed to momentarily transmit itself to his teammates, who suddenly found the confidence to get the ball on the ground and pass it instead of heaving it forward.

They were almost instantly rewarded when Robb passed to Mortensen inside the area, who cut inside and buried a shot into the corner of Grosics' goal. It was a goal that England scarcely deserved yet desperately needed. The incessant roar of the crowd that followed every England attack from Mortensen's goal to half-time suggested that the Wembley patrons sensed that they could be about to witness a truly improbable, yet quintessentially British comeback. Shortly after his Blackpool teammate had made it 4-2, Matthews found the space to jink through and set up the third part of the Tangerine triumvirate, Ernie Taylor, up to this point almost completely anonymous, who slipped as he shot and saw the ball gathered by a grateful Grosics.

Then it was the turn of Robb, the brightest of the England forwards, who was able to get a shot away from just inside the area, only for it to be charged down. Out of nowhere, England had the wind in their sails and it was Hungary's turn to look somewhat dazed. All of a sudden, there was tension in the Hungarian ranks where only minutes ago there had been nothing but elan and elation. When Puskás played in Budai, only for the winger to slice his shot wide with just Merrick to beat, Wembley bore witness to the first Puskásian eruption at his teammate's failure to add a fifth goal. Wolstenholme wryly noted, 'Fortunately the cameras weren't on Puskás because he showed Budai what he thought of that effort.'

Still England came, belief now coursing through their veins. A long, high ball split the Hungarian defence and seemed destined to land at the feet of Mortensen, only for Grosics to showcase his trigger-happy tendency to leave his line and clear the ball with a flying volley. For the first time in the game, England could be described as camped inside the Hungarian half, thoughtfully passing the ball instead of wildly punting it. Leo Horn's half-time whistle scarcely could have come at a more inopportune moment.

★ ★ ★

As the mist which had hung over London that morning rolled in to further envelop Wembley, the two teams gathered in their dressing rooms. Harry

Johnston appeared shell-shocked, completely at a loss as to how to perform even a modicum of his defensive duties when faced with the typhoon of Hungarian forwards and the restless presence of Hidegkuti. He would later write, 'The tragedy was the utter helplessness ... of being unable to do anything to alter the grim outlook.'[6]

Wright had told Johnston that surviving until half-time was key, for the 15 minutes with Winterbottom would set the matter straight and help England reorganise. But if the England defence expected a piece of divine intervention from their coach, undoing decades of footballing orthodoxy and Danubian evolution, none was forthcoming. George Raynor had impressed upon Winterbottom and Wright in a meeting in a Vienna coffee house after Sweden's game with Hungary that to stop Hidegkuti from drawing Johnston completely out of position, other players would need to mark the Hungarian, depending on where he was on the pitch.[7] While the former portion of this tactical advice had made it to Johnston and prevented him from haring around the pitch in pursuit of his man, the latter part clearly hadn't – if Johnston wasn't picking Hidegkuti up, nobody was.

Matthews, who had made his feelings about Winterbottom's tactical suggestions in the past abundantly clear, bemoaned the fact that 'nothing was said about [Hidegkuti] and no one was given the specific job of picking him up, a bad mistake in my opinion'.[8] Winterbottom was uncharacteristically bullish when defending his inaction at half-time: 'This idea that half-time discussion resolves anything, and the manager has only to get stuck in and tell the players to pull their socks up, is a load of nonsense.'[9] There was no miraculous solution to the Hidegkuti question, and no hopeful suggestions about how England could haul themselves back into contention against a clearly more talented and tactically inventive side.

The one kernel of comfort to which England could cling was the fact that they had exhibited a ruthlessness in attack that, despite their two-goal advantage, the Hungarians couldn't claim to have matched. The issue was that while England had been more clinical, scoring both of their clear-cut chances, the Hungarians had enjoyed so many opportunities that even while they had been uncharacteristically wasteful, they'd still been able to beat Merrick on four occasions. Being incisive was all well and good, but it counted for nought if the England attack did not have the opportunities with which to wield their mercilessness in front of Grosics' goal, or if the Hungarians continued to create openings at will. Despite their strong end to the half, the England players waited out the break in a sombre, funereal atmosphere, before grimly trooping out for the second period, condemned men on the long walk to the gallows.

Even with the Hungarian players acutely aware that the job was only half done, the mood in their dressing room was jubilant. Sebes warned his men that 'the English will never give up, it isn't in their nature. We need to kill them early so be wary and do your jobs', but he was careful not to overstate the need for caution, knowing that the ease with which Hungary were cutting through the England back line meant that attack remained the most effective manner of defence.[10] If the Hungarians were experiencing any added anxiety now that their dream of defeating England was within their grasp, they were doing a consummate job of hiding it. Lóránt, Buzánszky and Lantos spent the break ribbing Grosics for allowing two of England's handful of serious attempts on goal in and threatening to beat him should he concede any more.

★ ★ ★

For a brief moment as the second half began, the sun broke through the murk. If England hoped this respite in the gloom was an omen, they were quickly dissuaded. Winterbottom's team attempted to pick up where they'd left off, but their fears about the inopportune timing of the half-time period proved prescient. Under Sebes' instruction, Hungary appeared far calmer and less frantic, more confident in their superiority. There was no need to try to eviscerate England – playing sensibly and keeping the ball would do much of the Hungarians' work for them, as their opponents inevitably tired as they continued to chase the game.

The Hungarians stuck doggedly to their defensive task and sought to launch counter-attacks when the opportunity struck, rather than attacking pell-mell with almost all outfield players. The result of this shift in emphasis rendered England largely inert as the sun retreated and the conditions became increasingly soupy. The spaces they'd been able to find at the end of the first half seemed to have disappeared. Wolstenholme's reference to Matthews as 'Shuffling Stan' was a telling indication of the speed to which England's attacks slowed now that they faced the massed ranks of Hungary's defence. Zakariás, nominally a half-back, increasingly resembled a second centre-half alongside Lóránt, while both Budai and Czibor began dropping back frequently to help their respective full-backs.

As if their task wasn't Herculean enough already, England were dealt a further blow when Mortensen forced a save but was knocked out cold in the process, eventually being hauled off the pitch by the towering figures of Grosics and Lantos. The Blackpool striker, who had appeared sharp on the few occasions that the ball had found its way to him, was a diminished presence for the rest of the match.

With barely 5 minutes gone in the second period, any hopes of a concerted effort by England to haul themselves back into the game had faded markedly. Hungary lacked the intensity and speed with which they'd attacked earlier in the game, but Hidegkuti continued to evade Johnston and the constant move-ment of his fellow forwards, particularly the irrepressible Czibor, meant that even at half-speed, the England defence seemed utterly incapable of tracking runs or stopping what, for the Hungarians, were simple passes.

Bozsik rolled a ball in to Puskás, in a similar spot from which he'd humiliated Wright and scored his first goal. This time, rather than shoot, the 'Galloping Major' (as he'd be dubbed by the British press) bamboozled Johnston and placed a ball perfectly onto the Golden Head of Kocsis, who was once again denied a goal, this time by a stupendous save by Merrick, every bit the equal of the one Grosics had made in the first half, tipping the goal-bound header onto the post.

It would be a reprieve that lasted only seconds. England failed to clear their lines and the ball fell to Bozsik who, despite having netted just three times in his forty-four caps for his country, elected to shoot. The ball flew with such velocity that by the time the television camera operator managed to catch up with it, it was already bouncing out of Merrick's goal.

Nobody in the Hungarian side, not even Kocsis, who was becoming more desperate to get a goal of his own with each passing minute and missed chance, could begrudge Bozsik his goal. While others got the plaudits – Hidegkuti for his intelligence, Kocsis and Puskás for their goal scoring, Budai and Czibor for their energy and directness, Grosics, the defence and Zakariás for their ability to blunt attacks – Bozsik was easier to overlook. But everybody in the side understood how pivotal he was. His goal was not just a personal vindication, but one for the entire national team project.

Bozsik's goal put the game beyond any reasonable doubt. Shortly after-wards, Wolstenholme reminded British fans that Hungary had been undefeated for two years while England had, famously, never lost at home to a Continental side, 'so one record has to go – unless of course, it's a draw', but few watching harboured any serious hopes that England would find a way to score a further three goals while simultaneously stumbling across the solution to halt the Hungarian attack. Whereas up to this point, the England players had, at the very least, looked determined to hassle and disrupt the Hungarians whenever they could, after Bozsik's goal the shoulders slumped, the heads dropped, and players were wont to stand with hands on hips or half-heartedly stab at the ball as it swung mesmerically from cherry shirt to cherry shirt.

It was little surprise when Hungary added their sixth goal, still only 11 minutes into the half. Kocsis nodded a high ball down to Puskás, who was in more and more space as Johnston and the other England defenders attempted desperately to stick with Hidegkuti at all costs. Puskás brought the ball under his spell effortlessly before floating a half-volleyed cross over the defence and onto the boot of the onrushing Hidegkuti, who had shaken his marker and ghosted in at the far post to slam the ball home and complete a historic hat-trick. It was the first hat-trick England had conceded in more than twenty years, and only the second scored by a player from a nation other than Scotland. Such was Hungarian commentator György Szepesi's delirium in relaying the astonishing scoreline home that a nearby punter, amused by the foreign journalist's apoplexy at the events on the pitch, offered Szepesi a dram of whisky to settle his nerves.[11]

If England had appeared somewhat dumbfounded at times during the first half, they now appeared positively stupefied, wandering about aimlessly like men who had just been caught unawares by an aerial bombardment in the trenches. They did, somehow, manage to grab a third goal, although it required a significant helping hand from the Hungarian defence. A loose ball into the box seemed destined to be gathered by Grosics or cleared by Buzánszky, but they both left it for one another, allowing Robb to steal in. Though the winger was moving away from goal, Grosics, out of position and, like many of the best goalkeepers, never far from a moment of eccentricity, opted to lunge at the ball, taking Robb out in the process and gifting England a penalty.

Alf Ramsey, the veteran, wasted no time in stroking the ball into the corner, but the complete absence of celebrations from the England players and the brief, muted cheer from the crowd told the story of the match. There was no prospect of Ramsey's penalty triggering a stirring comeback. Instead, it was the death rattle for the era in which England's national football team could claim to be the greatest international side, the team that had taught the world the game and therefore could never be usurped.

★ ★ ★

For such an eventful and tumultuous game, the last half an hour was a non-event. Hungary appeared satisfied with their six goals and they passed up several extremely presentable opportunities to add to their tally. England, exhausted from their frantic exertions to stem the crimson tide in the first half, tried half-heartedly to breach the Hungary defence, but found Grosics and his defence in no mood to repeat the charitable mistake that had given England their penalty.

In a way, the lacklustre end to the match was a crueller fate for the millions of English fans across the country, watching and listening in disbelief as their team unravelled before them. Had the game kept up its breakneck speed and the teams continued to trade goals, the exhilaration of the spectacle would have helped to mask the nature of the defeat. Instead, with England's opponents certain of victory, England had to endure a further humiliation as Hungary casually kept them at arm's length. Even a knock to Grosics' arm, caused while attempting to save Ramsey's penalty, which was bad enough to eventually force him off to be replaced by Sándor Gellér, did nothing to inspire a late England show. For the Hungarian fans listening in raptures hundreds of miles away, nothing could dampen their spirits.

Even before Leo Horn had blown his whistle, several of the Hungarians had raised their arms aloft in anticipation. When full-time did officially arrive, some appeared scarcely to know what to do with themselves, as the enormity of their achievement sank in. The England players appeared stunned, before recovering themselves and congratulating their opponents. The crowd, which had been left in a stunned silence since Ramsey's penalty, save for the occasional grumble when Stan Matthews was brought to an unceremonious halt by a foul, rose to applaud the Hungarians from the field. Even the most partisan of supporters, those who had strolled into Wembley that afternoon in the expectation of seeing yet another Continental upstart with ideas above their station put firmly in their place, could not begrudge the Hungarians their victory or even focus their ire on the England players. There would be time for recriminations later. The manner of Hungary's victory, the wondrous style of play, the sheer gulf of the winning margin, meant that as they filtered out of the Empire Stadium into the misty London evening, the 100,000-strong crowd were thinking of only the team in cherry red.

12

THE TWILIGHT
OF THE GODS

For both the victors and the losers, the Match of the Century ought to have been the beginning. For Hungary, despite the marvellous success they'd enjoyed before the match, such comprehensive triumph at Wembley represented their ascent to a higher step on the sporting ziggurat. There was now no question that they were football's strongest nation; the only debate was how long they could sustain their dominance.

England, meanwhile, should have been shaken to the core, forced into a period of introspection that challenged every assumption that the national team had been built upon. Even the national press, normally so readily armed with an arsenal of excuses for England's missteps, came up empty handed. Bob Ferrier in the *Daily Mirror* wrote, 'Shed no tears for England. Seek no excuses. There were no excuses. England's record, unbeaten at home in ninety years of football, was shattered yesterday.' The *Daily Herald*'s Tom Philips declared that any blame apportioned to the players was misplaced – 'It's the system that's dead from the toenails up' – before looking for some philosophical solace, musing, 'We may yet bless the day that Hungary massacred England.'

Salt was added to the wounds by the Scottish press. The *Dundee Courier* reported with scarcely concealed glee that England had 'gained some revenge' on the Hungarians in the hours after the match by beating them in a mixed international table tennis match. The *Guardian*'s Pat Ward-Thomas lauded Hungary's performance as 'probably the finest exhibition of attacking play that has been seen in an international match in Britain', and noted that one of the Magyars' chief weapons had been Nándor Hidegkuti, who, despite his hat-trick, 'was often seen in his own goalmouth'.

The deep-lying centre-forward innovation was also pinpointed by Geoffrey Green in *The Times* in a write-up which has endured as one of Green's finest pieces of work. Beneath a subheading announcing 'a new conception of football', Green invoked the imperial mindset, extolling the 'foreign invaders' Hungary for reducing England's involvement in the contest to nil. Indeed, England were not so much an opposing team as a sacrificial victim, 'strangers in a strange world, a world of flitting red spirits'. In an age when much football reportage remained perfunctory at best, Green summoned up an epic, poetic verdict for the match: 'Here, indeed, did we attend, all 100,000 of us, the twilight of the gods.'

The FA were faced with a dilemma: embrace change and face the prospect of relinquishing some of their shadowy omnipotence in aid of once again making the England team the most feared in the world, or dig their heels in, stick their fingers in their ears and cling on to power, despite the detrimental effect such a course of action would inevitably have on the team's fortunes. Winterbottom and the players, meanwhile, had no opportunity to cleanse their palates of the bitter aftertaste of the Hungarian defeat. After their historic loss, England were forced to endure a wait of more than four months before their next game, a trip to Hampden Park to face Scotland. Playing the Scottish was a return to terra firma for England, who could rest assured that they wouldn't have to cope with any new-fangled tactics or players roaming where they weren't expected. However, never before had England faced their fiercest rivals off the back of such humiliation, and they were acutely aware that their northerly neighbours would like nothing more than to compound their misery.

To nobody's surprise, the FA, overlooking the tactical nature of England's Hungarian debacle and glossing over the role that they played in the team's institutionalised complacency, took a scythe to the team. Of the eleven who had been chastened by Puskás and Co., six were never to play for their country again. Both debutants, George Robb, the man who had only turned profes-sional in 1953 and had been drafted in as a last-minute replacement for the injured Tom Finney, and Ernie Taylor, called up in an attempt to harness some of Blackpool's Wembley magic, would never again be selected.

It wasn't just the junior England players from the Hungary match who felt the FA's wrath, however. Perhaps most predictably, Harry Johnston, who had been pulled from pillar to post by the movement of Hidegkuti and the other Hungarian forwards, found his sporadic time with the national team at an end. Forevermore, Johnston would be the name most keenly associated with Hidegkuti in the English footballing psyche. However, this legacy is a somewhat undeserved one. Johnston was, after all, the latest in a line of central defenders who had been trialled as a replacement to Neil Franklin, not a mainstay of the team. He was also 34, with his best years firmly behind him. He was a symptom of England's malaise, not a cause.

Nor was it hugely surprising that Alf Ramsey, who would also turn 34 before the Scotland fixture, had made his final bow. He had been a mainstay of the team since 1950, but his reputation as a cerebral defender, who made up for his lack of natural ability with an astute reading and understanding of the game, was now counted against him. In the perverse logic of the FA, if Ramsey was considered the brains of the England defence, what good was he, given he had been unable to solve the Hungarian riddle?

This line of thinking, focusing on individual shortcomings rather than the wider picture, wasn't unique to the FA. The English footballing public and press, so long accustomed to seeing matches decided not by tactics but by less tangible factors such as desire and gusto, could not see the wood for the trees.

Even Ramsey's international teammates were guilty. Matthews would darkly refer to 'a few players who were favourites with the selectors, I believe primarily because they said the right things before games and at the post-match banquets', who the Hungarians had exposed as lacking the 'sufficient quality to play at this level'.[1] It's likely that Matthews wasn't referring specifically to Ramsey when he said this. Well respected though he was, Ramsey was known as a shy, somewhat diffident figure, hardly the avuncular company man Matthews was taking aim at. He may instead have been referring to Bill Eckersley, another who felt the axe fall, following that misty November afternoon. Eckersley, a more outgoing and jovial presence in the team than Ramsey, had earned seventeen caps, despite playing in an extremely average Division 2 Blackburn Rovers side. With the demise of Ramsey, there was a sense of inevitability about Eckersley's international career drawing to a close as well, with the Blackburn man having played the bulk of his England career alongside the Spurs defender.

Perhaps the harshest post-Hungary exclusion was dealt to the third of Blackpool's four representatives in the match. Though starved of service and playing at centre-forward for just the fourth time for the Three Lions, Stan Mortensen had looked a threat every time he got the ball, worrying the Hungarian defence with his pace and the possibility that he could, at any moment, unleash one of his cannonball shots. He had taken his goal well, and his quiet second half could be attributed directly to his being knocked out early in the second period. Though far from the archetypal English centre-forward and on the verge of his 33rd birthday by the time England faced Scotland, there is a lingering sense that the man who had registered a remarkable twenty-three goals in twenty-five caps had more to give, if only he'd been afforded the opportunity to do so. Above all others, Mortensen's international exile appeared indicative of a staggered FA, up against the ropes and desperately swinging in the hopes of landing a punch on the cause of England's stunning demise.

Even with such vituperative blood-letting, there were some who felt the FA didn't go far enough in culling the players they saw as responsible for giving up England's proud, undefeated home record against Continental teams. Many were heavily critical of Merrick, although apart from perhaps Puskás' deflected second goal and Bozsik's strike from outside the area, it's difficult in retrospect to find much wrong with the goalkeeper's performance. The criticism of Merrick who, like Eckersley, would earn all his caps while playing in the Second Division, fell on deaf ears in the immediate aftermath of the Hungary match. As it transpired, fate had other, arguably crueller intentions for the end of his international career.

★ ★ ★

What was truly remarkable about the period between the Hungary defeat and the Scotland match was the lack of introspection from the FA, the players, managers and coaches, the press and fans about what had truly happened at Wembley that afternoon. Even allowing for their technical superiority on the day, it was patently obvious that the Hungarians had had the match half-won before they even set foot onto the field, thanks to their tactical innovations exposing decades of English systemic lassitude and hubris. On numerous occasions throughout the match, Kenneth Wolstenholme had excitedly remarked upon how deep Hidegkuti was playing, how Zakariás was willing to retreat at the first sign of danger to act as an auxiliary centre-half, how Czibor and Budai switched wings with effervescent abandon.

Gusztáv Sebes had been able to spring his trap by playing on the fact that English tactics had seen no significant tinkering since Herbert Chapman added his third back to counteract the 1925 alteration to the offside rule. The Hungarian deep-lying centre-forward was not a microscopic adjustment to the norm. There had been teams who had toyed with the W-M orthodoxy versus England before, notably Hugo Meisl's Rest of the World side that England had played just weeks earlier, and Argentina who, in the warm-up game on England's tour earlier in 1953, had deployed the roaming José Locasia against Bolton centre-half, Malcolm Barrass.

Hungary's approach, however, lacked any such subtlety. From the very first seconds of the match when Hidegkuti had received the ball midway inside the England half and, entirely free from the attentions of Johnston, had the freedom to turn, advance and fire into the top corner, it was readily apparent to anyone with even a passing interest in the game what was different about Hungary's formation. And yet, nothing happened.

What should have triggered a national crisis of confidence in the state of the English game, the way it was taught and the gatekeeping that had allowed such a logjam of innovation, instead caused nothing of the sort. English pride was dented. The loss provoked, in the words of Brian Glanville, 'an orgy of self-criticism'.[2] Yet, the willingness to ask the searching, difficult questions about what had led to the erosion of the enormous advantages England had once held in international football was non-existent.

With hindsight, the parallels to the decline of the British Empire are legion. In both imperial ambition and football, at their peaks, Britain and the England team had enjoyed such power that it had bred a supreme arrogance. This vanity made the notion that their grasp would ever weaken almost unfathomable. When the crown did begin to slip, rather than taking swift, corrective action, the response was akin to the ostrich burying its head in the sand, refusing to countenance the unavoidable truth.

While these delusions of grandeur were chiefly responsible for the inaction in English football, there were other factors. Ironically, if the game had been more closely fought and Hidegkuti's movement the difference between success and failure for England, it might have cast the spotlight on Sebes' tactics. As it was, Hungary were so vastly superior (indeed, it's difficult to envisage the Magyars not winning even if they had deployed a straightforward W-M to match England and relied solely upon the superior talent of their players) that there was an insinuation that attempting to learn anything from such a ruinous defeat was pointless.

More fundamentally, everyone involved in England's humiliation could point elsewhere at who should have taken the reins and guided the beautiful game through this crisis. The players, who had been schooled in the W-M, could quite reasonably assert it was down to their managers and coaches to provide tactical guidance. Club managers up and down the land depended on keeping favour with their owners and chairmen, and so needed assurances that they would be given enough time and patience to implement such changes. Club owners, even those involved directly within the FA, argued that the performance of the national team was not their concern. Why should they risk the performances of their team in order to lay the groundwork for the England side? Their job was to keep punters coming through the turnstiles and the coffers topped up, neither of which seemed to have anything to do with tactics.

Attendances in the 1953–54 season, though not matching the peak seen shortly after the end of the Second World War, suggested interest in football across all four divisions was in rude health, with an average attendance across the leagues of more than 17,000, a number that has never since been matched. This delineation between national and club teams was bolstered when, just over a year after Hungary's visit, Honvéd, with the same elastic attacking philosophy as the national team, were beaten 3-2 by Wolves at Molineux in a floodlit friendly. The men in the FA, like Stanley Rous and Walter Winterbottom, whose attentions were entirely focused on the national team, meanwhile, could point back to the youth coaches and club managers who steadfastly refused to entertain ideas beyond training and tactics the way they had been taught for decades. Winterbottom would later explain his position: 'I could not just get a team of players and say, "Look, lads, this is the way you're going to play." The clubs had to get it so the players were used to it.'[3]

It's difficult not to sympathise with Winterbottom's point. He was a rare example of a manager in the English game who believed in the value of coaching and, particularly after the Hungary match, tactics, even if he perhaps lacked the acuity and support that had led Sebes, assisted by Gyula Mándi and Márton Bukovi, to Hungary's tactical epiphany. Winterbottom shared a greater kinship with coaches, rather than those officially in charge of tactics at even the country's biggest clubs, who he denigrated as 'cheque-book managers'[4] and whose primary concern was their club's finances, rather than the manner in which their team played or even their success.

By 1953, Winterbottom's enthusiasm for attempting to impart tactical wisdom upon his charges had been beaten out of him, to a degree. Earlier run-ins with the likes of Tommy Lawton, Raich Carter and Stan Matthews had made it readily apparent that by the time a player received the fabled call from the national team, he was rarely willing (and, perhaps, entirely unable) to adjust the formula that had seen him reach the pinnacle of an English player's career.

Winterbottom's scornful analysis of the misplaced role that club managers were playing in the English game was borne out over the next few years by the sheer lack of innovation demonstrated by clubs when it came to tactics. Despite having been given a crash course in how susceptible the W-M was to even the most basic of alterations by the Hungarians, sticking their heads above the parapet and breaking with tactical tradition was something that virtually no English league club was willing to do. So ingrained was the twin belief in English football's infallibility and the unalterable brilliance of the W-M that owners, managers, players, coaches and fans alike did not see the value in being the team that risked it all and became the first to step out of line.

There would be one major exception, however. Towards the end of the 1953–54 season, Manchester City's reserves went on a remarkable run, recording twenty-six games unbeaten. Away from the scrutiny of fans and the prying eyes of City's owners and board members, two City reserves, forward Johnny Williamson and half-back Ken Barnes, had lobbied the team to attempt to replicate the Hungarian model, with Williamson playing the part of Hidegkuti. The results were such that the first team manager, Les McDowall, called the first team in for an early pre-season and declared they would be implementing a new system, named for the man who would replace Williamson in the deep-lying role – the Revie Plan.

City had languished in the lower reaches of the First Division for three seasons, and when they lost their first match with Don Revie playing deep 5-0, the number of rival chairmen and managers eyeing the Citizens smugly must have been legion. Swiftly, however, City improved. Revie, a relatively slow forward who had always relied upon his wits to make up for what he lacked in natural gifts, enjoyed the best top-flight goal-scoring season of his career and was awarded FWA Footballer of the Year. City finished a much-improved seventh in the league and reached the FA Cup Final.

Winterbottom called Revie up for the first of six England caps to face Northern Ireland in October 1954 and utilised him in a watered-down version of the role. Nonetheless, the rest of the team's lack of familiarity with the system – Revie was the only City player in the side – saw the experiment fizzle. In the words of Jon Henderson, it was like 'an orchestra without a conductor'.[5]

The year after, City finished fourth and returned to Wembley, winning the third FA Cup in the club's history. This, however, was to prove the high-water mark of the Revie experiment, which foundered as the player and McDowall's relationship deteriorated. Revie was eventually sold to Sunderland in 1956.

While the likes of Matt Busby at Manchester United began to blur the lines between club manager and head coach, gradually achieving the autonomy today associated with the job of manager, it would take several years and a taciturn former England defender named Alf Ramsey to truly kick-start the tactical revolution in English football.

★ ★ ★

In Hungary, the atmosphere had an altogether different mood. After a fractious summer in which a growing portion of the population had joined protests against the government of Mátyás Rákosi, emboldened by the Kremlin's policy of de-Stalinisation, which had led to a power-sharing system with Imre Nagy, the country had come together for the match. Thousands in the factories had worked extra hours earlier in the week in order to be given the afternoon off to follow the game. Budapest's historic streets were deserted, as every available radio was tuned to the breathless commentary of György Szepesi. Department stores, shops and restaurants attempted to entice customers in by promising they would be broadcasting the match. Policemen took to stopping passing cars and ordering them to roll down their windows and turn their radios up to full blast. Those unfortunate enough to be working in the mines during the game had score updates relayed via scrawled notes that were lowered into the pits in buckets – many depending on this rudimentary form of reportage must have assumed their better-informed colleagues on the surface were playing a cruel joke on them as Hungary racked up the score.

If the listening masses back home could scarcely believe their ears, for the Hungarian players, what followed the match felt equally dreamlike. Despite all their success in recent years, crushing England in such a manner was like nothing they'd experienced before. By the time Szepesi made his way to the team's dressing room, he expected to find them in celebration – instead, he walked into a hushed atmosphere, the players physically and emotionally spent from the match. It didn't take long for the reality of what they'd achieved to sink in, aided by a ghost from the past.

Jimmy Hogan was, by 1953, 71 years of age, his serious involvement with first-class football over. He was still, however, coaching the youth sides at Aston Villa, and it was in this capacity that he attended Wembley on that foggy November day to bear witness to the seeds that he had planted decades earlier blossoming in such spectacular fashion. Hogan told Sebes that his team had played 'the kind of football today I dreamed the Hungarians might one day be able to play'.[6] Sebes repaid the compliment, telling the press, 'We played football as Jimmy Hogan taught us. When our football history is told, his name should be written in gold letters,'[7] while Sándor Barcs added, 'Your Jimmy Hogan taught us the old Scottish style more than twenty years ago. You seem to have forgotten it.'[8] The man who had spent his career butting his head against the glass ceiling of English football had at last achieved the ultimate vindication.

A delegation of England fans graciously cheered the Hungarian team as they departed from Victoria Station, perhaps partly out of sheer relief to see the back of their vanquishers. If the team's spirits had been boosted by their arrival in Paris after their muted departure from Budapest before the match, the reception they received upon arriving back in the French capital was of an entirely different magnitude. Puskás remembered the hysteria among the French was such that it was as if 'they themselves had won'.[9]

Everywhere they went – including to a show and a French league game – they were the centre of attention, with the main event grinding to a halt and the Hungarian team feted as returning conquerors would have been in feudal centuries past. Thousands attempted to cram into the small stadium where the Mighty Magyars played another exhibition game and cruised to a 16-1 victory.

From Paris, the mania that greeted the team only increased. An even bigger crowd met the squad when they reached Vienna, as thousands of those who traditionally treated Hungary as their greatest rivals – including Austria's own national players – set aside partisan differences in acknowledgement of a truly historic achievement.

It was when the team entered Hungarian borders, however, that the extent of the celebratory homecoming they would be subjected to became apparent. Not content with welcoming the players on their return to Budapest, hundreds travelled to the tiny border village of Hegyeshalom to be the first to welcome their returning heroes back to the country. From there, the train laboured through every provincial station, with thousands desperate to delay the train's progress until the team had been sufficiently showered with gifts and worship.

The joy over the team's performance, melded with the hopes that Mátyás Rákosi's regime and its insidious attempts to undermine Hungarian national pride might be coming to an end, bloomed as the team train wound its way to Budapest. The *Magyar* squad could have been forgiven for thinking that, by the time they reached the capital, there would be none of their countrymen left to greet them there. Instead, an estimated crowd of more than 100,000 crammed in and around Keleti Station, still pockmarked with bullet holes from the bloody battle between the Nazis and the Soviet forces, to see the exhausted players and coaches disembark. Naturally, government officials wasted no time in delivering glad-handing speeches, attempting to equate Sebes' team's historic achievements with the work of the government, but few in the crowd had any interest in anyone but the footballers.

★ ★ ★

In spite of the psychological albatross now hung around the necks of the England team, they returned from Scotland with the spoils, winning 4-2 in their first game following the Hungary debacle. The next month, the team travelled to the Continent for a short preparatory tour before their second foray into the World Cup. The first match, in Belgrade against an extremely strong Yugoslavia, saw England deliver a stirring rearguard action, a stance few in the white shirts of their country had ever been asked to adopt and one which they had appeared utterly incapable of performing against Hungary. It took an 87th-minute winner for Yugoslavia to break English hearts, but the players, including yet another new centre-half, Luton Town's Syd Owen, could take encouragement in their newfound ability to frustrate opposition teams with defensive obstinance.

Much as Hungary's deceptively poor draw with Sweden had softened English hearts and minds before the mauling at Wembley, however, the narrow defeat to Yugoslavia perhaps lulled England into a greater confidence in their defensive prowess than was warranted, as they travelled to Budapest for the return match with Sebes, Puskás, Hidegkuti and Co. Since Wembley, Sebes' men had enjoyed a relatively relaxed schedule in between Nemzeti Bajnokság seasons, earning a comfortable 3-0 win over Egypt in Cairo before recording their second win in a row in Vienna against Austria. The return match with England would be their last game before the World Cup began in mid-June.

If the November match at Wembley had represented a historic changing of the guard, then the May match at the newly completed Népstadion was a brutal affirmation that what had happened in London was not an anomaly. Such was the clamour for tickets that even those struggling to make ends meet resorted to paying vastly inflated prices on the black market, and some fans even snuck homing pigeons into the ground, which they then used to fly their already-used tickets back to friends still waiting outside.

Hungary played with just one change from the Golden Team of Wembley. László Budai was replaced by József Tóth, yet another sparkling young talent from Hungary's apparently endless conveyor belt of players. England's team, meanwhile, retained just four names from the Wembley match, as the selectors stuck staunchly to their decision to banish certain players, ignoring the possibility that those who had already suffered at the hands of the Hungarians would at least have 90 minutes of familiarity and could perhaps help mitigate what the press were anticipating would be another defeat.

Tom Finney would note ruefully years later that such a test 'didn't seem to be the right occasion for experimenting'.[10] The *Daily Herald*, in a declaration that would have been unthinkable months before, stated that an England victory would be the 'biggest shock of post-war European football'.

Winterbottom's side had only five men with more than seven caps to their names: Merrick, the ever-present central pairing of Wright and Dickinson, Ivor Broadis and Finney, who'd missed the first match through injury. The highly inexperienced appearance of the England team was in stark contrast with Hungary, for whom only Tóth had fewer than twenty-two caps. Stanley Matthews, the one Englishman who Sebes had singled out as worthy of a place in his team from the Wembley match, missed out, much to the disappointment of the Hungarian fans (the cover of the match programme featured an anonymous white-shirted English player who bore a more than passing resemblance to the Blackpool star). Even the Iron Curtain had failed to stop the Wizard of Dribble's mystique from filtering through.

England hoped that the determined, backs-to-the-wall approach that they'd taken against Yugoslavia was proof of a new, pragmatic era for the team, where they could accept the need for attritional, defence-first performances against certain opponents. Hungary wasted no time puncturing those notions in spectacular style. The deadlock lasted just 8 minutes before Mihály Lantos fired a free kick directly into the net. Puskás bundled in a second on 22 minutes, before Sándor Kocsis, the one Hungarian for whom the Wembley experience was as frustrating as it was joyous, finally got his goal against England, expertly volleying in from a Puskás pass. The Three Lions could feel grateful to be just 3-0 down at half-time. Even though the Hungarian threat was now far more familiar, England's continued failure to get to grips with Nando Hidegkuti's dropping deep and the forward line interchanging meant the Magyars remained every bit as evasive and otherworldly as when they'd emerged from the Wembley fog.

The barrage continued in the second period, the Hungarian lesson lasting until the very last significant piece of action of the match. Hidegkuti was once again given the freedom of the Népstadion to pick up the ball, turn and charge at the English defence, before rolling a perfect through-ball to Puskás, who finished with aplomb. The goal made it 7-1, a scoreline that consigned England to their heaviest ever defeat in international football, the same fate England had condemned the Magyars to in 1908.

The match lacked the element of surprise of the first meeting and, for the English fans and Fleet Street pressmen, the immediacy of the Wembley setting, but there was no getting away from the fact that Hungary had stamped their supremacy over England in emphatic fashion. It was, in the words of Finney, 'thoroughbreds against carthorses'.[11] Decades of ignoring the national team's gradual demise, of dismissing the World Cup and Olympics as illegitimate claims to footballing glory, of adding caveats to preserve their proud, undefeated home record, could not mask the naked truth – not only were England no longer the best team in the world, they might not even be second rate.

Now that Hungary had sent the first domino of England's self-perception tumbling, who could honestly say where the nation's nadir would lie? Unfortunately for Walter Winterbottom and his increasingly rag-tag team, their next hurdle would be a stern examination of just how far they'd fallen down the pecking order.

★ ★ ★

The 1954 World Cup took place in an unseasonably hot Switzerland. After ignoring the early editions of the competition and their calamitous first participation in 1950, England travelled to the Continent for the first time feeling the competition's weight of expectation. Hungary had proved categorically that England were no longer the supreme force in world football, yet as Britain continued to grapple with the existential question of where the nation's place in the wider world lay as the empire disintegrated, Englishmen increasingly looked to the national team for a sense of international purpose, a potential source of restored pride and an affirmation of the country still playing a leading role.

To do so meant looking to the international teams and competitions that England had so recently scorned. The Home Championship, once the key staple of the national team's calendar, had taken on an introverted, parochial character in the increasingly globalised world of international football, a shift which marked the beginning of the end of the competition. The sense of desperation was palpable: Clifford Webb, writing in the *Daily Herald*, described the World Cup as 'a last chance for the English football system. If we are beaten the bottom will have dropped out of everything.'

Hungary, meanwhile, entered the tournament as overwhelming favourites, unbeaten for more than four years in official games. Even though the England team rolled out in Budapest had been slapdash and inexperienced, crushing them with such ease had been yet another feather in the *Magyar* cap. England may have suffered from delusions about their place in world football for some time, but it was a misapprehension shared across the globe. A team that could humiliate the old masters at will was a fearsome prospect indeed.

From the first round of matches, the tone of Hungary's group was set, as they demolished South Korea 9-0 and West Germany, who Hungary would play next, enjoyed a 4-1 stroll past Turkey. Despite their geographic proximity, Hungary had not played a German team since the war, having enjoyed a relatively even record against the Germans previously. For West Germany, the prospect of facing the Hungarian Golden Team was a daunting one, and Sebes' men didn't disappoint, achieving a remarkable 8-3 victory and laying down a marker for the rest of the tournament. The only blemish was an ankle injury to Puskás, which would cause him to miss the bulk of the competition.

To some bemusement, the West German manager, Sepp Herberger, had fielded what appeared to be a significantly weakened team, but such was Hungary's momentum, few were particularly surprised by the scoreline. Many assumed Herberger had simply wanted to protect his best players from a morale-sapping humiliation and to give his side a ready-made excuse for what had seemed an inevitable defeat. Fuel was added to this theory when Germany still escaped the group by beating Turkey again, this time in a play-off.

England, meanwhile, could watch with a degree of satisfaction as Hungary continued to make light work of every team they faced. The vindication they felt for Hungary's continued success, however, was not something that translated to their on-field performances. After the Népstadion rout, the FA had once again gone back to the drawing board for the World Cup squad, recalling Nat Lofthouse and Stan Matthews and abandoning their resolve to turn the page on the team of recent years for fear of the World Cup becoming a complete fiasco.

England had been handed a relatively kind draw, only having to play hosts Switzerland and Belgium and avoiding groupmates and two-time champions, Italy. Even with this promising draw, the same glaring defensive deficiencies that had been exposed against Hungary were exploited by the Belgians. England had defeated their opponents eleven times in their thirteen previous meetings but were indebted to Lofthouse and the rest of the attack for a laboured 4-4 draw after extra time. To make matters worse, Switzerland scored a surprise victory over Italy, meaning that anything less than a win in their second group game would take England's destiny out of their hands.

Despite Matthews and Lofthouse missing the game, a competent 2-0 victory over the host nation provided England safe passage to the knockout stages. The match with the Swiss was most notable for the redoubtable Billy Wright being moved from half-back to centre-half, a switch made initially out of desperation but that would ultimately prove something of a masterstroke. After years of incessantly trialling and then discarding central defenders, Wright was found to possess all the qualities that England had been searching for in their long quest for a replacement for Neil Franklin at the heart of the defence. Though already 30, Wright would go on to secure more than forty caps in his new international role.

Even with the solution for the centre-half conundrum found directly under their noses, England would be afforded just one more match in Switzerland, as they were drawn to face the reigning champions Uruguay, who had beaten England 2-1 the year before and had bulldozed a hapless Scotland 9-0 in the group stages. Ultimately, after the Hungary games, which had both culminated in a whimper from a team that knew they were well and truly whipped, England's 4-2 defeat to Uruguay was a far more creditable showing. However, the fact that the national team were able to take heart in the manner of a defeat was demonstrative of just how far they, and the English public's opinion of them, had fallen.

When Finney scored in the 67th minute to make the score 3-2 in Uruguay's favour, England had the wind in their sails, just as they did in the closing moments of the first half with Hungary at Wembley, and looked for all the world like they could produce the sort of heroic fightback that had been a mainstay of British folk legend for time immemorial. These hopes were dashed when, with England committing more of their players forward, Uruguay broke and put the game to bed with their fourth goal. It was a valiant effort, one that was reflected in the press. Geoffrey Green in *The Times* lauded England's display as 'all flags flying and all their guns firing, to show at last that there is no degeneracy of spirit deep down in English football'. Yet, despite the praise being heaped on the defeated Three Lions, there was an inescapable sense of inevitability about the defeat, which would have been utterly incompatible with England's footballing prestige before the first Hungary loss. The *Guardian* questioned whether England could ever hope to compete on the world stage while persevering with 'what her Continental critics with such surprising unanimity call stereotyped, conservative, primitive methods'.

★ ★ ★

Hungary's progress, meanwhile, was no less eventful. Drawn against Brazil in the quarter-finals, the world's attention focused on what promised to be a classic encounter. Even before their ascendancy to the status of footballing demigods, Brazil already had a reputation for wondrous entertainers. Hungary, of course, by now needed nothing in the way of introduction. However, what should have been a match of sheer beauty descended into infamy, described by Sebes as 'a battle; a brutal, savage match'.[12]

Hungary, without the injured Puskás, raced into a two-goal lead within 7 minutes, but it was their third goal, scored after Brazil had pulled one back, that triggered a remarkable series of events. Venerated English referee Arthur Ellis, who would later reflect on the game not as a football match, but as 'a battle of politics and religion', awarded Hungary a penalty which was duly dispatched by Lantos.[13] The Brazilian officials and journalists, incensed by the decision, swarmed the pitch and had to be dispersed by police.

But despite the field being cleared, the Brazilian players had reached the point of no return, even as Julinho hauled them back into contention with a superb goal to make the score 3-2. Shortly afterwards, Nílton Santos fouled Bozsik, and the two men came to blows, leading to both being sent off. From there, the match descended into farce.

Brazil's Humberto was sent off for a crude kick at Gyula Lóránt. By the time Kocsis put the game beyond all doubt with his second goal of the day, there was no question of Brazil letting bygones be bygones at Ellis' final whistle. Upon their semi-final berth being confirmed, the Hungarian players embraced and Grosics cartwheeled from his goal, but the *Magyar* celebrations would be short-lived. Brazilian fans, journalists and officials once again stormed the pitch. In the tunnel, what Sebes remembered as 'a small war' broke out, with bottles and boots flying through the air; one bottle split Sebes' head to the extent he required stitches.[14] At one point, in a desperate attempt to restore some order, Puskás effectively took a hostage, bundling one of the Brazilian players into the Hungarian dressing room. 'He was terrified,' recalled the team captain, 'and I ended up letting him go.'[15]

After the chaos of Brazil, Hungary faced Uruguay in the semi-finals. Many saw this match as being the actual final. The other semi would be contested between West Germany, who Hungary had brushed aside so emphatically, and Austria, who, despite possessing a talented team, had been shown repeatedly during recent years to be categorically weaker than the Hungarians. Should Hungary overcome the South Americans, it appeared they would have surmounted the most difficult hurdle. If the reigning World Cup Champions could become the first team in more than thirty matches to defeat Hungary, meanwhile, it was almost impossible to see them succumbing to whoever they met in the final.

After the meeting with Brazil had left such a sour taste, Hungary's match with Uruguay provided a footballing masterclass, with the natural fluidity of the South Americans' game – a characteristic imported to Latin America and encouraged by, among other luminaries, Hungarian coaches like Dori Kürschner and Imre Hirschl – proving a more natural foil to Hungary's roving deep-lying centre-forward than the static, staid English approach.[16] Despite an increasingly unfamiliar look to the team as injuries took their toll following months of near uninterrupted team selections, Hungary grabbed the early impetus and looked in command. Czibor put Hungary ahead, before Hidegkuti netted almost as soon as the second half began. With just 15 minutes remaining, it appeared that Sebes, Gyula Mándi and Márton Bukovi, who after being refused the chance to work with Sebes by the Hungarian government years before had finally been granted permission to travel officially with the team, had worked their magic again.

Suddenly, however, the Uruguayans made a breakthrough, in part aided by the oppressive heat that was more natural to them than the Hungarians (four days before, Austria and Switzerland had played out a farcical game, later known as the Heat Battle of Lausanne, where players had suffered from hyperthermia in the 40-degree heat). Juan Hohberg scored twice, his second with just 4 minutes to go, to take the match to extra time and shatter the Hungarian morale. Uruguay came desperately close to taking the lead early in extra time, but the reprieve seemed to breathe new life into the Magyars, for whom two crosses within 5 minutes both found the Golden Head of Kocsis. The striker, who would finish the tournament as top scorer with a remarkable eleven goals, made no mistake with either opportunity. Hungary were in the World Cup Final.

Remarkably, there they would meet West Germany again. After escaping their group, despite the crushing defeat by Hungary, the West Germans had gathered a head of steam, enjoying a professional 2-0 success against Yugoslavia, followed by a huge 6-1 win over Austria, undoubtedly the best result of their short post-war era. All three national teams – West Germany, East Germany and Saarland – spawned by the break-up of Germany, had been banned by FIFA until after the 1950 World Cup. The West Germany team had played just eighteen games together before the World Cup, fourteen fewer matches than Hungary's unbeaten run stretched to by the time the two met in the final, and few had given the team's nucleus of semi-professional players much hope of advancing far into the tournament. However, their fairy-tale run now appeared at an end. Faced with a repeat match with Hungary, their prospects of success appeared impossibly slim.

The main question that dominated the lead-up to the match centred on whether Puskás' ankle, injured in Hungary's earlier group match with Germany, would heal sufficiently in time for him to play. While Hungary were desperate for their captain and talisman to return to the field and lead them to glory, in many ways, the matter seemed largely academic. Hungary had come through the battle with Brazil and the technical challenge of Uruguay without Puskás. What could the West Germans, who had looked so hopelessly overmatched just two weeks before, possibly hope to achieve, even if Puskás failed to recover in time?

As ever, Sebes, Mándi and Bukovi sought to leave no stone unturned in the seven days between beating Uruguay and facing the Germans. However, some factors were out of the punctilious trio's control. As well as assessing Puskás' injury until the eleventh hour, Sebes was resigned to once again changing his team, something he was loath to do and had successfully avoided for much of the previous two years, as knocks and fatigue caused by the relentless World Cup schedule took their toll. Budai was patently too exhausted to play another game, and his usual replacement, József Tóth, was injured, leading to Sebes asking Czibor to start on the right for the national team for the first time, while Mihály Tóth came in on the left wing.

Puskás was eventually passed fit but, along with the rest of the team, endured a sleepless night before the final, as the Swiss National Brass Band Competition kept the players awake into the early morning by playing almost directly outside the team's hotel. Hungary's preparations were then further disrupted when the thronging crowds outside Bern's Wankdorf Stadium prevented their team bus from reaching the ground, leading to the players having to disembark and force their way inside.

After weeks of baking hot weather, the day of the final saw a huge rainstorm break over the city, drenching the pitch and playing into the hands of the Germans who, despite operating a fluid attack inspired by Hungary (called the 'Herberger whirl', after the team's coach), could not hope to match Hungary's freewheeling passing. Furthermore, the Hungarian boots, which had inspired Billy Wright's mockery just months before, were vastly inferior to the revolutionary Adidas ones worn by the Germans, which featured interchangeable studs that allowed them to be adapted for different conditions.

It wasn't just the attack that set Herberger apart from many coaches of the day. By the final, it was clear that he had never intended to try and win the Hungary match, preferring to protect his best players from what he anticipated could be a demoralising loss. Sebes and his coaches were well aware that the team Germany played in the final would bear little resemblance to the one they'd beaten so comfortably a fortnight earlier. Ultimately, six of the German players who began the final hadn't featured in the group match.

However, unlike England, who had shot themselves in the foot in Budapest by making wholesale changes when they would have benefited from turning to players with at least some familiarity with the Hungarian system, Herberger aimed to turn this potential weakness into a strength. This he did through careful analysis, with his players, of Hungary, a pre-match exercise still rarely practised with any degree of precision in those days. The Germans who, despite their flexible attacking line, still adhered closely to the classic W-M, painstakingly studied a recording of Hungary's victory at Wembley to learn how best to counter Hidegkuti's movement. This, combined with the fact that the Hungarians had no experience of playing against half the

German team, gave Herberger's charges a crucial edge. As Puskás would later reflect, despite the West German tactics being close cousins of those deployed by England, 'our [deep-lying centre-forward] tactic did not have the same devastating effect that it had at Wembley. The Germans ... seemed to know exactly what to expect.'[17]

With several minutes gone, the final seemed to be following the script. A blocked shot from Kocsis fell fortuitously for Puskás to bury the ball past German goalkeeper, Toni Turek. Two minutes later, Turek was picking the ball out of his net again, after a calamitous defensive mix-up allowed Czibor to roll the ball into the net unchallenged. At 2-0 down with scarcely 8 minutes gone, West Germany could have utterly capitulated. Instead, they staged a remarkable comeback, pulling the first goal back on 10 minutes and finding an equaliser soon after through winger Helmut Rahn. Hungary were stunned, but nonetheless took back the initiative for the remainder of the half, with Hidegkuti, shepherded throughout by right-half Horst Eckel, denied by both the post and a spectacular Turek save.

The theme continued into the second period, with Germany clearing off the line on multiple occasions, Turek making save after save and Kocsis smacking the crossbar with a header. The longer Hungary's domination lasted and the more times Germany were able to repel them, the greater the belief in the crowd, a sizeable proportion of whom were German, that the underdogs might be able to pull off one of international football's greatest upsets. With 6 minutes remaining, Rahn ranged forward, jinked inside to wrong-foot Lantos and stroked a shot beyond the reach of Grosics. Hungary continued to attack with abandon and seemed to find a leveller in the 88th minute, only for linesman Sandy Griffiths (a Welshman, who had refereed Hungary's previous game with Uruguay) to rule the goal out after English referee William Ling had given it.

As Germany collected their trophy, the defeated Hungarians watched on in stunned disbelief. The ever-analytical Sebes looked at the cold, hard facts of the matter – 'During the ninety minutes, the Germans had eight shots and scored three goals; we had twenty-five shots and scored twice, with one disallowed'[18] – but even he couldn't quite rationalise the defeat. He alluded darkly to the fact that it was 'odd that we always seemed to get British referees',[19] suggesting that the pall cast over British football by Hungary's success had influenced the officials.

The fatalistic Grosics would never shake the 'enormous, personal sense of loss' following the final, suggesting that rather than a bizarre aberration, perhaps the match had exposed 'a deep self-conceit in the team that had never showed itself before'.[20] Puskás, meanwhile, remained demanding yet matter of fact, even though he admitted he could have 'murdered' Griffiths for disallowing his goal, which in the Galloping Major's recollection only happened when the Hungarians were back in the centre circle, a full minute after he'd put the ball in the net.

'In the end, we deserved what we got,' reflected Puskás, decades later:

We should never have relaxed after going two up; we should have pressed on then, looking for the third to kill the game off. The defeat wasn't the result of any element of our training or preparation. It was our own fault: we thought we had the match won, gave two stupid goals away and let them back into it.[21]

The recriminations would continue long after the game. It would later be suggested that Adi Dassler's studs weren't the only piece of scientific innovation that the German team had benefited from. Syringes were allegedly found in the drains of the West German dressing room, while reports suggested that several of the German players appeared jaundiced and vomited after the match, hinting at possible abuse of performance-enhancing drugs.[22]

Whether or not Germany had enjoyed some clandestine assistance, there was no escaping the fact that Hungary had stumbled at the last hurdle. To do so after such an unprecedented run of success – on the very same pitch where Hungary had truly discovered the potential of Hidegkuti playing deep, no less – was utterly devastating. As Grosics recalled, 'It shattered the myth – our legendary status – and neither the experts nor the general public at home could bear it. It's more than forty years ago now, but if someone was to wake me up tomorrow morning and remind me of that match, I'd burst into tears.'[23]

13

GOODBYE, ENGLAND!

The Hungarian team returned home after having conquered England in 1953 to jubilant scenes, the likes of which Budapest and the rest of the country hadn't seen since before the Second World War. As the country convulsed in joy, the exhausted players were toasted and celebrated, granted pay rises, bonuses and military promotions. It was, from an objective point of view, a scarcely believable reaction to a football match that hadn't even happened within Hungary's borders, and yet, given the context of political tyranny and post-war deprivations, it made perfect sense.

The disparity between Hungary's triumphant homecoming in November of 1953 and their return following the World Cup, some eight months later, could hardly have been starker. So relentless was their progress through the competition that, by the time the final arrived, the Hungarian press and public treated the match as more a coronation than a contest. When West Germany emerged triumphant, the sheer shock ripped through Hungarian society like an earthquake.

The team avoided travelling to Budapest for fear of a mob, the political suspicions surrounding Gyula Grosics were resurrected by police and Gusztáv Sebes' son was beaten up at school.[1] Just as Mátyás Rákosi had profited from his relationship with the team during their numerous successes, so too did he now bear the brunt of the nation's heartbreak, with thousands taking to the streets, their anguish at the loss in Bern morphing into vehement anti-Soviet protests.

Hungarians could at least console themselves with the knowledge that the majority of their team would still be young enough to appear in the next World

Cup, in 1958 in Sweden. Few would have imagined that they'd already seen the apex of their beloved Golden Team's achievements. So, 1955 continued in the same vein as the years before, with Hungary looking dominant, although their sheen of pure invincibility had been lost in Bern to West Germany.

In 1956, the small cracks began to widen and become fissures. Hungary lost away in Turkey, then were held at home by Yugoslavia. They then lost for the first time ever at the Népstadion, 4-2 to Czechoslovakia, having won the previous six games against their old imperial neighbours. The loss would prove decisive in the ongoing edition of the Central European International Cup, and was followed by another defeat, against Belgium.

Hungary had lost as many games in four months as they'd done in the preceding seven years. The run, combined with the political events engulfing the country at the same time, led to Gusztáv Sebes' removal. After working for a time in sports administration, he would quietly live out the rest of his days in Budapest, teaching the school children who played near his home the basics of the beautiful game and showing them scratchy films of the two matches with England.

The sudden fallibility of the national team seemed to mirror the increasingly turbulent and unpredictable political situation Hungary was engulfed in. Imre Nagy's power-sharing arrangement with Rákosi had, at the time of the Match of the Century, offered hope for a less-tyrannical future. In some ways, that promise had held, but in others, it had simply plunged Hungary into greater uncertainty. Rákosi still pulled the strings and when Nagy refused to dance, the government descended into internecine civil war. After months of battling and counterintuitive governance – Nagy was instrumental in the release of many political dissidents from prison, while Rákosi attempted to reinstate the disastrous agricultural collectivism policy – the bull-headed Rákosi eventually succeeded in ousting Nagy. It was a pyrrhic victory that doomed Rákosi, as he failed to detect the change in direction that Nikita Khrushchev was instigating. The new Soviet Secretary was seeking to mend bridges with Tito and distance himself from the Stalinist brand of totalitarianism that Rákosi still aped.

★ ★ ★

In spite of the continued meddling of the selection committee, the England team did gradually begin to mimic one aspect of the Hungarian team – the gradual centralisation of a group of players at a single club. After enduring wilderness years following the Second World War, when the unusable, bombed-out carcass of Old Trafford served as a metaphor for the club's diminished state, Manchester United had emerged (along with Wolves) as the country's most exciting team, under the stewardship of Matt Busby, the first truly modern manager. Busby was a master teambuilder, understanding exactly when the moment had arrived to break up teams and reconstruct them. In the mid-1950s, he began this cycle again, creating a youthful nucleus as exciting as any team in British history. They were called the Busby Babes, and it wasn't long before several of them had made themselves all but impossible to ignore for the selectors.

It was as much by accident as it was design on England's part, but nonetheless, powered by this Mancunian core, the Three Lions delivered several stirring performances. Brazil were defeated 4-2 in May 1956, despite Walter Winterbottom's team conspiring to miss two penalties. Later that month, England travelled to Berlin, where they beat reigning World Champions West Germany 3-1. Geoffrey Green hailed the win as signalling that England were 'on the way back into the picture with their young men at a time when Hungary and Germany, the world champions, are going over the hill with their stars. So, the cycle of football is changing once more.' On both occasions, three United stars played, with another two in reserve. Even allowing for all of the systematic, structural shortcomings of the England team of that era, there was a sense that the Busby Babes might be capable of hauling the country back into contention.

Then tragedy struck.

On 6 February 1958, mere months before the World Cup, the Manchester United team plane crashed at Munich Airport while attempting to take off in treacherous conditions, claiming the lives of twenty-three on board, including eight players. The tragedy shook the entire nation to the core, and England, without the likes of Duncan Edwards and Tommy Taylor, sleepwalked to a group-stage exit at the World Cup.

Though no longer quite as naive as when Hungary had crushed them five years previously, England's tactics remained too static, giving savvy opposition managers ample opportunities to pick them apart. Milovan Ćirić, the coach of Yugoslavia who masterminded a 5-0 win over England in a warm-up match for the 1958 World Cup, an eerie echo of the humbling 7-1 in Budapest before the 1954 competition, summed up the ease with which his players had held England at bay: 'Why is everything with England number 10? ... Number 10 takes the corners! Number 10 takes the throw-ins! So what do we do? We put a man on number 10! Goodbye England!'[2]

★ ★ ★

For both Britain and Hungary, 1956 was a defining year. History has a habit of making fools of those who attempt to write it too quickly. What can, at the time, appear an event of incalculable import is often nullified and mitigated into insignificance in the grand scheme of things.

Equally, apparently innocuous happenings can ultimately prove catalysts for huge, landmark moments. Nobody predicted that a minor aristocrat being assassinated in Serbia could precipitate the deadliest conflict in human history, nor that one woman refusing to sit at the back of a bus in America could have seen a huge upheaval in civil rights.

The Suez Canal affair proved to be one of those rare, non-wartime events that felt huge as it occurred and has only become more and more pertinent. In an attempt to oust Egyptian President Gamal Abdel Nasser and regain control of the recently nationalised Suez Canal, Britain, France and Israel invaded, a show of strength that in centuries past would have been insurmountable. Instead, the three were forced into a humiliating withdrawal, due to pressure from both the USA and Soviet Union, underlining the new world order. By the end of the century, Suez towered above other losses and indignities that Britain had suffered as the nadir of her standing as a world power.

In a remarkable fluke of history, as the Suez Crisis was unfolding, events no less dramatic were occurring on the streets of Budapest. Three months earlier, despite Mátyás Rákosi's desperate, doomed attempts at appeasement, the tide had turned against him and, by extension, the Soviet Union's meddling in Hungarian affairs. Rákosi was replaced, but instead of the popular, progressive Imre Nagy, another sham election saw another Soviet puppet, Ernő Gerő, elected. Then, in October, Poland achieved a landmark democratic victory when, despite Khrushchev's best efforts, they had succeeded in electing Władysław Gomułka, their equivalent of Nagy. Hungarian students took to the streets of Budapest to show solidarity with their Polish brethren and demand the Soviet Union loosen their iron grip on Hungary. Several attempts to stymie the protest, which quickly swelled to more than 200,000 people, failed, with multiple incidents of the police and army laying down their weapons and joining the protestors. For a jubilant few days, it appeared that the revolution had succeeded. Nagy was re-elected, and Soviet forces appeared poised to withdraw. However, the joy of the Hungarian people was to be short-lived. Fearing humiliation, the Kremlin performed an about-turn and, using the full might of the Red Army, crushed the revolution, reimposed a Soviet-backed regime and forced Hungary back into Russian control.

With mass arrests swiftly following and the light of freedom at the end of the long tunnel suddenly snuffed out, tens of thousands of Hungarians decided they had no option but to take their chances and flee. Among them were several of the nation's beloved Golden Team. Having enjoyed a last hurrah by inflicting upon the Soviet Union their first home defeat, a result which fed the anti-Soviet feeling in Budapest, many of the players associated with the national team seized upon a slice of good fortune that saw Honvéd playing abroad on a tour as the revolution broke out and elected simply not to return home.

Ferenc Puskás, Sándor Kocsis and Zoltán Czibor, three of the six players still playing regularly who remained from the Match of the Century, all took the heartbreaking decision to abandon Hungary while they still had the chance. Czibor enjoyed a brief, successful spell with Barcelona with Kocsis, who maintained his prodigious goal-scoring exploits. Both played alongside László Kubala, who himself had defected as Rákosi had first risen to power. Predictably, however, it was Puskás who experienced the greatest success, forming a devastating one-two punch alongside Alfredo di Stéfano at Real Madrid. Puskás won five league titles with Real and was the top goal scorer in La Liga four times.

It was in the European Cup, however, that he earned his greatest accolades and went some way to righting what he felt to be the wrongs of the 1954 World Cup Final. He won the title three times, with perhaps his greatest moment coming in the middle triumph, where Real surgically dismantled Eintracht Frankfurt 7-3 and Puskás scored four.

Puskás, Kocsis and Czibor represented Hungary's past and present. The crushing of the Hungarian Uprising also robbed the team of its future. A few months before the Match of the Century, Hungary had won the under-18 FIFA Youth Tournament, a victory that signalled the sense of perpetual momentum building around Hungary's ability to produce world-class players. As the Soviet forces rolled into Budapest, many players of that same generation were away at an under-21 UEFA competition. None of them ever returned.[3]

Shorn of the next generation, with the line broken, the national team entered into a long, decrepit decline. Two years after the attempted revolution, they were knocked out of the World Cup group stage by Wales. Though they would win two further Olympic gold medals in the 1960s, the competition was, by that point, dominated by those with a looser interpretation of amateurism than the major football nations and had been completely eclipsed by the World Cup. In the premier tournament, Hungary fared far worse. They would qualify for just five of the next sixteen World Cups. Never again would Hungary come close to matching the superlative achievements of the Golden Team.

The story of the *Aranycsapat* didn't completely end with the revolution, however. At the same World Cup where the depleted Hungary were overcome by the Welsh, Brazil recorded their first title, powered by a young player named Pelé and playing a 4-2-4 formation that had arrived in the South American nation with a Hungarian coach named Dori Kürschner.[4] Between Kürschner's influence and the Hungarian Golden Team's example and willingness to challenge the status quo, Brazil were able to capitalise upon their immense promise. From then on, the orthodoxy of the W-M was on borrowed time. Soon, global football had awoken to the possibility of different tactical formations carrying equal, if not greater importance to the players who stepped onto the pitch. While it's impossible to trace the vast delta of modern football back to one trickling source, every team which has succeeded and inspired by throwing out the rule book, from the Total Football Dutch of the 1970s to the Pep Guardiola-led Barcelona wonder team of the 2000s, owes a debt to Hungary's greatest generation and the men who coached them.

★ ★ ★

On the England team's return from the 1958 World Cup, Walter Winterbottom's son's first words to his father were to demand an explanation as to why he hadn't elected to play Bobby Charlton. It was at this moment that Winterbottom knew his days as England manager were numbered. The first generation of players under his charge had ridiculed and resented Winterbottom for his belief in the possibilities of coaching, his attempts to improve players, even those already of an international standard, and his contention that through tactics and inter-player synergy, a team could become greater than the sum of their parts. Ironically, it was these same chief footballing passions that were now serving to undermine him as others, even in the myopic, superannuated world of British football, began to overtake him.

Though something of a visionary in many respects, Winterbottom ultimately lacked the oratory skill to rouse his players from the depths of despair, the arm-around-the-shoulder paternal instinct, and the tactical genius that set apart the greatest managers of the day. The men entering the game in the late 1950s and early 1960s who did possess these skills owed much to Winterbottom's tireless proselytising of the virtues of such a manager, even as they now eclipsed him. It was inevitable that, just as the likes of Jimmy Hogan and George Raynor had inadvertently brought about the humiliation of their home nation, so too had Winterbottom's life work set in motion the movement that would ultimately see him replaced.

Fittingly, it was one of those forged in the crucible of the Match of the Century that took the reins and led England to their first and, to date, only major triumph. Alf Ramsey had been powerless to stop the Wurlitzer of Hungarian attackers on that day in 1953, and his helplessness had cost him his international career. His club career had wound down just two years later, and he'd immediately taken up the managerial role at Ipswich Town, who had just suffered the ignominy of relegation to the Third Division. With the vision of Hungary's orthodoxy-smashing style seared into his mind and his experience of making up for his technical and physical shortcomings with a contemplative, cerebral view of the game, Ramsey set about building a team with the foundational mantra of the W-M not the be all and end all. The result was two promotions and, in 1962, a League Championship in Town's very first season in the top flight.

Fittingly, to truly break the tactical logjam that had afflicted English football since the death of Herbert Chapman, Ramsey had to kill its chief darling – the winger. By the time he took over from Winterbottom as England manager, shortly after his title success with Ipswich, the formation that Ramsey typically favoured was effectively a 4-1-3-2 and was known as the 'Wingless Wonders'. Believing wingers didn't offer enough cover defensively, perhaps inspired by years of being left high and dry by his attacking teammates, Ramsey simply eradicated the position of Matthews, Finney, et al. He replaced the traditional positions with a second striker, a central triumvirate of attacking midfielders who could help congest the centre of the pitch when not in possession, a modern back four and a dedicated defensive midfield destroyer, the one single role that England had missed the most when faced with Nándor Hidegkuti's marauding.

It wasn't only in the tactical realm that Ramsey detected deficiencies from his playing days. His appointment was subject to full control over team selection, something which caused simmering resentment among those in the FA who had enjoyed the final say on the England team dating back to the very first international. Ramsey's instincts, both on and off the field, proved to be faultless. Just three years after Ramsey took the job, England were at last, incontrovertibly, Champions of the World.

Sustained success at international level has been elusive to all but the very best generations of players, and so it proved to be the case with Ramsey's England team. The boys of 1966 aged, Ramsey's tactical edge was matched by equally innovative coaches elsewhere, and England's time as World Champions came to an end. Even so, there was mass consternation when he was sacked by the FA after England had failed to qualify for the 1974 World Cup in West Germany, a move which was widely interpreted as driven by vindictive spectres in the shadows of the FA's Lancaster Gate headquarters, who had never forgiven Ramsey for exposing them and their selection committee as an exercise in foolhardy vanity.

★ ★ ★

Football has come to act as a cipher for the modern world. Ancient scores are settled and international friendships are forged in major tournaments. National teams have come to assume their home's character, their history, their culture. Brazil play with effervescent freedom and exuberance; Italy with unbridled passion and a flair for the dramatic. Hungary's Golden Team was a beacon of hope during the dark days of the Rákosi regime, a beacon that was snuffed out at the same time as the attempted revolution of 1956.

The same can be said of the England national team which, since the 1950s, have often found their fortunes intertwining and dovetailing with those of the country and, more widely, Britain. The 1960s, the team's pinnacle, coincided with the point in time when Britain enjoyed a high cultural water mark. London was the epicentre of the psychedelic era, while the Beatles and the Rolling Stones, both quintessentially British, were arguably bigger than Jesus. The team's decline in the 1970s, culminating in the disastrous exit of Don Revie as manager, occurred as Britain endured her economic Winter of Discontent.

The heady 1990s zeitgeist, with Blair and Britpop, owed an enormous debt of gratitude to England's efforts at Italia '90, followed up in the home tournament of Euro '96.

These broad strokes have been mirrored at the micro level in the players. There is no question that England has continued to produce world-class individual footballers, just as it has brilliant innovators in other fields. Tim Berners-Lee's creation of the Internet may eventually have an impact greater on humankind than Crick and Watson's discovery of the double helix, mere months before Hungary faced England in 1953. Collectively, however, England as a football side has suffered from many of the same maladies that have afflicted the country at large in the decades since the Second World War: an inflated sense of self; a national nostalgia that occasionally borders on parochialism; a reluctance to countenance collaboration or to borrow from others for fear of appearing weak.

After the Hungary match, the rational, circumspect response would have been a period of probing, inevitably painful introspection, which could not have failed to upturn the systemic failings and blockages in the country's approach to football. Instead, the national team blundered forward, and save for the brief, enlightened reign of Ramsey, never truly capitalised upon the vast resources at its disposal.

For the best part of the forty years after the Match of the Century, England ploughed on, heedless of changing tactics and the improving preparation and habits of teams elsewhere. Things did improve in the 1990s, when Bobby Robson dared to introduce a sweeper at Italia '90 and Arsène Wenger taught English football that perhaps pasta was more conducive to a professional athlete than pints. However, rather than seizing the initiative, seeking out new, innovative approaches and leading from the front, the FA and their national team managers were generally guilty of lagging some years behind, consistently looking to emulate the style and set-up of the most recent tournament winner while other major nations instead searched for ways to dethrone the new champions.

Often, managers would utilise aggressive, attacking formations in qualification matches or friendlies with relative minnows, knowing only a swashbuckling, crushing victory would placate the baying masses. Invariably, this lack of competitive practice meant England then found themselves hopelessly unprepared and overmatched once they reached the knock-out rounds of a tournament and faced a team of equal or greater ability.

It was no coincidence that when England did eventually reach another final, fifty-five years after their World Cup triumph, they did so under the managerial auspices of Gareth Southgate. During the Euro 2020 qualification campaign, Southgate alternated between a 4-2-3-1 and 3-4-3, formations that attracted the ire of press and fans who deemed him overly cautious, a man cowed into conservatism by his own personal demons – namely a decisive penalty miss in Euro '96. As the tournament played out, however, it became clear that Southgate, an ex-England defender who had suffered a devastating humiliation, a distinction he shared with Ramsey, had turned weakness into strength, swapped popular clamour for steely eyed clarity. By forcing his team to become accustomed to more defensive, pragmatic formations throughout qualification, irrespective of the quality of the opposition, Southgate had built a team more capable of meeting the robust challenges of first-class international football than the England of previous generations. It was evidence that the English footballing establishment might at last be learning the lessons taught them by the Magical Magyars over half a century before. However, another of Hungary's lessons was the need to adapt to situations as they arose. Eventually, Southgate's England became arguably too wedded to this conservatism and began to underutilise a truly exceptional generation of attacking talent. Nothing underscored this better than when, in a Nations League match at Molineux in 2022, England suffered a humiliating 4-0 defeat, their largest home reverse since the Match of the Century. The team that inflicted this stinging riposte, just months before a critical World Cup campaign? Poetically, it was Hungary.

★ ★ ★

The Match of the Century incontrovertibly changed football history. The psychological force field surrounding the England team, in as much as it still existed by 1953, was completely destroyed. No longer was there a sense of insurmountable strength about teams from Britain and a feeling that, without them, the World Cup lacked legitimacy. After Hungary, every nation was free to envisage the prospect of becoming the irrefutable best in the world, and to do so while playing sparkling, pell-mell, attacking football. The match also foreshadowed the geopolitical clout of the game, just as Cold War tensions between the Soviet Union and the West were reaching unprecedented heights.

At a point in time when many in Britain still wrote the sport off as the pursuit of the working classes, unworthy of intellectual interrogation, the defeat to Hungary sent shockwaves around the world. It was a milestone in the establishment of football as a truly global sport, one which could hold meaning off the pitch as well as on for billions of people. Though Hungary possessed several outstanding talents, Sebes' team was a pertinent example of the team being stronger than the individual, a rarity in the W-M era, and in Britain in particular, where wingers were celebrated above all others and Tom Finney was said to play alongside 'ten drips' at Preston. More pertinently, it destroyed the monolith of British football and, in doing so, awoke the rest of the world to the notion that the English way of doing things was not necessarily totemic.

Within ten years of the match, tactics on the international stage had gone from being an inconsequential afterthought to being the dominant piece of the puzzle of success. Hungary, with a stronger team and smarter tactics, had eviscerated England, but even teams not blessed with the likes of Puskás, Kocsis, Hidegkuti and József Bozsik could use tactics to bridge the manpower gap.

The Match of the Century, in short, may very well have been the most important match in the history of football. The beautiful game we know today owes a great deal of that beauty to that foggy November day in 1953. As the old adage goes, those who do not heed the past are doomed to repeat it. England, in a typically English display of obstinance, may only just be beginning to heed its lessons.

NOTES

Chapter 1: The Engineer and the Count

1   G.R. Burnell, *Supplement to the Theory, Practice and Architecture of Bridges* (1982).

Chapter 2: The Old Masters

1   Simon Jenkins, *A Short History of England*, p.216.
2   *Ibid.*, p.72.
3   Arthur Hopcraft, *The Football Man*, loc. 57.
4   Rory Smith, *Mister*, subtitle.
5   Charles Emmerson, *1913: The World Before the Great War*, p.30.

Chapter 3: Pomp and Circumstance

1   Rory Smith, *Mister*, p.155.
2   Brian Glanville, *England Managers*, loc. 213.
3   Brian Glanville, *Soccer Nemesis*, p.34.
4   Tim Marshall, *Prisoners of Geography*, p.110.
5   Bob Ferrier, *Soccer Partnership*, p.59.
6   Rory Smith, *Mister*, p.166.
7   Brian Glanville, *England Managers*, loc. 319.
8   Jon Henderson, *The Wizard*, p.51.
9   Jonathan Wilson, *The Anatomy of England: A History in Ten Matches*, loc. 804.
10 Brian Glanville, *Soccer Nemesis*, p.101.
11 Tom Finney, *My Autobiography*, p.188.
12 *Ibid.*, p.213.
13 Leander Schaerlaeckens, 'Chasing Gaetjens', espn.com.
14 *Daily Herald*, 3 July 1950.

Chapter 4: The Young Pretenders

1 Charles Emmerson, *1913: The World Before the Great War*, p.94.
2 Jonathan Wilson, *The Anatomy of England: A History in Ten Matches*, loc. 1261.
3 Brian Glanville, *Soccer Nemesis*, p.71.
4 Norman Stone, *Hungary: A Short History*, p.115.
5 *Ibid.*, p.122.
6 David Bailey, *Magical Magyars*, p.29.
7 Norman Stone, *Hungary: A Short History*, p.134.
8 *Ibid.*, p.149.
9 *Ibid.*, p.172.
10 *Ibid.*, p.176.
11 *Ibid.*, p.182.
12 David Bailey, *Magical Magyars*, p.59.
13 Ferenc Puskás, Rogan Taylor & Klara Jamrich, *Puskás on Puskás,* p.90.
14 Bill Kristol, conversation with Garry Kasparov.
15 Jonathan Wilson, *Inverting the Pyramid*, p.68.
16 Stanley Matthews, *The Way it Was*, p.117.
17 Brian Glanville, *Soccer Nemesis*, p.103.
18 Jonathan Wilson, *Inverting the Pyramid*, p.85.
19 Brian Glanville, *Soccer Nemesis*, p.116.
20 *Ibid.*, p.103.
21 Ferenc Puskás, Rogan Taylor & Klara Jamrich, *Puskás on Puskás*, p.90.
22 *Ibid.*, p.34.
23 David Bailey, *Magical Magyars*, p.46.
24 Ferenc Puskás, Rogan Taylor & Klara Jamrich, *Puskás on Puskás*, p.34.
25 *Ibid.*, p.85.

Chapter 5: Thinking the Unthinkable

1 Jonathan Wilson, *The Anatomy of England: A History in Ten Matches*, loc. 1282.
2 Jonathan Wilson, *The Names Heard Long Ago*, p.179.
3 Jonathan Wilson, *The Anatomy of England: A History in Ten Matches*, loc. 601.
4 Brian Glanville, *Soccer Nemesis*, p.137.
5 Rory Smith, *Mister*, p.7.
6 Jonathan Wilson, *The Names Heard Long Ago*, p.279.
7 *Ibid.*, p.285.
8 David Bailey, *Magical Magyars*, p.102.

Chapter 6: Mr Sebes, It's Time We Arranged a Match

1 Péter Fodor, 'Erasing, Rewriting, and Propaganda in the Hungarian Sports Films of the 1950s', *The Hungarian Historical Review*, Vol. 6, No. 2 (2017).
2 Ferenc Puskás, Rogan Taylor & Klara Jamrich, *Puskás on Puskás*, p.45.
3 *Ibid.*, p.64.

4 David Bailey, *Magical Magyars*, p.89.
5 *Ibid.*, p.33.
6 *Ibid.*, p.92.
7 *Ibid.*, p.81.
8 Ferenc Puskás, Rogan Taylor & Klara Jamrich, *Puskás on Puskás*, p.46.
9 Jonathan Wilson, *The Names Heard Long Ago*, p.311.
10 Ferenc Puskás, Rogan Taylor & Klara Jamrich, *Puskás on Puskás*, p.41.
11 *Ibid.*, p.94.
12 *Ibid.*, p.44.
13 David Bailey, *Magical Magyars*, p.84.
14 Ferenc Puskás, Rogan Taylor & Klara Jamrich, *Puskás on Puskás*, p.42.
15 *Ibid.*, p.45.
16 Jonathan Wilson, *The Names Heard Long Ago*, p.313.
17 Ferenc Puskás, Rogan Taylor & Klara Jamrich, *Puskás on Puskás*, p.67.
18 Jonathan Wilson, *The Names Heard Long Ago*, p.311.
19 David Bailey, *Magical Magyars*, p.115.
20 Ferenc Puskás, Rogan Taylor & Klara Jamrich, *Puskás on Puskás*, p.69.
21 *Ibid.*, p.70.
22 *Ibid.*, p.69.
23 *Ibid.*, p.71.
24 *Ibid.*, p.72.
25 *Ibid.*
26 *Ibid.*, p.9.
27 *Ibid.*, p.75.
28 *Ibid.*, p.74.

Chapter 7: Island Supremacy

1 Tom Finney, *My Autobiography*, p.181.
2 Jon Henderson, *The Wizard*, p.186.
3 Bob Ferrier, *Soccer Partnership*, p.17.
4 Alf Ramsey, *Talking Football*, p.17.
5 Tom Finney, *My Autobiography*, p.236.
6 Bob Ferrier, *Soccer Partnership*, p.14.
7 David Tossell, *The Great English Final*, p.97.
8 Nat Lofthouse, *Goals Galore*, p.89.
9 Ferenc Puskás, Rogan Taylor & Klara Jamrich, *Puskás on Puskás*, p.69.
10 *Ibid.*, p.71.
11 *Ibid.*

Chapter 8: Brave New World

1 James D. Watson, *The Double Helix: A Personal Account of the Discovery of the Structure of DNA*.
2 Albin J. Zak III, *I Don't Sound Like Nobody: Remaking Music in 1950s America*.

3 Mick Conefrey, *Everest 1953*, p.xii.
4 Godfrey Hodgson, *America In Our Time: From World War II to Nixon*, p.18.
5 David Goldblatt, *The Game of Our Lives*, p.24.
6 David Carlton, *Churchill and the Soviet Union*, p.200.
7 Joshua Rubenstein, *The Last Days of Stalin*, p.139.
8 Norman Stone, *Hungary: A Short History*, p.190.

Chapter 9: Uncorking the Stopper

1 Stanley Rous, *Football Worlds*, p.190.
2 Alan Hoby, *Sunday People*.
3 Stanley Rous, *Football Worlds*, picture inlay.
4 Ferenc Puskás, Rogan Taylor & Klara Jamrich, *Puskás on Puskás*, p.76.
5 *Ibid.*
6 *Ibid.*
7 Jonathan Wilson, *The Anatomy of England: A History in Ten Matches*, loc. 804.
8 Stanley Rous, *Football Worlds*, p.71.
9 Jon Henderson, *The Wizard*, p.6.
10 *Ibid.*, p.188.
11 Jonathan Wilson, *The Anatomy of England: A History in Ten Matches*, loc. 1193.
12 *Ibid.*, loc. 1217.
13 *Ibid.*, loc. 1204.
14 *Ibid.*

Chapter 10: The Silence Before the Storm

1 David Bailey, *Magical Magyars*, p.120.
2 Ferenc Puskás, Rogan Taylor & Klara Jamrich, *Puskás on Puskás*, p.77.
3 Jonathan Wilson, *The Names Heard Long Ago*, p.313.
4 Ferenc Puskás, Rogan Taylor & Klara Jamrich, *Puskás on Puskás*, p.77.
5 Rory Smith, *Mister*, p.195.
6 Ferenc Puskás, Rogan Taylor & Klara Jamrich, *Puskás on Puskás*, p.78.
7 Rory Smith, *Mister*, p.196.
8 David Bailey, *Magical Magyars*, p.93.
9 Ferenc Puskás, Rogan Taylor & Klara Jamrich, *Puskás on Puskás*, p.78.
10 *Ibid.*, p.79.
11 *Ibid.*
12 *Ibid.*
13 Stanley Matthews, *The Way It Was: My Autobiography*.
14 Jonathan Wilson, *The Anatomy of England: A History in Ten Matches*, loc. 177.
15 Ferenc Puskás, Rogan Taylor & Klara Jamrich, *Puskás on Puskás*, p.80.
16 *Ibid.*
17 John Ludden, *The Magical Magyars: 6–3*, loc. 148.
18 Ferenc Puskás, Rogan Taylor & Klara Jamrich, *Puskás on Puskás*, p.80.

19 John Ludden, *The Magical Magyars: 6-3*, loc. 169.
20 Ferenc Puskás, Rogan Taylor & Klara Jamrich, *Puskás on Puskás*, p.81.

Chapter 11: The Match of the Century

1 Bob Ferrier, *Soccer Partnership*, p.73.
2 Jonathan Wilson, *The Anatomy of England: A History in Ten Matches*, loc. 1466.
3 Ferenc Puskás, Rogan Taylor & Klara Jamrich, *Puskás on Puskás*, p.82.
4 Geoffrey Green, *Soccer in the Fifties*, p.285.
5 Ferenc Puskás, Rogan Taylor & Klara Jamrich, *Puskás on Puskás*, p.82.
6 Harry Johnston, *The Rocky Road to Wembley*.
7 Rory Smith, *Mister*, p.196.
8 Stanley Matthews, *The Way It Was: My Autobiography*.
9 Ferenc Puskás, Rogan Taylor & Klara Jamrich, *Puskás on Puskás*, p.84.
10 John Ludden, *The Magical Magyars: 6-3*, loc. 242.
11 *Ibid.*, loc. 255.

Chapter 12: The Twilight of the Gods

1 Jonathan Wilson, *The Anatomy of England*, loc. 1494.
2 Brian Glanville, *Soccer Nemesis*, p.165.
3 Jon Henderson, *The Wizard*, p.250.
4 *Ibid.*
5 *Ibid.*, p.259.
6 Ferenc Puskás, Rogan Taylor & Klara Jamrich, *Puskás on Puskás*, p.86.
7 Jonathan Wilson, *The Names Heard Long Ago*, p.318.
8 Jonathan Wilson, *The Anatomy of England: A History in Ten Matches*, loc. 1583.
9 Ferenc Puskás, Rogan Taylor & Klara Jamrich, *Puskás on Puskás*, p.88.
10 Tom Finney, *My Autobiography*, p.194.
11 *Ibid.*
12 Ferenc Puskás, Rogan Taylor & Klara Jamrich, *Puskás on Puskás*, p.101.
13 *Ibid.*
14 *Ibid.*
15 *Ibid.*
16 Jonathan Wilson, *The Names Heard Long Ago*, p.6.
17 Ferenc Puskás, Rogan Taylor & Klara Jamrich, *Puskás on Puskás*, p.105.
18 *Ibid.*, p.106.
19 *Ibid.*
20 *Ibid.*, p.107.
21 *Ibid.*, p.106.
22 Brian Glanville, *England Managers*, loc. 483.
23 Ferenc Puskás, Rogan Taylor & Klara Jamrich, *Puskás on Puskás*, p.107.

Chapter 13: Goodbye, England!

1 Jonathan Wilson, *Inverting the Pyramid*, p.94.
2 Brian Glanville, *England Managers*, loc. 514.
3 Jonathan Wilson, *The Names Heard Long Ago*, p.360.
4 *Ibid.*, p.6.

BIBLIOGRAPHY

Bailey, David, *Magical Magyars: The Rise and Fall of the World's Once Greatest Football Team* (Pitch Publishing, 2019).

Burnell, George Rowdon, *Supplement to the Theory, Practice and Architecture of Bridges* (J. Weale, 1852).

Carlton, David, *Churchill and the Soviet Union* (Manchester University Press, 2000).

Conefrey, Mick, *Everest 1953: The Epic Story of the First Ascent* (Oneworld Publications, 2013).

Davis, Pete, *One Night in Turin: The Inside Story of a World Cup that Changed our Footballing Nation Forever* (Yellow Jersey, 2010).

Davis, Wade, *Into the Silence: The Great War, Mallory and the Conquest of Everest* (Vintage, 2011).

Emmerson, Charles, *1913: The World Before the Great War* (Vintage, 2013).

Ferrier, Bob, *Soccer Partnership: Billy Wright and Walter Winterbottom* (Heinemann, 1960).

Finney, Tom, *Tom Finney: My Autobiography* (Headline, 2004).

Glanville, Brian, *Soccer Nemesis* (Secker & Warburg, 1955).

Glanville, Brian, *England Managers: The Toughest Job in Football* (Headline, 2008).

Goldblatt, David, *The Game of Our Lives: The Meaning and Making of English Football* (Penguin, 2015).

Greaves, Jimmy, *The Heart of the Game* (Little, Brown, 2009).

Green, Geoffrey, *Soccer in the Fifties* (Allan, 1974).

Hamilton, Duncan, *The Footballer Who Could Fly* (Century, 2012).

Henderson, Jon, *The Wizard: The Life of Stanley Matthews* (Yellow Jersey, 2013).

Hobsbawm, Eric, *Age of Extremes: The Short Twentieth Century 1914–1991* (Abacus, 1994).

Hodgson, Godfrey, *America in Our Time: From World War II to Nixon* (Princeton University Press, 2005).

Hopcraft, Arthur, *The Football Man: People & Passions in Soccer* (Aurum Press, 2013).

Jenkins, Simon, *A Short History of England* (Profile Books, 2011).

Johnston, Harry, *The Rocky Road to Wembley* (Museum Press, 1954).

Kynaston, David, *Family Britain, 1951–1957* (Bloomsbury, 2010).

Lamming, Douglas, *An English Football Internationalists' Who's Who* (Hutton Press, 1990).

Lofthouse, Nat, *Goals Galore* (Stanley Paul, 1954).

Ludden, John, *The Magical Magyars: 6–3* (CreateSpace, 2017).

Marr, Andrew, *A History of Modern Britain* (Picador, 2009).

Marshall, Tim, *Prisoners of Geography: Ten Maps That Tell You Everything You Need To Know About Global Politics* (Elliott & Thompson, 2015).

Matthews, Stanley, *The Way it Was: My Autobiography* (Headline, 2001).

Puskás, Ferenc, Rogan Taylor & Klara Jamrich, *Puskás on Puskás* (Robson Books, 1998).

Ramsey, Alf, *Talking Football* (S. Paul, 1952).

Rous, Stanley, *Football Worlds* (Faber and Faber, 1978).

Rubenstein, Joshua, *The Last Days of Stalin* (Yale University Press, 2016).

Smith, Rory, *Mister* (Simon & Schuster, 2016).

Stone, Norman, *Hungary: A Short History* (Profile Books, 2019).

Tossell, David, *The Great English Final, 1953: Cup, Coronation & Stanley Matthews* (Pitch Publishing, 2013).

Watson, James D., *The Double Helix: A Personal Account of the Discovery of the Structure of DNA* (Scribner, 2011).

Wilson, Jonathan, *Inverting the Pyramid* (Orion, 2009).

Wilson, Jonathan, *The Anatomy of England: A History in Ten Matches* (Orion, 2010).

Wilson, Jonathan, *The Names Heard Long Ago* (Blink Publishing, 2020).

Winner, David, *Those Feet: A Sensual History of English Football* (Abrams, 2013).

Zak, Albin J. III, *I Don't Sound Like Nobody: Remaking Music in 1950s America* (University of Michigan Press, 2012).

Periodicals

Athletic News
Belfast News-Letter
Daily Herald
Daily Mirror
Daily Record
Dundee Courier
Guardian
The Hungarian Historical Review
Nepssport
The People
Sports Argus
The Sunday People
The Times

INDEX